Artillery
in the
Great War

Artillery
in the
Great War

Paul Strong and Sanders Marble

Pen & Sword
MILITARY

First published in Great Britain in 2011
and reprinted in this format in 2013
PEN & SWORD MILITARY
An imprint of
Pen & Sword Books Ltd
47 Church Street
Barnsley, South Yorkshire
S70 2AS

ISBN 978 1 78303 012 5

Typeset in Ehrhardt by Phoenix Typesetting, Auldgirth, Dumfriesshire

Printed and bound in England
By CPI Group (UK) Ltd, Croydon, CR0 4YY

Pen & Sword Books Ltd incorporates the Imprints of Aviation, Atlas,
Family History, Fiction, Maritime, Military, Discovery, Politics, History,
Archaeology, Select, Wharncliffe Local History, Wharncliffe True Crime,
Military Classics, Wharncliffe Transport, Leo Cooper, The Praetorian Press,
Remember When, Seaforth Publishing and Frontline Publishing

For a complete list of Pen & Sword titles please contact
PEN & SWORD BOOKS LIMITED
47 Church Street, Barnsley, South Yorkshire, S70 2AS, England
E-mail: enquiries@pen-and-sword.co.uk
Website: www.pen-and-sword.co.uk

Contents

Dedicated to
Lieutenant-Colonel Ernest Ian Elphinstone Strong,
Royal Artillery (1919–1949)

Maps

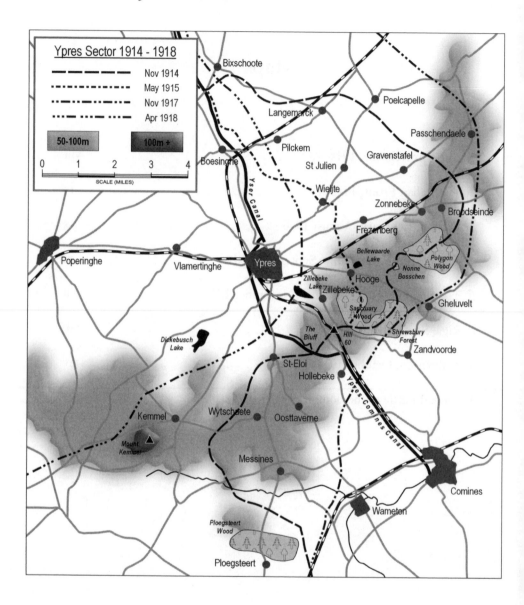

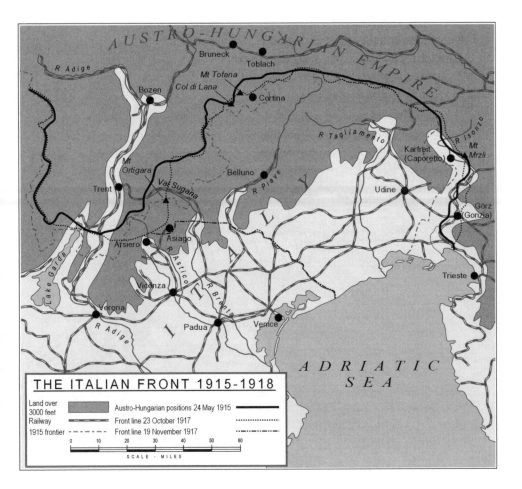

THE ITALIAN FRONT 1915-1918

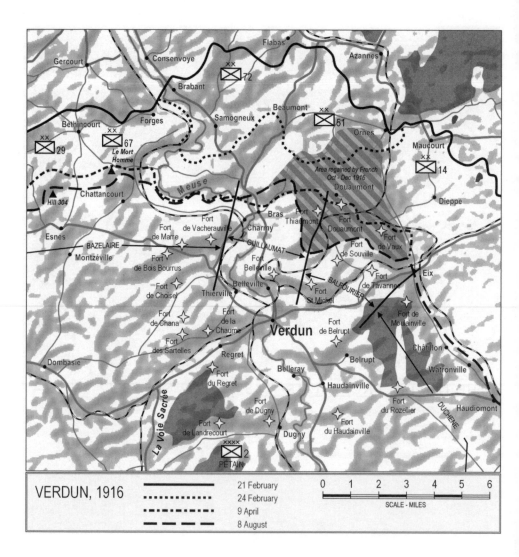

VERDUN, 1916

————	21 February
··········	24 February
·–·–·–·	9 April
– – – –	8 August

SCALE - MILES

0 1 2 3 4 5 6

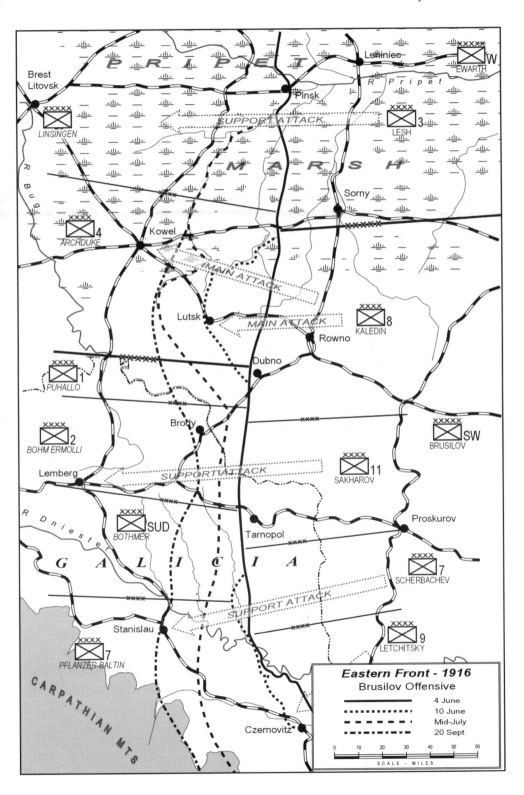

Brest Litovsk

PRIPET

Letliniec

R Pripet

EWARTH W

LINSINGEN

LESH 3

MARSH

Sorny

ARCHDUKE 4

Kowel

SUPPORT ATTACK

MAIN ATTACK

MAIN ATTACK

Lutsk

KALEDIN 8

Rowno

PUHALLO 1

Dubno

Brody

BOHM ERMOLLI 2

SW BRUSILOV

Lemberg

SUPPORT ATTACK

SAKHAROV 11

BOTHMER SUD

Tarnopol

Proskurov

GALICIA

SCHERBACHEV 7

SUPPORT ATTACK

Stanislau

LETCHITSKY 9

PFLANZER-BALTIN 7

CARPATHIAN MTS

Czernovitz

Eastern Front - 1916
Brusilov Offensive

	4 June
	10 June
	Mid-July
	20 Sept

0   10   20   30   40   50   60
SCALE - MILES

THE SOMME - ADVANCES IN THE BRITISH SECTOR 1 July - 18 November 1916

0	2	4	6

SCALE KM

Front line, 1 July 1916
Front line, 17 July 1916
Front line, 13 September 1916
Front line, 18 November 1916

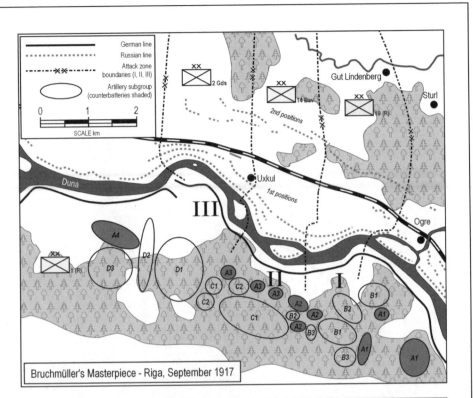

Bruchmüller's Masterpiece - Riga, September 1917

Organisation and Missions of German Artillery							
			Batteries				
Group	Subgroup	Mission	Field Guns	Heavy Guns	Lt Field Howitzers	Hvy Field Howitzers	Hvy Mortars
A	A1	Neutralise the enemy artillery	5	5	- -	2	- -
	A2		6	- -	- -	1	- -
	A3		7	1	- -	- -	- -
	A4		7	1	- -	1	- -
B	B1	Lay fire on first line positions for 19 (Res) Division assault	4	- -	8	6	3
	B2	Lay fire on second line positions for 19 (Res) Division assault	- -	- -	3	3	- -
	B3	Lay down fire barrier to the East	9	2	- -	- -	- -
C	C1	Lay fire on first line positions for 14 Bav Division assault	6	2	7	10	5
	C2	Lay fire on second line positions for 14 Bav Division assault	2	2	3	3	- -
D	D1	Lay fire on first line positions for 2 Gds Division assault	5	- -	7	7	2
	D2	Lay fire on second line positions for 2 Gds Division assault	1	- -	5	3	- -
	D3	Lay down fire barrier to the West; provide fire support for 1 (Res) Div in case of Russian attack	6	2	- -	- -	- -

Source: Maj D T Zabecki, USAR ("Der Durchbruchmueller" - Field Artillery, August 1990)

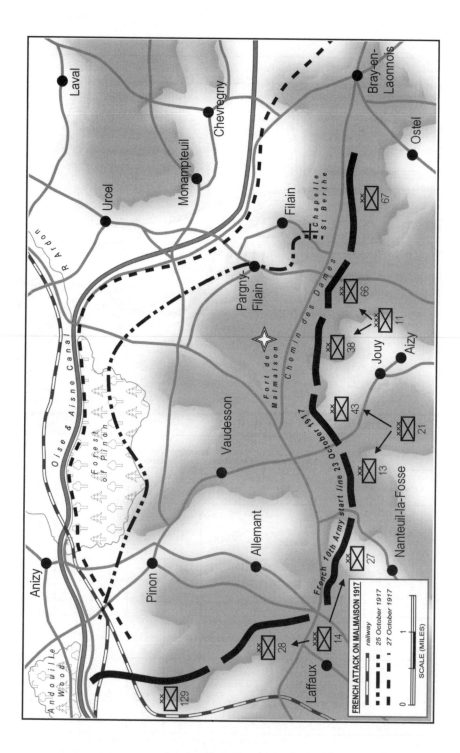

Laval

Chevregny

Monampteuil

Urcel

R. Ardon

Bray-en-
Laonnois

Ostel

Filain

Pargny-
Filain

+ Chapelle
St Berthe

C h e m i n   d e s   D a m e s

Fort de
Malmaison

Jouy

Aizy

XX
67

XX
66

XXX
11

XX
38

XX
43

XXX
21

XX
13

Oise & Aisne Canal

Forest
of Pinon

Anizy

Vaudesson

Allemant

Pinon

French 10th Army start line 23 October 1917

Nanteuil-la-Fosse

XX
27

Andouille
Wood

XXX
14

XX
28

XX
129

Laffaux

FRENCH ATTACK ON MALMAISON 1917

railway

····· 25 October 1917

– – – 27 October 1917

SCALE (MILES)

0   1

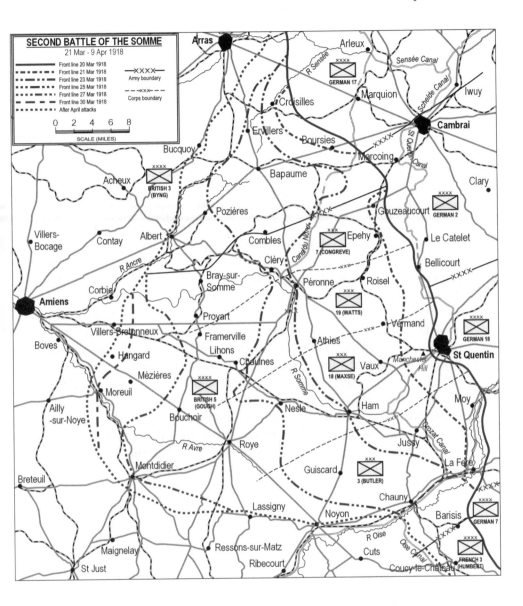

Introduction

It is often said that the First World War was an artillery war and that shell-fire caused over half of the battlefield casualties; Jonathan Bailey, for example, notes that shellfire and trench mortars together caused 58.51 per cent of Britain's casualties in the Great War. Many of the tactical innovations during the war were in direct response to the impact of artillery on the battlefield – usually inspired by the enemy's own innovations, a process known as reciprocal development, where organisations develop and counter new technologies and organisational structures in a continuous competitive process. Yet the artillery's direct influence on both the planning and the conduct of operations has rarely been examined. There are numerous excellent books on guns, munitions and technology, many volumes dealing with individual battles that mention artillery's role in a specific operation, and a number of memoirs by artillerymen (which can sometimes come across as dry recitations of their most successful fire-plans). The best on artillery are those by Jonathan Bailey and Bruce Gudmundsson, but these deal with the wider evolution of artillery rather than specifically focusing on the events of the Great War. Perhaps many modern authors have been deterred from looking at the role of the artillery by the grim technical processes involved in industrialised, impersonalised killing and have therefore preferred to focus on the 'more human' story of the infantry caught up in the terrifying environment created by the war in the trenches.

In this volume, we aim to start filling that gap. We examine each year of the war and look at key and representative battles on various fronts to explore how the constant process of reciprocal development affected both the conduct of operations and the people actually fighting the battles. We try to draw together the changing technologies of artillery and shells, and the innovations that affected accuracy such as mapping, sound-ranging and aerial observation. We also look at how military doctrine directly affected artillery and more generally at how artillery was fitted (or was not) into the evolving combined arms doctrine. We also examine how artillery was organised and commanded, because there were important differences that influenced its effectiveness. By looking at different countries and different theatres, we try to show how different armies faced varied circumstances and came up with unique solutions. Looking at a single nation's military progress reveals only one learning curve associated with the particular circumstances in a given theatre, and thus inevitably fails to demonstrate the complex evolutionary processes at work. It would also fail to counter the assumption by some modern historians (and much of the popular media) that commanders in the First World War were less generally able than those who faced far less challenging circumstances in other wars.

We would like to acknowledge the assistance of those who read draft sections of the book, including John Lee, Tim Ratcliffe, Howard Body, Kathryn Walls and Patrick Rose, and those who kindly allowed us to quote from their work. We particularly want to thank Paul Evans and the staff of the Library of the Royal Artillery Museum who opened up the Aladdin's cave of archival material in the Royal Artillery's remarkable collection, and Tim Ratcliffe who provided the superb maps and illustrations.

Given the enormity of the subject and the limited space available, faults and omissions inevitably remain and these are entirely our responsibility. We also want to thank Rupert Harding who allowed this project to go on longer than he wanted, yet helped us throughout! And to our families, who saw less of us as we worked on this, our thanks.

Prologue

The Battle of Le Cateau

After the thundershowers that covered II Corps' retreat, Lieutenant General Sir Horace Smith-Dorrien took the calculated risk to stand and fight on 26 August 1914 instead of continuing to withdraw. With four German corps plus cavalry marching forward, a gap opening on the right flank between II Corps and Sir Douglas Haig's I Corps, and only a weak French covering force on the left flank, II Corps faced a stiff fight as dawn broke. The encounter would go down in history as the battle of Le Cateau.

II Corps had three infantry divisions in the line, deployed along a ridge, and they would fight two different types of battle. The 5th Division, on the right, had an open flank, and Smith-Dorrien's orders to stand and fight arrived late, so the troops had less time to select good positions and dig in. The 3rd Division (centre) and the 4th Division (left) had more time to pick their positions carefully and dug themselves in a bit with the rudimentary 'grubbers' the men carried. With mist covering the ridge during the night, the men of the 5th Division ended up selecting positions that were on the forward slope – when daylight came, they were able to see the enemy but their positions were visible to the enemy. This left the 5th Division in a weak position. The division's artillery commander, Brigadier General John Headlam, compounded the problem. Following standard pre-war British practice, he decentralised his forces and attached a brigade of field guns (each brigade comprising three six-gun batteries) to each of the infantry brigades. Ordinarily, Headlam would still have the field howitzers (another three batteries) and the single heavy battery of 60-pounder long-range guns under his command, but he also split up the howitzer brigade, sending one battery to the 3rd Division and one battery forward, keeping only one battery, plus the heavy battery, as a reserve. Not only did the 5th Division's artillery get split up, but it deployed far too far forward, in many cases amid the infantry.

In contrast, the 3rd and 4th Divisions deployed the bulk of their guns well behind the infantry and out of sight of the Germans. They would have to rely on signals (wig-wag flags, couriers or telephone messages) to know where and when to fire and they would have a harder time adjusting their fire or switching targets, but they were under cover and harder for the German artillery to hit. The trade-off was somewhat less firepower in exchange for better odds of survival, and surviving one day meant being able to provide firepower tomorrow. A few guns were deployed forward, up with the infantry, but staying silent until the advancing Germans were close enough to blast with shrapnel; some of these forward guns were disguised with corn stalks, since the crops had been cut but not gathered.

The forward guns were sited there for various reasons. Beyond the inevitable communications problems, most guns had only a modest range. Battles were expected to be fought at fairly short ranges, and the British 18-pounder field guns had been optimised accordingly: the guns were built for high-velocity but low-trajectory firing and could not elevate more than 16 degrees, which restricted their range to about 3.7 miles. That expectation and design encompassed another assumption: that shrapnel would be the key munition. (The actual weapon of artillery is the shell: guns, howitzers, mortars and rockets are simply delivery mechanisms.) Shrapnel lost effectiveness as the shell's velocity dropped, and since the Royal Artillery believed so heavily in shrapnel the lack of long range hardly bothered them. Indeed, so strongly did they believe in shrapnel over high explosive (HE) that the 4.5-inch field howitzer had its HE shells designed to match the ballistic performance of shrapnel, although that reduced their bursting charge and thus effectiveness. II Corps had no heavy artillery (6 inches and over) at Le Cateau because the British Army was divided in its thinking about the employment of artillery in modern warfare: there were sieges and field battles, and the two did not mix. Heavy artillery was only for sieges, and the Siege Train (four batteries of 6-inch howitzers and two batteries of 9.45-inch howitzers) was still mobilising in Britain. A final expectation was that artillery should fight right up in the front line; the honorable thing was for the gunners to risk their lives alongside the infantry (and cavalry), and that was the only way to attain the recognition and glory of being in combat. This idea harked back to the Napoleonic wars, and while it had been beaten out of the Royal Artillery in the Boer War, it had crept back into the thinking.

Reports note that the 5th Division gunners whistled while they deployed their guns alongside the infantry. They would be fighting alongside their comrades, just as their predecessors had done for centuries. One of the brigade commanders told his subordinates 'fight it out here; there will be no retirement', but they were facing new battlefield conditions. Indirect fire would replace direct fire as the leading cause of casualties in the Great War, and why that happened can be seen on the battlefield of Le Cateau.

As the gunners prepared themselves, the Germans were moving south and west. They had found the seam between II and I Corps, and *III Korps* was feeling its way forward. But the Germans also saw the 5th Division troops on the ridge. The 72nd Infanterie Regiment moved into Le Cateau, catching some British rearguard piquets. The British flank was obvious to the German commanders and two more regiments moved into action to turn the flank while three more pinned down the 5th Division from the front. More troops were ordered to move deeper into the British rear, but they moved slowly through the day and did not influence the battle. Meanwhile, as the flank attack unfolded, German artillery observers did their job from the hills north of Le Cateau. From about 6am there was ruthlessly methodical German fire moving from target to target on the ridge, preparing the way for the infantry attack. The British guns fired back, aiming at the German muzzle-flashes about 5,000 yards away, and managed to silence some of the German guns – but only some of them and only for a time. More German artillery arrived (and deployed) and German counter-battery fire began to tell. High explosive and 'universal' shells (a German compromise between HE and shrapnel) were bursting over the British positions, hitting command posts, cutting telephone wires, killing and wounding; soon direct hits were knocking out some guns. Nevertheless, the remaining British guns opened fire when the German infantry started advancing, although all they could do was force the Germans to spread out. A few casualties and a little delay were about all that was inflicted on the Germans, and they may have been willing to pay the price to learn more about the British defences. By 9am the Germans were feeling their way around the British flank and preparing their frontal assault, and had perhaps 200 guns deployed in an arc around the men of the 5th Division.

From 9am to noon the battle raged fiercely. A British pilot noticed more and more German guns moving forward, but there was nothing he could do about it. The Germans were shelling the British batteries and, since the guns were up close to the infantry, the infantry collected some of the near-misses. But the British gunners stayed in action, blasting away at the German infantry; one German infantry officer paid tribute to their gallantry: 'Regardless of loss, the English artillery came forward to protect their infantrymen and in full view of our guns kept up a devastating fire.' The Germans tended to march into action in companies and then deploy into skirmish lines, and the advancing companies made easy and juicy targets, and for a time one British battery was blasting a German platoon with every round fired. On the receiving end, the Germans complained that 'as we went forward only dead and wounded were to be seen in our firing line'. During lulls in the infantry attack, the gunners would switch back to bombarding the German gun positions. Some batteries fired off their ammunition, and wagonloads had to be brought forward from the ammunition columns. About noon the Germans paused to regroup, while their drumfire bombardment continued. The British infantry was learning to tell the 'whizz-bang' 77mm field guns apart from the booming 150mm howitzers, which burst with black smoke and earned the nickname 'Jack Johnson' after a heavyweight boxer.

If Headlam could have surveyed his position at about 1pm he would have found his right and centre savaged; over half the guns were out of action as German shells slammed in from front and flank. An observer described the 'throb of noise from our left flank. We all looked instinctively in the direction of Le Cateau where the Montay spur was overhung by a bank of white and yellow smoke, punctuated by angry flashes.' The 5th Division's left was better off, with most guns still in action and the two batteries in the rear busy firing at German artillery. On the right flank German machine guns were only 500 yards from the British infantry; a subaltern in 122 Battery, RFA described the 'pop-pop-pop-pop of a machine gun and a perfect hail of bullets'. Another German assault might break the line. Smith-Dorrien was hastily consulted and the division was ordered to pull out; II Corps had given the Germans a bloody nose and bought time to continue the retreat. Now they had to solve the problem of getting the guns back from the forward positions under relentless German artillery and small-arms fire.

Headlam saw that the 5th Division's position was now untenable and he ordered the horse teams forward to withdraw the guns. Men of the 1/Royal West Kents stood and cheered, waving their caps, as the horse teams trotted forward. Shells were still falling, and several teams were blown to bits on their way forward, men and horses scattered by shellfire, mangled and screaming. A few batteries had picked positions in folds in the ground and they typically escaped lightly, but several batteries were up forward in the open. As the horse teams swept over the crest of the ridge, the Germans redoubled their fire. In some cases infantry and machine guns were close enough that bullets punched through the gun-shields, and small-arms fire added to the rain of shells. Few guns could be extracted; some had taken direct hits, others had too few men left to hook them into the limbers, and sometimes – despite the most gallant efforts – the hail of fire was simply too much. Gunners fired off the last rounds from guns that could not be withdrawn, then smashed the sights and pulled the breechblocks to deny the Germans anything more than a trophy. As the German infantry finally started forward, some groups were silhouetted on the ridgeline offering the British reserve batteries easy pickings. One 'mob' eight deep was hit with a flurry of howitzer shells. British observers saw the group 'disperse' but what they would not have seen was individual soldiers being blown apart.

The net result was the loss of 27 guns, over one-third of the 5th Division's total. At least 22 artillery officers and 180 other ranks were lost, along with 257 horses. The gunners (and of course the infantry) had fought with great gallantry, and the Germans never managed to organise an overwhelming attack. II Corps had fought to win time, to check the German advance so the retreat could resume, and they succeeded in creating a 'stopping blow' that forced the German 1st Army to slow its advance. The British withdrawal started at about 2pm, and the Germans resumed their advance the next morning, allowing the BEF enough of a head start that it would not be overwhelmed by superior numbers and firepower. The next morning the infantrymen showed their appreciation of the gallant gunners, and the battlefield effectiveness of the guns: 'Exhausted as they were by the long night march, many men stepped from the ranks as they marched past to give a silent pat to the guns drawn up by the roadside.'[1] But regardless of the 5th Division's gallantry, need they have suffered such heavy losses? Was there a more effective way to fight than deploying the guns up with the infantry and literally fighting side by side?

Unlike the 5th Division, the guns of the 3rd Division, in the centre of the line, were deployed in depth, Brigadier General Frederick Wing making the best use of the terrain. Instead of pushing the guns forward, all except four were deployed behind the ridge; those four were used as direct support guns, and all four were written off. The gunners' role was to wait silently until the British outpost in the village of Caudry had been pushed back and the first major German attack developed. Then they would open up and blast away. They were expendable, but they would defeat an attack and shatter the attacking battalions.

The early German shelling did little damage in the 3rd Division zone except for knocking out telephone lines, obliging the observation posts to send messages back by galloping messengers – not much different than communications a century earlier. But in return the British guns could not find the German batteries either and both sides fired fairly blindly; at one stage a German airplane flew over and apparently dropped a message back to the German gunners, because their accuracy improved for a time. Infantry targets were another matter, and the British guns could readily hit the advancing German infantry. Their movement was slowed, but never stopped; there were simply too many Germans and if they were willing to take risks they could filter forward in skirmish lines. Not even a month into the war, the infantry's enthusiasm was undimmed, with casualties correspondingly high. As the morning wore on, German counter-battery shelling continued, not so much aimed fire as simply searching places where the British batteries might be. The German 5.9-inch (150mm) howitzers were an unpleasant surprise, especially for infantry in villages: in stout houses they were generally immune from field guns but these heavy howitzers could literally pulverise buildings. But this level of firepower was only useful if there was a target. The infantry, grouped together in the villages, could be hit, but the British guns were scattered behind the line and were thus tougher targets; German fire thus only 'flecked the landscape'. This searching fire was expensive in ammunition and time, and the British guns remained in action, hitting German infantry at ranges as close as 2,000–3,000 yards, but the Germans nonetheless closed in on Caudry.

By 1pm the Germans had taken Caudry and were moving past Inchy. The 8th Infantry Brigade had only a thin line, but the artillery (including a British howitzer battery that simply fired on Inchy, needing no more specific target) held the Germans. In mid-afternoon, as the 5th Division was struggling to get its guns away, a German attack was massing around Inchy but the four forward guns (camouflaged until then) now opened up. They fired off several hundred rounds of ammunition, each shell showering the Germans with 375 shrapnel balls. The Germans were blown back, suffering terrible casualties, and were sufficiently disorganised to enable the British infantry (and the gunners from the forward sections) to withdraw with minimal loss.

The 3rd Division's withdrawal was straightforward. Artillery leapfrogged from its scattered locations to cover the retreat, and almost no guns were lost except for the forward sections. For all the damage they did to the Germans, the 3rd Division's artillery lost only three men.

Chapter One
1914

No country began the Great War with a fully developed appreciation of how artillery would function in a modern industrialised war. Only a few technical specialists proposed applying scientific principles to orchestrating artillery fire, usually described as fire-planning, and even fewer recognised the startling impact of a wide array of technical advances on the battlefield effectiveness of the artillery arm. Recent wars in South Africa, the Far East and the Balkans, all offering potentially useful examples illustrating the impact of both new tactics and technology, were more often used by leading theorists examining the future of warfare to 'prove' what they already believed than to explore the emerging character of conflict in the new century. Within a few weeks the Great War would overturn many of these assumptions, forcing both sides to innovate and counter-innovate at an increasingly bewildering speed. Historians looking at the evolution of the conduct of operations by specific armies have sometimes described this process as a learning curve but this term ignores the ways in which the opposing sides inspired and frustrated the designs of their opponents, and marginalises the cultural factors that encouraged or delayed development.

Each nation organised its armed forces to fit the strategies that it expected to use to secure its intended national objectives. Inevitably the pre-war development of artillery techniques and technology mirrored these assumptions in each of the war plans. Just as the overall strategies proved to be flawed, much of the equipment and tactical doctrine turned out to be short-sighted, and none of the belligerents appreciated the difficulties they would face in keeping the artillery synchronised with their operational plans and supplied with adequate ammunition. This chapter briefly reviews these assumptions and the immediate reaction of the artillery officers to the shattering of their pre-war illusions during the first months of the war.[1]

Germany and 'The Guns of August'

Given Germany's perception of encirclement by powerful opponents and the challenge created by her formidable military objectives, the effective

1

application of artillery firepower was central to her entire war plan. The *Großer Generalstab* (Great General Staff) was all too aware of the threat from Russia and France and had good reason to believe that Britain would be hostile even if Germany observed Belgian neutrality. A long war against those countries' combined wealth, industry and population was assumed to end with Germany being ground down, so German strategy, immortalised as the Schlieffen Plan,[2] became one where she knocked out one of her opponents before dealing with the others. With Russia's territory being so vast and her army's mobilisation slow, France became the target almost by default. In 1870 the Prussians had been able to attack France head-on because the French had few modern frontier forts, but by 1900 the French had both refortified their frontier and increased the size of their army to fill the gaps between the upgraded defences. If the Germans repeated their 1870 manoeuvres they would simply smash into the French defensive system and the offensive would stall just as the Russian steamroller gathered momentum in the east. Due to the rough terrain in southern Belgium (principally the wooded hills of the Ardennes), the Germans began examining the option of a wide outflanking manoeuvre through Belgium. Belgian neutrality was guaranteed by international agreement, but the Belgians knew that their neutrality depended more on being ready to fight back than on what the Kaiser had derisively dismissed as 'a scrap of paper'. They upgraded the fortifications around the key border city of Liege, the main communications hub for the area, and thus a key part of the German war plan hinged on rapidly defeating the dozen forts covering this one city.

Established around 1890 under the direction of the highly regarded Dutch-born fortress engineer Henri Alexis Brialmont,[3] the Liege forts were built to resist 210mm artillery, and although there had been some recent refurbishment, most of this was cosmetic and much of the core of the *enceinte* (defensive system) had not been upgraded with reinforced concrete. The layout of the detached forts had been designed to protect and support a strong infantry force with casemated artillery (some 400 guns), but in turn required infantry to cover the roughly 4 mile gaps between them.[4] In 1914 the Belgians assigned a reinforced infantry division to this role but the Germans had also made special preparations. Several brigades of assault infantry were kept at full war strength, earmarked for operations against Liege. More importantly, they were assigned a powerful siege train of extraordinary siege mortars.

The Krupp works had designed a 420mm (16.2-inch) mortar that fired projectiles weighing over a ton. However, the mortar itself weighed 175 tons and could only move by railway, so it was hardly the offensive siege piece the Germans needed to crack Liege. As a result, a more mobile 42.6-ton version was designed that could move at 7km per hour on roads; these improved siege mortars could lob 800kg (1,760lb) shells a distance of around 9km.[5] Only five of these behemoths were ready in August 1914 and the Germans had to borrow four batteries of Austrian 305mm howitzers to augment the siege train. The Germans also deployed a few naval gun barrels in bespoke gun carriages, including the 380mm *Schwersteflachfeuer*. The need for a steady supply of heavy guns was a consequence of both the wealth of fortified objectives outlined for destruction in the overall strategic plan and the effect of barrel-wear on the largest guns: a 105mm howitzer could fire 10,000 rounds before barrel-wear began to affect accuracy but a 42cm howitzer would wear out after firing only 100 shells. The fire-planning for these monsters was dominated by concepts developed by the coastal artillery, whose technical research into both ballistics and indirect artillery techniques was far in advance of anything developed by the field artillery. Many of these approaches had faded into obscurity before the war as increasing gun ranges made accuracy at sea problematic without complex and expensive mechanical computers, and a number of useful lessons were lost until similar challenges arose on the Western Front.

German troops crossed the Belgian border at dawn on 4 August and raced the 50km to Liege; by nightfall they were attacking Belgian pickets. The next day the Germans attempted to storm the forts with infantry, but they were mown down; General Bülow was thus forced to halt the Second Army while the cavalry and Emmich's Army of the Meuse commenced a grand encirclement of the city designed to both secure the lines of circum-vallation and isolate the individual forts. The Belgian troops between the forts recognised the danger and retreated, and by 7 August the gaps were large enough to enable Generalmajor Erich Ludendorff to lead a brigade of infantry into the centre of the town and capture the garrison commander; however, the forts continued to resist while they could. Unfortunately for the Belgians, the fort defences proved to be inadequate owing to the use of mediocre concrete – a fact the Germans did not trumpet at the time.[6] As the German mortars methodically hammered the isolated Belgian forts, a German battery commander described the effect of the heavy shells:

'The train is coming,' my telephone operator used to say. . . . Now it was time to direct the telescope upon the air just above the target; with a little practice the shell could be picked up in the air and the impact itself observed. . . . There was a quick flash, which we had learned at Kummersdorf [the German artillery testing range] to recognise as the impact of steel upon steel . . . Then an appreciable pause, during which the cupola seemed uninjured; then a great explosion . . . After a few minutes the smoke began to clear, and in place of the cupola we saw a black hole, from which dense smoke was pouring. Half the cupola stood upright, 50 metres away; the other half had fallen to the ground. The shell, fitted with a delayed action fuse, had exploded inside.[7]

The last of the Liege forts surrendered on 16 August, just as the Germans completed their mobilisation and deployment. In another ten days the Germans would be across Belgium, with the forts at Liege hardly hindering their advance. At the time the Germans crowed about their success but admitted they had not expected to penetrate the forts so quickly.[8] However, the Germans' ordinary 210mm (8.2-inch) mortars were almost as effective; the forts at Namur and Maubeuge were likewise crushed under their concentrated artillery fire.[9] These smaller shells did a fair amount of damage but they also demoralised the defenders, who must have feared to hear at any moment the roar of the terrifying Krupp mortars that had cracked Liege. By the end of the first phase of the Schlieffen Plan, the consensus was that the pre-war fort designs had performed poorly when pitted against the German onslaught.

There is no doubt that the Belgian forts were outdated; designed to withstand shellfire from black-powder artillery, they were helpless against the more modern and powerful shells. Obsolete weapons are often of little use, and obsolete forts proved more of a hazard to the defender because they were obvious targets and their outdated guns lacked the firepower to keep any attacker out of range. In the meantime the Germans had achieved what they had hoped for: the door to Belgium was open, their supply lines were clear for the Schlieffen Plan to start, and the 'Guns of August' had established their fearsome reputation.

Germany and France – 'right but repulsive' versus 'wrong but romantic'
In contrast to the huge siege guns, the German field gun assigned to the infantry divisions (the 77mm FK 96 n/a) was technically less formidable than the French 75mm or the British 18-pounder but was supported at the divisional level by an effective light howitzer, the 105mm FH 98/09.

German field gunners were expected to support any assault as closely as their opponents but the howitzer gunners were given basic instructions in how to conceal their positions (in defilade) and how to utilise the successful indirect fire methods that German liaison officers had witnessed in the Russo-Japanese War.

Unlike the Entente powers, the Germans intended to dedicate a proportion of their artillery to counter-battery missions, thus neutralising the enemy's artillery before the decisive infantry attack: the so-called 'gunners' duel'.[10] Counter-battery fire had proved effective in 1870 though the prewar regulations reminded artillery officers to keep close to the infantry to maintain close support: 'our own infantry [should] never have to do without the support of the artillery. Therefore, the artillery must not, in decisive moments, avoid even the heaviest infantry fire.'[11] To enable more effective close support at divisional level, from 1876 onwards the German Field Service Instructions stipulated that batteries should be organised into larger formations on the battlefield so that a higher commander could concentrate his guns more closely and perhaps decisively. Shrapnel shells, fired from the new generation of quick-firing guns, might not destroy a gun in a defilade position but were likely to kill gunners and horses out in the open, and this meant that counter-battery fire had to start at the range at which these projectiles became effective against the infantry (in 1914, between 5,000 and 7,000 yards); the Germans decided that the most practical solution was to use field guns to support the infantry and longer-ranged howitzers to eliminate the defender's batteries once enemy positions were identified.

At corps and army level the German military retained far larger numbers of heavy guns than their opponents, though these were usually assigned to the infantry divisions as soon as the operational *schwerpunkt* (decisive point) was identified. At corps level they deployed four heavy batteries of modern 150mm howitzers, the most effective heavy gun of the early years of the Great War.[12] It is important to note that howitzers fired a substantially more powerful shell than the field guns; on average a medium howitzer hurled twice the amount of high explosive a far greater distance, and with greater accuracy, for the same weight of gun carriage as the basic field gun. As described above, the Schlieffen Plan required the German army to smash through a range of enemy defences and established fortifications, and this requirement gave them a major advantage once the *grabenkrieg* ('war of the ditches') began. Yet much like the Entente powers, the Germans had no clear doctrine for dealing with a major European opponent armed with modern weapons, and their ammunition reserves were inadequate for a sustained conflict – as Bethmann-Hollweg, the German Chancellor noted, the coming war would be 'decisive – a brief storm'. Much of the German artillery doctrine was as outdated as that of any other army mobilising in August 1914: pre-war training still focused on mobility and gunnery deployment on manoeuvres still shared many characteristics with the cavalry. Much of the field artillery was expected to support the infantry closely, firing over open sights. These limitations were outweighed by the fact that detailed pre-war planning gave Germany more effective battlefield tools, in large enough concentrations, to allow her to dominate her opponents in the initial engagements.

The Germans thus had a technical edge over the Entente powers in the first few months of the war and this priceless advantage was maintained once the front line stabilised and Falkenhayn ordered the armies in the west to go on to the defensive while the Russian threat was addressed. In the west the German army focused on improving its defensive tactics and field fortifications, while on the Eastern Front they sought to capitalise on the greater opportunities for manoeuvre (and Russian technical and organisational weaknesses), with artillery proving the weapon most capable of counter-acting Russia's numerical advantage. German soldiers soon discovered ways of improving their survival chances against the weaker Allied barrages of the first months of the war, and the poor coordination of their opponent's infantry and artillery usually gave them more than enough time to get from the dugouts and bunkers to their assigned positions in the defensive system.

The training of German artillery officers was more focused on tactics than on the technology available to their batteries and this made them far more open to new ways of utilising innovative ideas and to developing ways of collaborating with the infantry.[13] This was a cultural advantage that was to give the Germans an edge in innovation until their opponents developed their own unique approaches to developing, collating and disseminating new ideas. Artillery officers were expected to understand the wider plan and adapt their own actions to support their overall commander's intentions. Their commanders were also given far more latitude during an evolving engagement, enabling them to adapt far more rapidly to a changing situation than their equivalents in other armies and to assign batteries to missions as required instead of having dedicated units. When firepower needed to massed, the operating division's artillery commander concentrated all the available batteries on the *schwerpunkt*; as Graf von Haslingen noted in 1910, 'if it is established where the decisive attack is directed, the artillery must place an overpowering fire there'.[14]

One deadly addition to Germany's formidable arsenal was the *minenwerfer* (mine launcher). This weapon was created specifically to deal with heavy fortifications after an analysis of the siege of Port Arthur suggested the need for a close-quarter infantry support weapon for clearing strongpoints, machine-gun posts and barbed wire. The first heavy variant, developed by the army's *Ingenieurkomitee*, was a 250mm weapon developed in 1910; a total of 44 of these deadly devices were available to the armies invading Belgium in 1914. These static but radically simplified muzzle-loading monsters gave the German army additional firepower against heavy defences in a deliberate attack, laying down shells that were relatively short-ranged but needing a carriage only a tenth the size of a howitzer firing a similar-sized shell. A medium (170mm) *minenwerfer* was ordered in 1913 and 116 of these were assigned to engineer units in 1914. The low muzzle velocity allowed the use of more powerful explosives than conventional guns and less expensive shell cases. Faced with an evolving *Stellungskrieg* ('fortress or positional war'), the Germans ordered vast numbers of *minenwerfer* from commercial suppliers but the delivery of significant quantities would take time and the engineers were often forced to jury-rig their own versions for immediate use, often working with designs that would have been familiar to medieval siege engineers.

Before the war the French army had developed a range of doctrines based upon the Gallic tradition of offensive élan on the battlefield. In theory, the predicted *offensive à l'outrance* would combine the latest advances in technology with the moral superiority of the French soldier when advancing on the enemy. The grand theorists included notable lecturers from the *Ecole Supérieure De Guerre*, such as Grandmaison and Foch, but the artillery contribution to the concept was far more sophisticated than is often portrayed by historians. General Hippolyte Langois, writing in 1892, saw the development of light artillery weapons, using the latest advances in quick-firing, as a natural complement to, and not a replacement for, what he saw as uniquely French approaches to the modern battlefield. If his broad thesis was correct, then the advance guards, coordinating with the artillery, would identify the enemy dispositions and hinder their deployment. The artillery would then dominate the enemy batteries, deluging them with a superior rate of fire. Once the enemy artillery was reduced in number, the French artillery would wear down the enemy infantry and then support the decisive attack.

While Langois rightly saw liaison as the key to success, he assumed that communication problems would require the artillery to operate within line of sight of the enemy and, where possible, to be deployed upon nearby high ground. Broadening his analysis, he noted that 'speed is the key quality for the attacker' and guns would thus need to be light as well as quick-firing so that they could be rapidly manoeuvred to the decisive sector of the battle-field; heavier guns would take longer to get into position and the relative weight of shells arriving on target within a given period would be reduced because larger shells took longer to load.[15] It was thus essential that the infantry had quick-firing field guns instead of relying on the relatively inaccurate (when compared to field guns firing over open sights) howitzers to get into position, thus enabling French commanders to retain the initiative in a rapidly evolving battlefield environment.[16]

When the famed *Mademoiselle Soixante-Quinze* (the 75) was introduced, it appeared to satisfy all of the operational requirements of the Langois model. It was the most advanced quick-firing field piece in the world, despite the seventeen-year lapse for imitators to catch up. With both a highly efficient 'long recoil' system (enabling the barrel to recoil and recuperate without disrupting the gun carriage) and an innovative breech mechanism, it could fire up to 12 rounds a minute without the gun being repositioned (it is estimated that a group of three batteries of four guns each could saturate 12 hectares with 100 shells a minute), and at rapid-fire it could fire 20 rounds per minute – so fast that it needed automatic fuse-setting gear. The 75 had poor elevation and fired a relatively light shell (weighing only 5.5kg) but even with these disadvantages, bursts of fire (*rafales*) from it were assumed to be sufficient to demoralise the enemy. With the 75 providing overwhelming firepower, the artillery was now expected to prepare for the attack with covering fire and then directly support the infantry (*appuyer l'infanterie*) as they dashed forwards with typical Gallic panache to inevitable victory.[17] This approach was summed up in a 1913 report entitled 'The Conduct of Large Units', which noted sagely that

> of all great nations, the military history of France offers the most striking examples of the great results that are produced by a war of attack, as well as the disasters which are brought about in a war which is conducted in a waiting attitude. Developed by us almost to the point of perfection, the doctrine of the offensive has won for us the most glorious successes . . . The passive defence is doomed to certain defeat; it is to be absolutely precluded.[18]

The French could outperform the German 77mm field gun, but as soon as heavier guns were deployed and commenced counter-battery fire, the 75 simply didn't have the range or the shell-weight to reply effectively. This oversight is particularly unfortunate when one notes that the pre-war Regulations for Service in the Field reminded officers that artillery was more effective in enfilade, firing, at inevitably longer ranges, into the flank of the enemy's 'centre of resistance'.[19] Even if the batteries were positioned directly behind the front line, the relatively light shell would make little impact on enemy entrenchments and none at all on the deeper bunkers.

The support for the 75 was at least as political as it was doctrinal. Reports of the increasing effectiveness of infantry firepower were ascribed to the inferior quality of the attacking troops – reports from the Russo-Japanese War even suggested that gun-shields made close support viable against rifles and machine guns – and the problems with communication were spun to show that the French doctrine was inherently more flexible than less audacious approaches to conducting operations. Where heavy guns were demonstratively superior, critics airily noted that it would be difficult to supply them with enough shells to influence the battle, commenting that the expenditure of ammunition at Port Arthur 'exceeded all expectations'.[20] In 1913 De Lamothe, who was closely involved in pre-war technical development, dismissed a new design for a 135mm howitzer: 'heavy cannon, encumbering and weakly provisioned, which will march in the rear of the columns . . . will be reserved for attack on large fortified positions'.[21]

When German developments appeared to undermine the central tenets of the Langois model, Joffre, while reviewing his command as Chief of Staff in 1911, presented a memorandum that suggested a light field howitzer to counter the German medium and heavy batteries.[22] Joffre wanted each corps to have its own artillery reserve but the *3ème Direction* of the *Etat Major De l'Armee* (General Staff) argued against his suggestion, citing a range of reports showing the 75 outperforming all other weapons; thus far fewer field howitzers were available in 1914 than Joffre had hoped.

In 1913 the French belatedly attempted to adapt their existing doctrine to allow for the analysis of recent conflicts and new technologies. Contrary to the assumptions of the *offensive à l'outrance*, the new recommendations noted that 'the power of the present armament makes any attack in dense formation delivered in daytime over open terrain impossible', and 'when the enemy has been able to arrange all his means of action, on terrain which he has organised, the general conduct of the engagement must be methodical'. The new guidance continued to focus on supporting the attack directly but noted the importance of ensuring 'convergence of effort' through effective liaison. The latter was assumed to include both direct coordination of the infantry and artillery and the wider dissemination of tactical and operational intelligence. The tactical notes also included sections on using terrain, the concealment of infantry and artillery positions and basic fortification. In theory, these ideas gave the French a doctrinal advantage over both their allies and their opponents – but the ideas were not widely disseminated. There were no central training schools that could evaluate and pass on the new approaches to battlefield planning, particularly to the junior officers and NCOs who would be essential to the success of the new system. Most senior officers were convinced that the pre-1913 regulations continued to have utility, a 'community of viewpoint' that enhanced *esprit de corps* but led to a focus on the already established 'unity of doctrine' that appeared to centre on France's instinctive advantage over the Teutonic horde.[23] Crucially the politicians were behind the 75 and the *offensive à l'outrance*, one breathtakingly pompous deputy remarking to his colleagues in 1908: 'you talk to us of heavy artillery. Thank God, we have none. The strength of the French Army is in the lightness of its guns.'[24]

By 1914 only a few officers recognised the risk of placing far too much reliance on one weapon system.[25] Henri Philippe Pétain was one of the officers convinced that the *offensive à l'outrance* was doomed by improvements in firepower and he gained a number of enemies when he expounded on his heretical ideas at the *École de Guerre* between 1901 and 1911. While watching part of the 1913 manoeuvres being conducted without artillery preparation, Pétain laconically observed that, 'I am sure that General Le Gallet intended, the better to impress you, to present a synthesis of all of the mistakes that a modern army should not commit . . . Let us first crush the enemy with artillery fire, and afterwards we shall win our victory.' Pétain's sarcastic certainty won him few friends and did little to advance the cause of innovation in artillery tactics. His truism, *le feu tue* (fire kills), should have served as a counterpoint to the ideas of Grandmaison but instead identified him as an officer with few prospects. Petain's opportunity would have to wait until the casualties proved his point but his tendency towards overconfidence in his own analysis would bear bitter fruit during the Second World War.[26]

Where heavier weapons were already available, they were still relegated to siege batteries to work with the specialist engineers or stored in fortresses. Fréderic-Georges Herr, an enthusiastic advocate of heavy artillery operations, ruefully noted as the war clouds gathered that 'it is quite rare that anyone thinks to make an allusion to their method of employment and their consequences for the final success'.[27] This reluctance to consider the utility of heavier guns is all the more remarkable when one considers that France's two main competitors during the early twentieth century, Britain and Germany, had both developed a range of modern heavy guns. Germany deployed 3,500 heavy guns in 1914 to France's 544 mostly obsolete field pieces. These few guns were organised into only five field regiments, totalling 308 artillery pieces, and none of these units was equipped with anything more modern than the Rimailho 155mm howitzer (1904).[28] The mortars were even more primitive, with some of the designs dating back to the 1870s.

In the first battles of 1914 the 75 caused devastation when it was properly employed, but the French soon discovered the effectiveness of German counter-battery fire. Under fire from howitzers, batteries of 75s were often withdrawn leaving the infantry to the less than gentle ministrations of the German 77mm field batteries.[29] Mysteriously, considering the doctrine of rapid fire, French stocks of ammunition in 1914 were relatively small, roughly 3,000 rounds per gun or 4 hours of firing at the maximum rate – an amazingly short-sighted policy decision considering the 75 was intended to be a rapid-fire weapon.[30]

Shellfire inflicted far higher casualties than had been predicted before the war and while the French saw hostile infantry as a primary target and recognised (before both their allies and their opponents) that local commanders needed to control key reserves, they neglected to realise the impact of German counter-battery fire, inflicted by heavy batteries directed by the officer responsible for the sector, on their own artillery. Foch, in August 1914, noted with some bitterness, 'the intense artillery fire, including that of heavy pieces, [that was] able to select emplacements that our artillery couldn't reach (when we ourselves attacked) . . . and the occasions when the progress of our attacks faltered in the face of artillery fire that our guns couldn't silence'. As a result of the weakness in heavy guns, the French infantry were pounded far harder than their allies in the early years of the war.[31] It is notable that the first big allied victory, on the Marne, occurred after the Germans had been forced to leave behind much of their horse-drawn heavy artillery support.

In the initial encounters the Germans proved demonstrably more skilful in using aviation to support artillery and the French infantry 'clearly had no conception of any necessity for waiting for artillery support'. A report dated 24 August, betraying an understandable level of exasperation from the *Grand Quartier Général* (GQG), noted that 'every time a strong point is to be taken, the attack must be prepared by artillery' and reminded the reader that this meant 'serious preparation'. Pascal Lucas suggests that the French army found repugnant the idea of digging in and regarded siege warfare as a specialist activity, remarking that few officers were even aware of the *Instruction on the Service of Artillery in Siege Warfare* of 1913 and even fewer recognised that the methodical ideas of the sappers and foot artillery offered lessons that might apply in the field.[32]

After experiencing for themselves the deadly effects of dedicated counter-battery fire, the French realised that this was a separate and dedicated mission for the artillery, and the First Artillery Programme of October 1914 saw the emergency redeployment of both existing (obsolete) heavy guns and new batteries of 105mm howitzers to this role while the Second Artillery Programme of November in the same year accelerated the production of 155s to provide a longer-ranged weapon.[33] Unfortunately, heavy casualties among trained staff officers meant that there were too few qualified officers available to discuss and pass on new doctrines to existing units, a problem shared by the rapidly expanding British army. Inevitably, the evolution of counter-battery techniques proceeded at a glacial pace – far too slowly to make a contribution to the first French offensives in Arras and in Champagne. Part of the problem was that enthusiastic proponents of *offensive à outrance* continued to dominate GQG.[34] As members of Joffre's staff, these individuals retained their influence and thus played a leading role in operational planning despite relations between GQG and the generals becoming increasingly strained.

A major problem for the French was that the heavy guns initially sent to reinforce the corps and army reserves were slow-firing weapons that couldn't hope to match the more modern German guns. After years of depending on destructive fire-missions by field gun batteries, the French found themselves forced to rely on an extended artillery preparation before launching an infantry assault as soon as they faced elaborate trench systems – an expedient that enabled accurate registration and what was seen as an acceptable level of destruction of pre-identified targets but also ensured that the Germans had plenty of warning of an imminent infantry attack.

The German deployment of *minenwerfer* impressed the French and they started evaluating equivalents of the new weapons. Joffre had personally noted their existence before the war began but had failed to convince his colleagues to authorise the necessary tests and development work which would have placed France on an equal footing with Germany. The earliest improvised versions were based upon nineteenth-century designs but the French soon started adapting their pre-war 80mm guns and introduced a spigot mortar in 1915 (the spigot meant that the explosives were above the barrel) that they called the *lance mines Gatard*. These basic mortars were useful but utterly outclassed and further designs were introduced and issued to the newly raised units of *artillerie de tranche*.[35]

French and German ideas collide: the battles in Alsace and Lorraine

A week before the British fought at Le Cateau, the French had already engaged large forces in Alsace and Lorraine, in the Battles of the Frontiers. These two provinces featured heavily in French war plans, not only because they had been lost after the Franco-Prussian War but because the French army was forbidden to breach Belgian neutrality. Wedded to attacking, and denied the opportunity to try a flank move, the French were determined to plunge straight ahead. The French army was organised and trained for conducting rapid attacks. Each division had twelve battalions (in four three-battalion regiments) and 36 guns, consisting of nine four-gun batteries in a *groupe* of three battalions. The two–division corps had four more battalions of 75s to reinforce wherever desired. Advance guards, coordinating with some artillery, were designed to identify the enemy dispositions and hinder their deployment. The artillery would then smother the enemy batteries, deluging them with a superior rate of fire. Once the enemy artillery was reduced, the French artillery would overwhelm the enemy infantry. This would open the way for the French infantry to charge without needing prolonged firefights to gain superiority before moving forwards. The artillery would open the door and the infantry would charge, with limited tactical nuance or training needed. Instead, the red-trousered infantry (*les pantalons rouge c'est la France!*), behind white-gloved officers with sabres, would fix bayonets and sweep forwards. This concept was hopelessly anachronistic but it was attempted again and again – with predictable results.[36]

The Germans, in contrast, were more pragmatic in both their training and their doctrine.[37] They had realistic training grounds and preached the heretical creed of tactical entrenchment. Their infantry divisions had the same organisation as the French, but one-third more field guns (because the Germans rightly assessed their 77mm gun as weaker than the French 75) and a battalion of 105mm field howitzers. The Germans had also recognised how fire and movement might work with modern weapons deployed:

skirmishers would find the enemy positions; infantry reinforcements, machine guns and guns would increase the pressure on those positions; and once the defenders were beaten down the decisive advance would begin. Doctrine made clear that troops should be aggressive but not hasty. As noted above, the heavy field howitzers, initially only sixteen per two-division infantry corps, were intended for counter-battery fire at the decisive-point of the attack.

The French troops had mobilised and concentrated according to Plan XVII, and now went into action. The first move was on Mulhouse, a small town on the upper Rhine. Two French divisions plus a cavalry division advanced cautiously and carelessly occupied the town before quickly retreating. Sloppy tactical reconnaissance failed to find the German infantry in the woods, an error that was symptomatic of French troops drilled for parade-ground warfare. The corps commander and the cavalry commander were duly sacked, the first of hundreds. Doctrine and training could not be changed as easily as the leaders and they would cause many more French casualties; the first month alone saw 260,000.[38] Mulhouse was only intended to secure the flank of the main French attack. First and Second Armies (totalling 21 divisions) were to drive northeast and clear the Germans from Morhange and Sarrebourg (Metz, a more strategic city, was seen as being too heavily fortified). This French move actually suited the Germans, who needed the French to be busy (and away from the intact railway lines) while the Schlieffen Plan unrolled across Belgium. While there were roughly equal German forces in the area, they were deployed back from the frontier to pull the French in.

Defensive detachments – some local reservists and *landwehr* – sometimes gave the French a bloody nose but were occasionally outflanked and captured. The Germans were typically entrenched and had good artillery support, the French often reporting they were outranged. However, it is more probable that the flat-trajectory 75s were unable to hit German guns and howitzers positioned on reverse slopes (i.e. behind hills), but regard-less, the 75s were away from the infantry they were supposed to be supporting. Reports came back that French attacks were being stopped by enemy fire: 'Our infantry has attacked with élan, but they have been halted primarily by enemy artillery fire and by unseen enemy infantry hidden in trenches.' The Second Army commander reported that attacks needed to be carefully prepared with infantry and artillery cooperation. This was hardly revolutionary (it was noticed on the second day of the fighting) but the pity is that it needed to be said at all. All Joffre could do was praise his infantry while saying that attacks would be even more effective (and less costly) if they were carefully prepared.

German troops were able to dodge French shellfire by pulling back into nearby woods (where French observers typically assumed that the Germans were *hors de combat*) or out of sight behind hills. The terrain also discouraged a rapid advance, with obstacles splitting the French columns.[39] Roads followed the valleys and the French infantry, under orders to advance quickly, rarely probed the wooded hills. As they advanced the French had to spread out, First Army heading in a more easterly direction and Second Army northerly. If that were not enough, three additional divisions were pulled from Second Army and switched to positions further north – which was exactly what the Germans wanted to prevent. After a week of advancing, the French arrived at the Germans' main defensive line around Saarebourg.

So poor was the French reconnaissance (and so blind their faith in their offensive plans) that they assumed the Germans were retreating. Fresh units of French infantry charged forwards again on 19 August. Private Frank Dolbau recalled: 'At our first battle at Morhange on the 19th of August, unsupported by artillery, against heavily fortified positions, we had attacked. We were shot down like rabbits because you know for them we were a real target, as we had red trousers on. When we were fired at we were like sitting ducks in the field.'[40] The division fed into the attack had been in reserve the day before, but this only meant that it was behind the line and had to make a night march before the planned dawn attack. Attacking at 04:00 without scouts, they overran the German picket line and pushed a mile up the Sarre valley. Then they hit the German main line, encountering entrenched infantry, machine guns, and pre-planned artillery fire to cover a long, open slope. The French were easily beaten off; they fell back and temporarily regrouped out of the artillery's main killing zone. By midmorning the Germans had formulated their new counter-attack plans and disseminated them; the heavier guns could still reach the French and the howitzers pummelled them before the German infantry pushed forwards. The French withdrew into Sarrebourg and the Germans, instead of bypassing the town, fought an expensive street battle but the French advance was over. They withdrew in decent order from Sarrebourg, but that was not what anyone had in mind. A little to the left, in the woods, two French regiments had taken their initial objectives, one by infiltration and one by bayonet charges, but they too came up against solid German lines (and artillery) and the third regiment could make no progress whatsoever.

Once they had consolidated their position, the Germans pressed forwards. It may have been too early (the Schlieffen Plan needed the French attacking into Lorraine) but the French were already withdrawing troops. The French had treated Sarrebourg as a local problem, and were stunned that the Germans were attacking there – judging by his journal, so was Joffre.[41] The 5am German bombardment contributed to their success and two French corps were in full retreat by nightfall. They had been defeated by roughly equal numbers, although the attacks were not tidy affairs: confused infantry abounded and their befuddled artillery shelled anything that moved. The Germans also captured a number of 75s.

The Germans pressed forwards, trying to pin down (or even destroy) the French forces so that they could not redeploy against the northern armies but they gained little ground and the action only increased the casualty lists on both sides; both sides wisely pulled troops from Lorraine for the critical sector further north as the Battle of the Marne unfolded. We need not review those operations and battles, since there were no significant developments for artillerymen except that almost everyone was finally recognising how crucial the guns were in both attack and defence, and both sides were increasingly deploying their supporting batteries far behind the front line to avoid counter-battery fire.

'Proper Soldiering': The Royal Artillery and the British Expeditionary Force

The Royal Artillery was organised to enable the British and Imperial army to fight across a range of battlefields and this led to an eclectic mix of weapons that left the British marginally under-equipped compared to the Germans but far more flexible than the French. The British army's experience in the Second Boer War had an enormous influence on its artillery doctrine, both John Du Cane and William Furse arguing that the quick-firing artillery revolution meant that indirect fire was now the dominant form; artillery casualties at Colenso were often cited to illustrate the danger of operating over open sights within range of enemy rifles. Ian Hamilton's *A Staff Officer's Scrapbook* on the Russo-Japanese War supported the view that artillery was becoming increasingly important in the battlefield but this insight was not reflected in army doctrine. The most important criticism, by Douglas Haig and others, was that communication on a mobile battlefield made indirect fire support problematic. The artillery had no champion in the General Staff and the highly flexible but chaotic structure of British brigades (collections of battalions drawn from many regiments) and the regimental system undermined combined arms approaches to training.

The three brigades of 18-pounders (each of 18 guns) gave the British a highly effective weapon; it was supported by a single battery of the far larger 60-pounders (usually dedicated to counter-battery fire) and a brigade of 4.5-inch howitzers. At GHQ level the British deployed some elderly 6-inch howitzers as the basis of a battering train but the need for heavier guns had been recognised and a formidable 9.2-inch howitzer design was in the pre-production stage in 1914. The technical manuals were impressive but the doctrine for using them was remarkably sketchy, as demonstrated at Le Cateau, where even British artillery brigades in the same corps deployed in different ways. Unlike the Germans, who focused on the division's *schwer-punkt,* and the French, who assumed they could mass their artillery at corps level as part of a grand plan, the British outlined vaguely theoretical roles for higher-level artillery commanders and assigned their divisions a mixed bag of artillery and let divisional commanders come up with solutions.

Training was not helped by the batteries being dispersed in peacetime, with only 27 of the 50 artillery brigades garrisoned as a unified unit. The *Field Artillery Training* manual of 1914 mentioned 'war of movement' and 'positional wars' but failed to define either to the level required to actually coordinate artillery brigades. Coordination was assumed in the manual but not described and, as General Herr had noted in the French Army, artillery was seen as 'an accessory arm'.[42] To compound the problem of undefined planning, Royal Artillery commanders (CsRAs or CRAs) had minimal staffs and no clear role in the organisation of the division, often being assigned the role of training officer instead of advising the planners or co-ordinating the fire-plan. While the manual stated that 'indirect laying . . . is the normal method employed in the field', gunners were well aware that their main job was infantry support, regardless of method. Inevitably, the most detailed sections focused on the 'spirit of close support' and on the artillery 'entering the ring', noting with approval 'the moral effect of batteries advancing boldly'.[43]

As with the French and Germans, coastal artillery officers led the debate on accuracy but were rapidly dispersed among the new heavy batteries and the urgent requirement for new doctrinal and technical tools vanished as industry focused on increasing the rate of production of the guns themselves. Ideas about coordination, including a paper by J.F.C. Fuller in 1913 (and a demonstration of tactical fire-planning in the same year) showed that the British were exploring the potential impact of new technology but the process was incomplete by 1914. There was no organisation designed to examine and disseminate new doctrine. Inevitably this lack of doctrinal focus on continuous fire-support meant that the infantry were left to their own devices as soon as they advanced beyond the range of the initial bombardment, and misunderstandings about the utility of artillery in a long war delayed the testing and introduction of innovations such as communication equipment, targeting processes and the development of an effective HE round for the 18-pounder.

Captain Henry Hugh Tudor, one of the Great War's most remarkable artillery officers, bitterly criticised pre-war artillery methods. He wrote a series of articles for the *Journal of the Royal Artillery* advocating improvements in coordination, targeting and the use of meteorological tables to improve accuracy but most were refused publication. Frustrated, Tudor pointed out to his superiors that even the basic 18-pounder had unresolved technical issues over the untabulated performance characteristics of its two main variants of shrapnel shell, a problem made worse by poor range-tables and inadequate fuses. The increasingly choleric Ordnance Committee informed him that 'if I got any [more] cranky ideas I had better work them out myself', a letter to the Director of Artillery was returned unread and Tudor decided to use a public lecture at the Royal Artillery Institution to air his views but fluffed his lines and was booed. Undeterred, he wrote a paper for General Archibald Murray, then General Officer Commanding 2nd Division, on German approaches to heavy artillery doctrine, noting that mobility was often the cry in peacetime but in wartime the demand was for 'heavy metal'. More practically, he wrote an article for the Royal United Services Institute on the performance characteristics of British guns and howitzers and also created data cards for battery commanders on each type of gun and handed them out to anyone who would take them, including the instructors at both Lydd (the School of Siege Artillery) and Woolwich. Tudor argued for manoeuvres to improve infantry–artillery coordination as the threat of war loomed but admitted in his memoirs that money was scarce and the public were understandably reluctant to support the funds needed to properly prepare Britain for war. While Tudor was remarkably prescient, it is difficult to avoid the impression that, like Pétain, his waspish personality alienated many of his colleagues.[44]

Even in 1914 the Royal Artillery was capable of some remarkable feats of innovation in artillery techniques but lacked the institutional structures and equipment to absorb lessons from other forces on the Western Front or to test and disseminate new methods. When the equipment was available and the officer was resourceful, the Royal Artillery demonstrated an impressive ability to innovate under fire. Lieutenant A.G. Bates can plausibly claim to be the first forward observation officer to call in a successful predicted indirect fire mission, using just a map and compass. Unable to observe his target directly, but equipped with one of the few accurate maps of the region, he coordinated his battery's initial fire missions on to German units crossing the bridge at Le Ferté Sous Jouarre during the Battle of the Marne.[45]

The British experience in 1914 was one of increasing frustration with the scale of the problem faced by the BEF. Most continental armies were no better equipped to fight a trench war than Britain's, but the British also had to contend with managing a massive expansion of the army at the same time as her experienced cadre of non-commissioned officers and specialists was bled dry on the Western Front. This became ever more important as the front line stabilised and the initial trench system was replaced by a more complex defensive system designed to resist artillery bombardment; it was protected by line after line of barbed-wire entanglements, draped like a murderous iron cobweb between the combatants, and secured by ever more complex networks of machine-gun posts and bunkers.

Above the Common Herd: Russia's Artillery

Although Russia produced a workmanlike, if cumbersome, field gun (the M1902 76.2mm Putilov) to support her infantry divisions, in contrast to the other combatants many of Russia's most modern field guns and howitzers were imported models and included weapons from France, Germany and Britain. Trapped by the same assumptions about impregnable fortresses that constrained some of the French and Belgian theorists, the Russian general staff (STAVKA) kept 2,813 modern heavy guns and 3,000 obsolete weapons in their border forts while only 240 were assigned to the field armies – transferring these guns to more mobile commands in the event of war was complicated by the fact that many of them were designed for static garrison mountings (including a number of Krupp-made 280mm guns purchased from the Japanese). Just before the commencement of hostilities, as part of the Great Programme for Strengthening the Army of 1913, Russia's heavy artillery reserve of eight pre-war field artillery brigades was reorganised into batteries of six guns. These reforms did not proceed smoothly, as the eight gun batteries of the Russo-Japanese War had provided ample opportunities for the traditional process of promotion by seniority and the smaller establishment was seen as an attempt to radically narrow the field for ambitious officers and as a way of giving positions to individuals with a lower-class background.

The Russian Artillery Committee was dubious about the role of howitzers in battle, implying in one report that such devices were a 'coward's weapon'. While the technical staff of the Artillery Officers' School made impressive advances in indirect fire techniques, attempts to get the infantry's view into the committee's more general discussions were adroitly dealt with by drowning all discussion in technical language and ensuring the relevant statutes left the artillery independent from interference at the highest level, allowing only direct collaboration with individual batteries. Further complicating this situation, the Russian artillery did not have a happy relationship with the infantry. It would not be an exaggeration to say that the humble infantryman was usually despised by his more educated counterpart in the artillery, the latter often seeing little purpose in collaborating with mere 'cattle'.[46] As soon as the Russian army mobilised, new heavy artillery batteries were established to support the freshly created infantry corps being marched resolutely westwards.

Karl H. von Wiegand, the Berlin correspondent of the United Press during the early encounters, noticed that the Russian artillery performed poorly when preparing for an attack, even when assisted by airborne observers.[47] On the Eastern Front both sides had roughly 8,000 guns by the end of 1914, while in the West 11,000 German guns faced 18,000 Entente weapons.[48]

Fighting on the Eastern Front shared many of the characteristics seen in the Western theatre but key differences emerged in the initial fighting in East Prussia. The Russian artillery received a disproportionately large share of educated enlisted men[49] and many bourgeois artillery officers considered their branch to be a technical elite.[50] The Russians had little heavy artillery outside their fortresses and even fewer howitzers – although that was due to a belief that indirect fire was less brave than direct fire and thus howitzers were therefore less soldierly compared to guns. The bright spot was the provision of modern field guns. The 76mm field gun, accepted in 1902, was fully fielded by 1911; the 122mm howitzer for corps and 152mm howitzer for armies were adopted in 1910, although fielding these guns would take time and the initial deployments were on a small scale. The average corps had only a single battery of 122mm howitzers and, while they threw a heavier shell than the German divisional 105s, there were fewer of them. The Russo-Japanese War had taught painful lessons about the effectiveness of indirect fire, and the Russians could do it (sometimes surprising the Germans in 1914)[51] but the infantry disliked such methods as the guns were less effective when firing indirectly and because the infantry resented the guns when they were not seen to be in a direct fire support role, creating further problems coordinating infantry and artillery.[52] STAVKA had forecast a short war and thus their reserves of shells were low, at around 1,000 per gun. The Russians had also largely ignored their reserve units, and their reserve divisions were thus sadly short of artillery, averaging only two batteries (16 guns) per sixteen battalions.

In 1914 the Russians advanced aggressively into East Prussia. For generations they had planned to defend in central Poland, partly due to a healthy regard for the quality of the German army. They had built a belt of fortifications in Poland and Lithuania, and had also deliberately left the border roads in poor condition.[53] The alliance with France had changed their overall strategy, and economic developments (and increasing confidence in the quality of their own forces) led STAVKA to contemplate seizing the initiative. The 1914 plan was inevitably the product of this shift in strategy with the initial attack coming from mobilisation areas that were safely behind the border; this meant they were far away from any potentially disruptive German strike, but inevitably left supply depots far away from the potential operational area.

The Russian army was also in the midst of overhauling its logistics systems, which were mediocre to begin with. The confusion of mobilisation did not help. When the Russians advanced (First Army under Rennenkampf would advance from Lithuania on 17 August, while Second Army under Samsonov mobilised around Warsaw and crossed the border on 22 August), they would face not only basic supply problems, but also increasing distances from their rail lines, inadequate roads and even poor farmland where there was little that could be foraged. Rennenkampf's army was quicker off the mark (it was both closer to the border and operating over better roads) and hit the Germans at Stalluponen. It was a short, sharp battle and had little result, but the Russian guns that were engaged quickly ran out of shells. (One Russian infantry regiment fired over 800,000 rounds of small-arms ammunition, and its supporting artillery fired 10,000 rounds – it was an impressive amount of firepower, but it would have exhausted the ammunition wagons of a whole corps.)[54] Rennenkampf telegraphed back that he needed over 125,000 shells to maintain operational momentum.[55] All the pre-war planners had advocated mobility and one way to achieve this was to carry fewer shells; in theory this meant fewer wagons (and thus fewer horses) clogging the roads behind the advance. As long as the supply lines were adequate, depots in the rear could feed the guns, and despite marching for a week before contacting the Germans the Russian

First Army was assumed to be close enough to the depots. In contrast, the German Eighth Army was reeling backwards, bewildered by the shock of real battle and unnerved by the threat of Samsonov advancing northwards from Poland to cut them off. When General von Prittwitz momentarily lost his nerve and planned a retreat, he unwisely shared his plans with the Great General Staff. Instant communications by telegraph were his undoing and the reply to his momentary panic was dismissal: a retired general named Hindenburg would be his replacement and an experienced officer, Erich Ludendorff, was assigned as his Chief of Staff.

The Germans still had to respond to the threat from Samsonov. A masterly redeployment of the entire army, initiated by Colonel Max Hoffmann, used the interior railways instead of roads but the Germans also took risks and stripped some troops away from fortresses. The strategy proved highly effective and enabled the Germans to break away from Rennenkampf's struggling army. Russian units were disorganised, and when cavalry reconnaissance reported a German retreat, they wasted time bringing up a siege train to crack the fortress at Konigsberg.[56] The net result was a slow and cautious advance by First Army.

Even without battle, Second Army had suffered. The long march (roughly 115 miles[57] in a week) had led to straggling, and the poorly organised supply trains had exacerbated the situation by forcing troops to disperse and forage. Scouting was poor – Rennenkampf was not alone in having sub-standard cavalry scouts – and troops and officers were nervous (of course, with the Germans redeploying, they had reason to be, but all they knew was that they were heading into the unknown with open flanks.) This led to rumours and, when a flurry of shots halted a patrol, the report came back that it was German civilians rather than troops.[58] Larger forces were deliberately left in the rear and reserve divisions were told to guard the flanks and supply lines; in the event so many troops were detached that Samsonov ended up with fewer guns in the front line than the Germans (he managed to scatter roughly 400 guns out of his original complement of 1,160). Most crucially, he was at the end of a tenuous supply line.[59]

When the German troops finally re-established contact with the Russians (the lines on maps are often deceptively simple, and the tired, hot, footsore infantry were marching through unknown fields and forests), they actually had more strength at the decisive point. Samsonov had spread out his forces to cover his exposed flanks and the Germans had slightly better intelligence and far better communications links (both physical, i.e. roads and railways, and electronic, i.e. telephone and telegraph lines) so they were able to coordinate their movements and concentrate. Thanks to the use of older reservists, Hindenburg's forces outnumbered Samsonov's (including roughly 4:3 in guns[60]) and he was able to outflank the Russians as well as concentrating more combat power for a series of attacks.

When *I Korps* punched into the Russians, it was in a deliberate attack with a 4:1 advantage in guns overall, augmented by a substantially greater weight of metal thanks to the 105s and 150s.[61] The Russian trenches at Usdau were simple straight lines and lacked any overhead protection, such as dugouts, so shells could rake along them. Having already suffered painful infantry losses earlier in the campaign, *I Korps* now slowed down its advance and used its guns as a battering ram to both damage and demoralise the Russians.[62] Samsonov's Second Army, a confused force with dwindling supplies (by now the horses were low on fodder, affecting their ability to haul anything, and the troops were running short of rations),[63] buckled under a series of uncoordinated blows. Samsonov's whole army had only 25 telephones and 130km of wire;[64] the signal network, such as it was, only ran from front to back, with Samsonov tenuously connected to his corps commanders, who then could not telephone either their neighbours or their subordinates. The attacks continued for several days, a grim necessity given the size of the armies but the Germans had enough supporting artillery to leapfrog it forwards and maintain some momentum.[65] The Germans completed their counter-offensive with the capture of around 100,000 prisoners and 400 guns.[66]

The victory at Allenstein, an engagement that Hoffmann mischievously renamed Tannenberg, was not solely a question of logistics and intelligence; pushing the Russians back was not a simple matter, and with solid supply lines the Russians would have maintained their morale and had access to far more firepower. Since ammunition was the key to firepower, and railways were the key to ammunition supplies, the dictates of military geography had shifted. Armies now needed to stay close to railway lines (and in time they would build miles of light-gauge tracks) because of the ravenous appetite of the artillery. German units also benefited from having closer collaboration with their artillery and the Russians found that the German army was a far more cunning opponent than the Austro-Hungarians.

The strategic lesson learnt at Tannenberg was fairly straightforward, and few of the mistakes were repeated in the battles that followed. As Hindenburg was sending his victory telegram to the Kaiser, he was already redeploying his forces to face Rennenkampf. With Samsonov as a salutary lesson (and with better supply lines), Rennenkampf rapidly fell back under German pressure and the focus on the Eastern Front switched to the Austro-Hungarians and Russians sparring in Galicia.

Without a Coherent Strategy or the Tools to Fight: Austria-Hungary

In the Austro-Hungarian army the artillery was considered to be the province of intelligent but essentially bourgeois officers. As a result, the technical prowess of the artillery arm was taken for granted by successive Chiefs of Staff and the Austro-Hungarians started the war with moderate numbers of obsolete guns and far less practical experience than their opponents. The technical weaknesses were further exaggerated by delays in the fundamental reform of the artillery caused by the shrill insistence of the Hungarians on their own dedicated units and the continuous process of reorganisation which all too often descended into stopgaps that further weakened the artillery arm. At the same time the popular and institutional image of the artillery was dominated by the legend of the 'Battery of the Dead' at Sadawa in 1866, a wilfully misunderstood example of deployment too close to effective infantry fire that made emulation of the original battery's pointless sacrifice tragically inevitable in the brutal first encounters in 1914. The impact of this event magnified the commonly held pre-war assumption that the artillery should provide close support for the infantry and elevated what military logic suggested was irrational stubbornness in the face of overwhelming fire into an unofficial doctrine sanctified by the blood of heroes.

The Empire's political complexity and resulting lack of funds forced her to update and improve on existing bronze technologies instead of expanding her domestic steel production. As a result, at the start of the Great War only one facility at Skoda was capable of turning out steel barrels. Much of the development and technical review work was conducted by the remarkably efficient *Technisches und Administratives Militär-Komitee* (TMK). Although the TMK rarely had the funds to put new designs into production, they encouraged companies to proffer designs and reviewed many more prototypes than any of the other major powers. Unusually, detailed specifications were only issued in reaction to key innovations abroad, thus allowing original solutions to emerge while maintaining technical parity with potential opponents. The problem was that while the Austro-Hungarians had lots of advanced designs ready to put into production, the units marching into battle in 1914 were under-equipped and Austro-Hungarian manufacturers were woefully unprepared to provide the guns and ammunition that the army desperately needed.[67]

Internal disputes with Hungary had led to the creation of a three-part army, the Hungarian *Honvéd*, the Austrian *Landwehr* and the *Kaiserlich und Königlich* (Imperial and Royal or Common Army). Reducing the political impact of the new Hungarian units on the artillery arm required the byzantine manoeuvre of reducing the guns per division across the entire army and assigning the extra guns to the corps artillery reserve so that they could remain under the exclusive control of the Common Army. This innovation, only partially reversed in the final months before the war, reduced battlefield effectiveness without appeasing the Hungarian nationalists. A brief flash of political sanity kept training under the control of the Common Army schools and this ensured that quality was maintained. Corps artillery was organised on the same lines as the field guns of the divisions, with six-gun batteries, but these units were equipped with howitzers. Mountain artillery, a vital asset in the Balkans and during any potential conflict with Italy, was organised into independent regiments that could be allocated to divisions or corps as required. Siege units were where the Austro-Hungarians allocated the most impressive product of the TMK's research programme, the formidable Skoda 30.5cm M.11 *Mörser* (siege howitzer). This massive weapon was originally designed to smash Italy's mountain fortresses and its huge blast on firing required the crew to take cover in nearby trenches. As noted above, the Germans soon found other uses for these guns as soon as it became apparent that Italy was staying out of the first phase of the war.

Austria-Hungary was probably the Great Power most firmly stuck in the nineteenth century, the Royal and Imperial Army still believing that firepower could be traded for moral qualities – leadership, discipline, morale and devotion. They were not entirely alone in this, for no army recognised how important firepower would become, but they were the most dramatic example of dislocation between national ideology and technology. The reasons for this confusion were mixed but largely the result of the Empire's fractured internal politics.[68] The military budget stagnated for years until 1912, when the outbreak of the Balkan Wars showed a need to actually do something, and an Army Bill was passed that was intended to increase the size of the army as well as funding more machine guns and more artillery (Austria had fewer guns per division than any other Great Power, and only in 1908 were the Austrian *Landwehr* and Hungarian *Honvéd* divisions actually allotted artillery).[69] Until the Army Bill, the basic problems of the military were maintaining existing manpower levels and purchasing modern equipment. Unfortunately for Austria-Hungary the new legislation came too late; it was not even designed to take full effect until 1915. Parliamentary wrangling was only part of the problem; the army itself underplayed firepower and technology in general.

The final pre-war exercises emphasised speed over firepower, with the rules sidelining artillery so much that the guns were often left behind in the rush to manoeuvre.[70] Annual training allotments were only about 250 rounds per field battery or 40 shells per gun – roughly 10 minutes' firing time.[71] Some units went to war without ever having fired a single live round, and even those crews who had learned how to fire their piece had observation officers who had never trained in indirect fire techniques.[72] Franz Conrad von Hötzendorf, the Chief of Staff, had risen to prominence on his reputation as a tactical expert (despite never commanding troops in combat), but he too underplayed the artillery. His analysis of the Franco-Prussian War claimed that artillery was not crucial to the results of every battle, and thus his decisions about the army focused on the infantry. While he did mention combined-arms work, he stressed the problems rather than advocating solutions. The 1911 regulations that were Austria's last pre-war opportunity to update doctrine featured the infantry advancing using their own firepower rather than effectively coordinating with the artillery. Infantry was seen as the dominant factor, with 'cooperation' essentially meaning the artillery doing what it was told – and taking the blame if that were not possible.

Austrian artillery equipment was a mixed bag.[73] The low budgets created by the unpopularity of military spending[74] interacted with sclerotic procurement cycles to delay modernisation. Austria had even bought what the authorities fondly assumed was a modern field artillery piece (based on spring-moderated carriage recoil rather than a recuperator) just before the French introduced the 75 and made all other artillery obsolete. Not only could the Austrians not afford new guns, it would have embarrassed the government to admit their mistake. Only in 1904 were quick-firing guns adopted, and even those were old-fashioned. They had bronze-steel barrels that were cheaper to manufacture but less strong and thus had a lower range; they also warped easily when hot, so the rate of fire was lower. The Austro-Hungarian field howitzers were equally obsolete, with 1899 models still in use; even the heavy field howitzers were out of date. Mountain guns were a minor bright spot; an excellent new design had been introduced, but only four of the 52 batteries had been re-equipped by 1914. Ammunition stocks were low even by comparison with rivals; field guns had about 500 rounds and howitzers 330, and most shells were shrapnel rather than high explosive. Manpower was also a problem. About 10 per cent of the army was artillery, but that included all training personnel and depots – and the artillery was about 12 per cent under-establishment, including static fortress artillery. The increased spending on Italian border fortresses raised the number of artillerymen but camouflaged the stagnant state of the mobile artillery. The army was forced to cut musicians and other non-combat personnel to bolster potential fighting strength in 1914. Even the excellent 30.5cm siege guns had been questioned in the Imperial Parliament. Conrad had approved these guns because of his inveterate distrust of Italy but their procurement had languished until the Balkan War crisis when the war minister finally ignored his parliament's furious attempts to delay the programme and ordered a dozen of these extremely useful pieces.

Strategically Austro-Hungary was caught between two opponents, Russia and Serbia.[75] There were thus two war plans, one for a war against Serbia alone and one for a two-front war. Both relied on an aggressive strategy; Austrian morale was assumed to be better than enemy morale and this advantage could be both exploited and improved by early victories. The plans depended on the final decision by the Chief of Staff, particularly the decision as to where to send the reserve force (the Second Army). In theory, it could either smother Serbia or drive into Russian Poland but it could not do both at the same time. Unfortunately for the Austrians, Conrad botched the decision and sent the Second Army south, then realised the Russians were advancing and had to wait for it to arrive before turning most units around and heading them into Galicia north of the Carpathians (in what is now Poland and Ukraine). The two objectives were to defend the Dual Monarchy (especially the city of Lemberg, now Lviv in Ukraine) and drive into Russian Poland but here too Conrad ended up making the worst possible decision. His initial plan to concentrate against Serbia meant a defensive deployment around 100 miles behind the Russian border but when he switched the emphasis to Galicia that meant switching to the offensive, so that Austrian troops had to advance that distance into their new positions. The Russians had fewer problems and completed their mobilisation without interruption and without the fatigue of additional marching.

The Galician front split into two halves, one facing east and centred on Lemberg, and one facing north and focused more on enemy concentrations than locations.[76] General Brudermann's Third Army was told to keep the Russians out of Lemberg by advancing and conducting an active defence.

These orders were hardly defensive (Brudermann was known to be aggressive) and the Russians were known to have a numerical superiority. Brudermann moved out smartly, while the Russians moved more slowly as their larger numbers of troops mobilised. Brudermann wholly misread the situation and thought he was facing only a small covering force so he attempted an ambush – only to find that the 'isolated corps' was in fact four Russian corps, coherent units that had advanced carefully and were organised for action. Unsurprisingly, Third Army did little damage and suffered heavily. The numerically superior Russian artillery was especially lethal; it was well positioned and accurate, and not only fired on the Austrian infantry, but also successfully suppressed the Austrian artillery. Careful positioning meant that the Russians could stay organised and maintain better infantry–artillery coordination than their opponents.[77]

Meanwhile, the Austrian First and Fourth Armies were heading north. They roughly matched the Russians at seven corps or about 350,000 men. Here the blundering was reversed, with Russian units moving without reconnaissance and beating themselves to a pulp against the Austrian Fourth Army; some 6,000 prisoners were taken along with 28 guns. In the second phase, Conrad weakened Brudermann and moved troops to outflank the northern Russians. This worked very efficiently, the Austrians rounding up 20,000 prisoners and 100 guns and driving the Russians back in disorder – but it was not the encirclement that Conrad had sought. Even when successful, the Austrians could be reckless: some infantry regiments made multiple frontal charges and failed to wait for support. Conrad put a positive spin on such poor coordination by claiming that the infantry was so eager to attack that it did not wait for the artillery.[78] Both the Russians and Conrad over-reacted. Conrad thought these opening skirmishes could be exploited and major damage inflicted on the Russians. The Russians feared exactly that, so they reinforced heavily, diverting troops who might otherwise have faced the Germans. The Austrians found themselves 'pursuing' what they thought was a defeated enemy, when in fact they were facing twice their own numbers.

While Conrad plotted ever greater successes, the pressure was taken off the Austrian eastern flank, partly due to the arrival of his Second Army to bolster the line and partly due to Russian caution. Conrad continued to interpret intelligence to suit his preconceptions and assumed that the Russians were demoralised and vulnerable. He ordered Brudermann to attack again. On 28 August Third Army again attacked bravely (too bravely) but ineffectively and achieved almost nothing. Units were disorganised by several weeks of hard campaigning, morale was shaken by the perceived mistakes of the higher command, while the higher command was genuinely confused and making increasing numbers of mistakes. The infantry knew all too well their tactical inferiority and were especially aware of their lack of artillery support.[79] Operationally Third Army had not been able to co-ordinate attacks by its corps and divisions so the piecemeal attacks all suffered, and tactically there was almost no infantry–artillery cooperation and the infantry often charged with no preliminary bombardment or covering fire during their attacks.[80] On 30 August, when the Russians went over to the attack, including preliminary bombardments and using heavy artillery to support their main assault, the Austrian infantry cracked. At the same time the northern sector was turning in the Russians' favour. They were closer to their supply depots, had fresh troops deploying, and had a 2:1 numerical superiority. Several Austrian tactical blunders exacerbated the growing crisis (such as the 15th Infantry Division moving through a swamp and getting hit from three sides) and retreat became inevitable.

Rain helped cover the Austrian withdrawal, but by mid-September the Austrians had lost some 350–400,000 men – around half of the forces they had deployed in Galicia; this was particularly bad news for an army that was reliant on high morale instead of adequate firepower. Some 100,000 of those casualties were prisoners. A post-war assessment of Austrian artillery pointed to numerous failures.[81] There was no counter-battery fire because it had never been considered necessary and thus gunners were inadequately trained in the appropriate techniques; while the gunners had tried their best, it often meant deploying the guns in open positions and trying to silence the Russian guns. However, there were more Russian guns, they had longer range, they could deploy in cover, they could use indirect fire and they could sustain higher rates of fire. As the Austrian batteries were grad-ually shelled to bits, the Russian numerical superiority grew, and the Austrian infantry felt even more let down. Moreover, there was no attempt to concentrate guns and achieve local superiority. Guns belonged to their division and were usually allotted to a brigade, regiment or battalion. Dispersing guns meant they came under the orders of relatively junior infantry officers, who probably knew even less about combined–arms work than more senior ones. Moreover, this dispersal was happening at the same time (and in the same place) that at least one Russian commander, Alexei Brusilov, was considering concentrating his artillery more and was using artillery inspectors at corps level as commanders.[82]

Fritz Kreisler, the noted violinist, was a reserve infantry officer.

Wounded in the first weeks of fighting against the Russians, he recorded his impressions of being under fire and the impact on the infantry of having effective support:

> The moral effect of the thundering of one's own artillery is most extra-ordinary, and many of us thought that we had never heard any more welcome sound than the deep roaring and crashing that started in at our rear. It quickly helped to disperse the nervousness caused by the first entering into battle and to restore self control and confidence.

Kreisler also noted that shells made distinctive sounds according to their calibre and approach angle, and suggested to his commander that he might be able to detect the locations of enemy batteries.[83]

The campaign in Serbia would be more traditional but equally far from what the Austrians had expected. Austria had long denigrated the Serb army as a poorly led and poorly equipped militia. However, reform of the officer corps and the purchase of new equipment (including French 75s) had substantially improved their quality and the Serbs had fought well in the Balkan Wars. When the assassination crisis turned into war, the Austrian commander Oskar Potiorek, who been the military governor of Bosnia when Franz Ferdinand was shot, was eager to punish Serbia and redeem his reputation. It was also suggested in Vienna that a defensive deployment might encourage Italy or Romania to threaten the Habsburgs over disputed border territories. With the Fifth and Sixth Armies, as well as those elements of the Second Army that had stayed on the Serbian front, Potiorek prepared to invade Serbia. He was still in charge of Bosnia, and his responsibility to defend that province may have influenced him to not attack directly across the Sava river but to assault Serbia from the north-west, despite the rough terrain, few roads and no railway.

The Serb army had almost doubled in size since the Balkan Wars.[84] However, Serbia had taken nearly 100,000 casualties and spent almost 300 per cent of her GDP fighting her neighbours and as a result the government had to postpone military repairs and replenishment to the extent that many guns, carriages and caissons were still in storage sheds, essentially unrepaired, in 1914. War with Austria had been considered a major risk but most of the Serbian army was deployed in Macedonia, in case the Bulgarians risked a Third Balkan War. Serbia could mobilise around 350,000 men, about half of them first-line infantry, supported by 617 guns. Only 381 of the guns were modern – French 75s – and some of the rest were black-powder pieces from the 1880s without recoil mechanisms or gun-shields. The theoretical organisation was 48 guns for each of the ten infantry divisions, but the five first-line divisions had around half that number and the five second-line divisions only a quarter. Most divisions did have a battery of good 120mm howitzers. There was some heavy artillery, roughly 40 pieces, and each of the three armies had a small artillery battalion.[85] The government had spent nothing on replenishing ammunition stocks; the one arsenal in Serbia could produce 250 shells per day but only 200 fuses and even less gunpowder. Thus Serbia and her colourful ally, the Montenegrin militia, needed external support to fight and survive even an extremely short war.

On the main front Potiorek had slightly fewer men and guns, mainly because the Second Army was being chaotically redeployed to Galicia.[86] The Fifth and Sixth Armies were not elite troops and many units were *Landsturm*, older third-line troops with little recent training and limited artillery. With the Second Army only around for a few days and the Sixth Army slow to mobilise, Potiorek nonetheless sent the Fifth Army over the broad, deep, fast-flowing Drina river into Serbia on 12 August. The Second Army would make a demonstration and the Sixth Army's mobilisation would at least be some threat to the Serbs. The Serbs, unsure of Austrian plans, had kept their forces centrally deployed and thus able to respond either to the north or the west. After two days, when it became clear that the northern front was noise and bluster while the real advance was to the west, Field Marshal Radomir Putnik swung his Second Army (four infantry divisions) into action. The key to the sector was Mount Cer, which dominated the Jadar valley just to the south and the Macka Plain to the north. Two Serb divisions marched from before dawn until after dark, covering some 60km, and smashed into the 21st Infantry Division. One Serb infantryman recalled:

> It was dark, with the torrential rain and volcanic thunder of a summer storm. The soldiers were exhausted by the day's march, and the artillery was stuck on muddy roads. The order came from the division commander that the summit had to be taken at all costs. Our soldiers jumped into enemy trenches. It was boiling as in hell, the soldiers yelling and shooting in all directions. Both sides brought up reinforcements, and the butchery continued all night long.[87]

Cer was an upland 4 miles broad and 12 long, with ridges and hills. The Austrians were scattered across the area, and fighting continued for the various bits of high ground. At night the Serbs' advantage in numbers helped, and on the morning of the 16th another Serb regiment arrived, along with the artillery that had been delayed on the muddy roads. The Austrian batteries were too far away for effective signalling, and the Serb guns could fire over open sights. The 21st Division lost over a third of its infantry and was flung backwards. With his centre forced back, Potiorek tried to swing his flanks forwards but the Serbs held and the Austrians had to retreat back across the Drina. The Serbs had lost around 17,000 men but the Austrian losses were 24,000 (including 4,500 taken prisoner) and 48 guns. The Austrian soldier Egon Kirsch wrote, 'Our army has been crushed and is running away in utter disarray . . . Drivers whipped their horses, artillery troops jabbed their horses with spurs, officers and soldiers shoved and squeezed through between the columns of wagons, or ran in bunches through the roadside ditches . . .'.[88] Austria had been embarrassed by a third-rate country, and the Allies trumpeted the result.

The defeat may have been humiliating but Austria had ample resources to renew the fight and reservists filled out the ranks. The Serbs had been promised munitions by both France and Russia but only if they took the offensive. Emboldened by their success, they probed into Austria while the Austrians regrouped but then had to pull back when the Austrians resumed the attack in mid-September. In the second offensive the Austrians were no more sophisticated but at least had better artillery support, with heavy guns and river monitors supporting the crossing. The Serbs used a forward defence and fought hard; the 21st Division was again in the centre of the attack and a senior Austrian artillery officer noted 'there was no cooperation between the infantry and the artillery, and also no plan of action for the infantry'. The Austrian official history makes little mention of this failure but had to admit that a considerable degree of un-certainty in the choice of tactics was typical of all Austro-Hungarian forces during the initial battles.[89] The Serbs had too little artillery to concentrate it but had great success in using harassing fire into the Austrian rear; this was disorganising and demoralising for the Austrian infantry. It did not help their morale that their own artillery, heavier and more numerous, could not manage effective counter-battery fire.

The Austrians were clumsy but stronger than the Serbs and ultimately wore them down. One of the Serb army commanders complained 'my soldiers are dying and I have no replacements', but Putnik was publicly more determined: 'If we lack artillery, we have to resist with rifles alone.'[90] In private, he appealed to the French and Russians for more munitions. The

French agreed to send 25,000 shells and to get the Greeks to send some as well. By October even Putnik was worried about shaky morale. This co-incided with one of the rare Austrian tactical victories: along the Paranica peninsula the 21st Division finally organised a timetabled attack with an adequate preparatory bombardment and with both the fire-plan and the infantry advancing on schedule.[91] This coordinated attack helped break the Serbs, who were already stretched too thinly and were losing men to disease as well as battle. Putnik was forced to retreat. Some 8,000 prisoners were taken, along with 42 guns, some of which had to be abandoned owing to a lack of draught animals.[92]

The Serbs broke contact, falling back southeast of Belgrade. Potiorek tried to be clever and swung some of his troops to the northeast to secure Belgrade and potentially outflank Putnik. Instead, the poor weather slowed the move, costing about a week and giving the Serbs time to regroup. Putnik called up gendarmes and frontier guards to fill the ranks and formed student volunteers into battalions. Ammunition was beginning to arrive from Greece, and Putnik decided it was time to either counter-attack or admit defeat. He issued an order appealing to the Serbs to defend their homeland and then stripped his northern flank for a drive to the west. Putnik had timed his moment well: Potiorek had driven his troops too hard and supplies were low. The chance to reorganise and rearm had given the Serbs an edge. First the Austrian XV Corps retreated, then XVI Corps had to conform. The change of fortunes was too much, and the Austrian with-drawal turned into a rout, compounded by a thaw in the weather which meant that wagons and guns were caught in the mud. No fewer than 43,000 prisoners and 142 guns were captured in December. The results were so embarrassing that even the Austrian official history admitted 'a serious diminution in the Dual Monarchy's prestige and self-confidence'.[93]

The Austrians had fought one of the last nineteenth-century campaigns. Firepower was low on both sides and thus morale was more important. In general, artillery mainly influenced morale: it encouraged the troops who had effective support and discouraged those who did not. The Serbs did not need much artillery, they only needed to let the Austrians fail to co-ordinate their own and thus throw their infantry into futile attacks. The Austrians' own official history acknowledged 'too little attention was paid to the cooperation of infantry and artillery',[94] and that sort of basic mistake was another nail in the Habsburg Dynasty's coffin: why should the troops trust an army so clumsy it could not even arrange combined-arms tactics?

In the initial encounters the Austrian divisional artillery commanders awaited orders and then raced off to deploy their guns. The lack of wire meant that any changes in the plan of battle had to be conveyed by sending written orders. Inevitably, the strong corps reserve was rarely placed where it would have the greatest impact and the obsolete Austro-Hungarian guns were quickly outmatched by more experienced or more numerous opponents. The 1899 regulations had advised against a 'meaningless advance into the effective fire of infantry', but the ghosts of 1866 still cast their baleful shadow and artillerymen were reminded that 'steadfast perseverance until the last moment is the duty of the artillery and ensures its honour, even if it is bought with the loss of its guns'.[95]

Racing towards the Sea and Stalemate

In October and November the war of movement on the Western Front came to an end after the French, British and German armies had spent weeks struggling to exploit each other's northern flank in a sequence of turning movements later described as the 'Race to the Sea'.[96] This jockeying for position resembled mobile warfare, with advance guards and rearguards, cavalry forces testing each other, and artillery being used in a direct support role, but space soon ran out as both sides closed in on the strategic communications hub at Ypres. Both sides wanted the city for its own sake and because control of the sector would determine whether the Belgian forces could hold on the Yser and thus retain one corner of their beleaguered country. Both sides piled in more troops and tried to keep attacking, but the Germans had deeper reserves of men and munitions and the battle increasingly became a series of German assaults on a thin Allied line.

The Belgians were so hard-pressed that they opened the sluice-gates and flooded the fields, partly because they were low on shells and partly because their elderly guns were already wearing out – but mostly because there were too few infantry to hold the line. French troops arrived in growing numbers and they usually had enough ammunition as Joffre cut back on operations elsewhere to focus on Ypres. Britain did not have the same level of forces elsewhere (overseas garrisons had been recalled, formed into divisions and sent to the continent) and ran desperately short of men and munitions as the battle unfolded. The Germans, like the French, pulled guns and shells from along the front. Like the British they were also mobilising new units (also without full allotments of artillery) but these were largely enthusiastic volunteers rather than regulars returning from overseas.

The battlefield was not ideal for artillery. Villages and copses were largely intact and the damp weather often produced ground fog or morning mist as autumn turned into winter. With the topography offering only low hills, church steeples were prime observation posts until the frenzied shelling knocked them down. The Germans deployed an observation balloon and both sides used observation aircraft as best they could in the mediocre weather. From the observation posts (OPs) telephones were used but the wires were easily broken by shellfire (or simply by horses' hooves when the wires were on the ground) and several times German troops used patriotic songs to let observers know their locations.

The details of the battle are not the focus here: the Germans had greater numbers but the Allies (especially the remaining British regulars) were of better quality. However, the battle should be seen as the tipping-point from mobile warfare to trench warfare, as numbers became even less important and firepower began to dominate the struggle. Even primitive trenches provided enough protection for a small number of men to survive a fierce bombardment; armed with magazine rifles and machine guns those few men could cut down most attacks. Obstacles, most notably barbed wire, gave them even more time to shoot so fewer men could decimate the attackers. The British had some trouble adapting to trench warfare as they sited their trenches on forward slopes. There were advantages to this (longer fields of fire and protection against shrapnel shells) but also serious disadvantages: they were within sight of the German observers and risked being buried by near-misses from high explosive (HE) shells. (Douglas Haig and his staff confusingly gave mixed advice on the placement of forward trenches.) British troops tried pulling back during German bombardments and reoccupying the trenches before the German infantry could arrive, but the Germans dealt with this by shelling the reserve positions – a first step in the back-and-forth exchange of tactics. Even the Germans had trouble coordinating infantry and artillery; typically the artillery bombarded the line and then lifted prematurely, leaving the infantry charging without covering fire. If the infantry were not motivated they might choose to send out patrols, ostensibly to report on the enemy positions but often winning a postponement of the assault, but if the infantry were motivated and the artillery ineffective then the battle could turn into a slaughter.

Trench warfare meant that the attacker needed more shells to have the same effect, and thus a battle could pull in guns and shells from along the front. The Germans had plenty of guns (including the 420mm monsters from Liege and Antwerp) and enough shells for the initial battles. In contrast, the British sent guns out of battle because there were not enough shells and there was no point in putting the gunners at risk if they could not fire back. Ammunition stocks were controlled by Field Marshal Sir John French himself, and guns were rationed to 50, 40 or even 20 rounds per day.[97] At one point the British planned a deliberate counterattack with special artillery support, but even that meant using less than 1,000 rounds.[98] Sometimes the sheer volume of German fire demoralised British troops not yet accustomed to prolonged bombardment, as when four battalions of the 7th Division pulled back from a salient at Kruiseecke after 36 hours of shelling, though it is worth noting that they fought off several infantry attacks before withdrawing. One gunner in the RFA described the experience as his battery retreated from Gheluvelt: 'We pass through a perfect hail of shells up the Menin Road. Awful time! How we got out is a mystery! Shells are bursting all over the place. My horse is wounded and nearly drops down with exhaustion . . .'.[99]

The battle ended when the Germans ran out of reserves before they could break the tattered remnants of the BEF, although the French were beginning to transfer enough troops to relieve the British and thicken the line. The battle showed not only that artillery was vital for attacks in trench warfare (and would become vital in defence as well), but also how hard it would be to develop tactics to make those attacks effective. In 1915 the starting point would be trying to produce more shells from more guns. However, guns were slow to make and factories had huge quality problems with accelerating shell production leading to a general 'shell shortage'. Eventually it became clear that even quantity would not solve the increasingly complex tactical problems posed by trench warfare.

Browbeaten and Weary of War: The Ottoman Empire

In August 1914 the Ottoman army was still in the midst of a complete reorganisation after the Balkan Wars with her German advisers alternating between good advice and outright intrigue in their efforts to embroil the Turks in a war that the wiser officers saw as a potential disaster for the Empire. Only half of her population were deemed (and proved) reliable, most of her guns and ammunition had to be imported (a route blocked by Serbia until 1915), her rail system did not link together all of her potential fronts (a situation made worse by the choke-points in southeast Anatolia), her pre-war planning and deployments were still based on a resumption of the Balkan Wars and only one of her corps (IX) had its allotted howitzer battalion. Once the Ottoman government decided to join the Central

Powers, the ill-equipped and poorly supplied Turkish army lurched into its assigned defensive positions before being sent on a series of inadequately manned misadventures along the frontier. Most of the corps were weak in artillery (the Third Army fielding 218 guns instead of the paper strength of 252, even after being reinforced with additional batteries) and many of the guns were a museum catalogue of obsolete weapons, many consisting of variants of the ubiquitous 75mm field gun.

The initial operations were not a success for the army or the Ottoman artillery. The Mesopotamian garrison proved inadequate even against an Anglo-Indian expeditionary force that was almost as weak in artillery, the assault on the Sinai collapsed during the attempt to cross the Suez Canal and the winter campaign in the Caucasus foundered after the Russians proved more capable and stubborn than expected and the terrain proved impossible for the field guns to make an impact.[100]

The Shell Shortage

By October and November the war in the West was slowing down, and on 1 October Joffre cabled the War Ministry that a shortage of shells restricted attacks. There was fierce fighting at Ypres but less elsewhere on the Western Front because neither side had the resources for more battles and it was becoming increasingly difficult to get those resources where they were needed most.[101] The French continued to attack throughout the winter, fully aware that having more guns and more shells would have meant they lost fewer infantry but grim political necessity required that some attempt should be made to recapture the provinces occupied by the Germans.[102] Overall, casualties had sapped units, especially the junior leaders needed to lead attacks. The troops knew they needed artillery support, and that there were not enough shells – the Germans had time to start digging in because the French lacked shells to attack in more places. By mid-November the Germans lacked shells too and they broke off the attack at Ypres not least because they were down to only four days' worth of shells.[103] The pre-war expectations had been of a short war and for a short war a sprint was not only sensible but necessary lest the enemy run faster and win. But sprinting made no sense for the long haul and all the combatants had to adjust. The shell shortage would affect strategy and policy for months and years.

The term 'shell shortage' was actually a convenient shorthand for a number of bottlenecks in the process of turning enthusiasm and raw recruits into well trained and properly equipped troops. Soldiers needed basic equipment, uniforms and rifles. They needed training and heavy weapons. Industry needed raw materials, reasonably skilled labour and proper equipment. Everyone planning for war had relied on stockpiles of weapons and ammunition, with the intention of stepping up the production of ammunition once war broke out, but nobody had planned adequate quantities of guns and shells and some short-term decisions made increases in production difficult. Putting skilled workers into uniform (either as conscripts or volunteers) reduced industrial output. The pre-war plans were fulfilled but they were utterly inadequate. Each government's first response was to order more production from state-run arsenals and issue contracts to private industry but that was only the first step. Sometimes industry was reluctant to respond; many industrialists knew that conversion would be expensive and they feared that if the war was over quickly they might not recover their costs. (Governments could advance money for conversion, but that required an extra decision and thus created a further delay.[104]) In Russia there were even political battles over using private industry, and for two years the War Minister issued contracts abroad – despite the shipping bottlenecks they faced – rather than offer contracts to private industry.[105]

Producing and operating artillery was actually far more complex than most ministers understood. A gun had moving parts with tight tolerances; it could not be manufactured overnight, and hasty construction led to malfunctions and accidents. For instance, in 1915 British factories made recoil springs from inadequately tempered steel, and by mid-1916 up to 20 per cent of 18-pounders were out of action due to broken recoil springs (this also reflected the problem of inadequate training because more experienced troops were better at maintenance). Shells were also complex to manufacture; even the apparently straightforward outer case could cause problems. Make the case too thin and the shell might burst prematurely, potentially as it was being fired; make it from cheap steel and it could be too brittle – with equally fatal results. The French deliberately chose quantity over quality and paid that price: in 1915 one 75 blew up for every 5,000 shells fired. The Germans temporarily used cast iron instead of steel; the weaker metal meant shell walls had to be thicker, thus reducing the payload. Once the shells were manufactured there were shortages of explosives; once the explosives were available companies had to learn how to fill shells. Once there were filled shells there had to be fuses. These complex devices had the smallest parts of all and had to be both robust enough to withstand the huge acceleration of being fired and delicate enough to function effectively.

Into 1916 some 35 per cent of British shells might be 'duds', partly because industrial mobilisation varied wildly; even cuckoo-clock makers were mobilised, making clockwork fuses.[106]

There were few alternatives. In theory, better tactics might use fewer shells but there had to be some shells with which to experiment and develop those tactics. Foreign orders might substitute for one's own inadequate production – the Turks remained dependent on foreign imports until the end of the war – but there were still problems getting the right quality and prompt delivery. American companies, with no stake in the war other than profits, might ship shells filled with sawdust rather than explosives. Foreign orders could also raise some very different issues, for example involving foreign exchange and gold reserves, something with which generals typically had little patience or experience. Captured weapons were sometimes pressed into use, especially by the Central Powers. These were generally adequate for quiet sectors but posed problems of ammunition supply since captured supplies would be finite and making more meant making less of something else. Older guns were also pressed into service, sometimes even coastal guns or naval guns, occasionally fortress guns, sometimes including elderly black-powder weapons. The British converted coastal guns into howitzers while the Germans turned coastal and naval guns into railway artillery.[107] The French pulled coastal guns (and coastal gunners) and fortress guns into the battle-line as emergency fire-power and heavy support for the beleaguered field batteries. They also dredged up hundreds of 1880s-vintage black-powder guns, of limited range and accuracy but with ample ammunition supplies, to tide them over until the production of modern weapons became adequate. Repairs also supplemented production, although not solving the problem of expanding armies. The Austrians, for instance, essentially stopped field-gun production in the second half of 1915 in favour of repairing existing guns. This was complicated by the Austro-Hungarians having forty-five types of gun demanding 200,000 shells a week, although shell production barely reached 116,000 in December 1914.[108]

A few new weapons were introduced, mainly mortars. Mortars offered several advantages over artillery pieces: they used fewer raw materials, had wider manufacturing tolerances, and could use new plant (and thus not disrupt existing contracts), while a low-velocity mortar bomb could carry proportionately more payload than an artillery shell. The disadvantage was substantially shorter range. Another new weapon, used partly to get around production bottlenecks, was poison gas.

There was generally no substitute for expanding the industrial base; this took time as complex production issues had to be resolved, from the production of machine tools to obtaining raw materials to retraining workers and shipping products. Thus Russian armies howled about shell shortages when there were hundreds of railway wagons, filled with shells, that the War Ministry had decided to hoard. It also involved governments in issues far from any general's pre-war thinking. Britain instituted licensing hours on public houses so munitions workers would not get drunk; social conservatives complained about females working in industry; and both generals and recruitment officials had to weigh up whether a skilled workman was more valuable in uniform or on the shop floor. Munitions shortages would affect the rate at which armies could be expanded: it was all very well to raise infantry battalions but those battalions would be no offensive threat until there was artillery to prepare the attack and support them. Another problem for armies and industry was the ever-increasing need for heavy artillery. As defences grew denser and deeper, attackers needed more and more heavy artillery, in some cases rising to 50 per cent of the guns assigned to an attack.

Operationally the 'shell shortage' would reduce the tempo of operations; there were attacks but these were either inadequately supported (and produced higher casualties) or there were pauses between attacks to build up ammunition stocks. The French (and especially British) shortages in 1915 allowed the Germans breathing space to drive the Russians out of Poland and Lithuania; the increased production of 1916 meant the French could fight at Verdun while the British could launch the Somme offensive and the bland phrase 'attrition warfare' would take on a new and terrifying meaning.

Chapter Two

1915

The winter lull gave both sides time to examine their strategic situation. The Allies had more resources, both in materials and especially in manpower, than the Central Powers but they were geographically separated and needed to coordinate their operations. They also had to *use* those resources to attack or the Central Powers would be able to target and defeat the Allies one by one. Coordinating three theatres (the Western, Eastern and Serbian) with four different national armies, each having unique military and political circumstances, would be difficult, if not impossible. Then there was the question of the Middle East, where the Ottoman Empire had joined the Central Powers. All the Allies wanted chunks of the Ottoman Empire and the alluring prospect of acquiring Ottoman provinces threatened to divert valuable resources. Some strategists suggested that the British and French were better off using their resources to attack the Turks (potentially opening a shorter supply route to Russia, as well as expanding their colonial empires) while others contended that this would lead to a ruinous waste of effort when forces should be concentrated against Germany.

The British army needed time for its Territorial Force divisions to prepare and Kitchener's New Armies to train from scratch. While the British reorganised, the French dominated the strategic debate on the Western Front. In the East, Russian military opinion was split between those who wanted to fight Austria, whom many assumed could be beaten by the Russians alone, and those who wanted to fight Germany, whom Russia clearly could not beat without assistance. Serbia had lost heavily in 1914 in both manpower and material, and the subsequent typhus epidemic meant that, although the Serbs had insignificant offensive potential during 1915, they would at least tie down some Austrian troops.

The Central Powers had fewer resources but occupied a central position that allowed better coordination. The Germans were obviously the major players, but they needed to support their allies. Without the Turks blocking the Dardanelles, the Allies could ship munitions to Russia and enable the Russians to fully utilise their manpower. Without the Austrians, there would be no holding the Russians back from overwhelming East Prussia. The strategic weakness of Germany's allies sometimes gave them the political leverage they needed to secure the support they wanted: Germany had little choice but to provide essential materiel – but every man, gun and shell diverted from the Western Front risked the main area of operations. The Germans therefore sought alternatives to numbers and explored various options, for instance thickening their defences and reorganising their infantry divisions. The former reduced their losses to Allied shelling, by forcing the Entente powers to conduct a lengthy preliminary bombardment before any attack; this meant there was no chance of achieving operational surprise (defences thus having both tactical and operational effects); the latter involved adding machine guns to the infantry regiments but pulling three battalions out of each infantry division. The German advantage in trench mortars, grenades, sniping and other trench warfare equipment and tactics meant they established an operational superiority over the Allies. In contrast, the Austrians were engaged in an appallingly costly (and appallingly badly run) winter campaign in the Carpathians, and could do little to reorganise their army. The Turks had only declared war in November 1914 and were still mobilising their army, but they were isolated from the other Central Powers and needed to conserve their strength.

The wildcard in the pack was the remaining neutrals. With front lines reaching right across the continent, neutral countries were the only flanks, and they were eagerly wooed by both sides. Italy was the largest and most powerful, Romania and Bulgaria enjoyed strategically important positions, and Greece was valuable because it controlled the supply lines to Serbia. The belligerents would spend much effort (and money) trying to sway these neutrals. The main campaigns were influenced by such diplomacy; attacks were used as evidence to prove to a wavering country that one side was winning. As the general staffs on both sides looked at their options for the spring, swayed to the various political and diplomatic pressures they faced and considered their shortages of troops, guns and shells, they knew that inaction was not an option.

Winter – Artois and Champagne

Dismayed by the heavy casualties of 1914, Joffre circulated a series of memoranda to his commanders that would lay the foundations for more methodically assaulting the formidable German defensive line based upon high ground and pre-registered artillery zones: 'Every time a strong-point is to be taken, the attack must be prepared by artillery. The infantry should be held back and should deliver the assault only from a distance where it is certain that the objective can be reached.'[1] Joffre had told the French President that the 'weapons of siege warfare' would not be available until later in the year, but GQG's Operations Bureau identified Artois and Champagne as potential sectors which could be attacked with operational effect during the winter. Assisted by a series of supporting attacks, the Tenth Army would attack Vimy Ridge in the Artois region and the Fourth Army would drive towards Mézières in Champagne.

In Artois the French attempted to conceal the main axis of their attack but had insufficient artillery to destroy the key strong-points in the German front line; with heavy rain rapidly turning the battlefield into a quagmire, the French made only minimal gains. The Fourth Army's General de Langle de Cary attempted to maintain momentum with a continuous series of assaults instead of one overwhelming rush but, until more artillery became available and coordination became more sophisticated, this tactic proved insufficient to shatter the defences. Recognising the limitations of his artillery, De Langle quickly switched to using artillery to prepare a succession of limited attacks against key locations he described as 'chosen points', instead of attempting to smash through the entire line in one desperate operation.

On 30 March an attack against the St Mihiel salient demonstrated the inherent weakness of infantry assaulting well prepared and carefully sited positions with inadequate artillery support. The infantry struggled through the mud to find only one breach in the wire. Moreover, the hilly terrain made it difficult for artillery observers to coordinate support against cunningly emplaced German machine guns positioned to take advantage of any attempt to flank the main strong-points – each of which was built with concrete casemates that were impervious to light artillery fire. The German defences at Les Éparges proved even more formidable and the French were initially stunned by the ferocity of the German counter-attacks – co-ordinated assaults that were supported by the rapid concentration of large numbers of artillery and minenwerfer.

The French were swatting at the Germans (with negligible effect) and the Russians and Austrians were bleeding and freezing in the Carpathians, while German attacks on the Russians in northern Poland gained ground (and inflicted around 100,000 casualties) but had little strategic impact. The British and French paused and planned to coordinate further attacks for mid-March, but the French were forced to defer their plans and the British were left to move alone or await development; they decided to attack alone, at Neuve Chapelle.

The Hurricane: The Battle of Neuve Chapelle

The French had been pressing for a combined Allied offensive on the Western Front, with an Anglo–French attack on the north and a French attack on the south of the German salient between the armies. However, late in the winter of 1914/15 the French had to drop out as their winter attacks had drained both munitions and manpower; that left the British.[2] Sir John French felt the BEF needed to prove itself to the French (especially in attacking, something the British had not done since September) and believed that an attack would improve morale in the BEF – the men were suffering from both frostbite and trench-foot through a cold winter, exacerbated by the lack of creature comforts in the trenches, while the Germans had the advantage in sniping, shelling and trench mortars.

Right from the start there was the question of whether the First Army (under General Sir Douglas Haig) would try to break through or whether they would make a limited attack to gain ground. Haig wanted a break-through, although he recognised that it could only go a few miles up on to Aubers Ridge. In theory, if the ridge fell it would force the Germans to pull back throughout the sector and establish new defensive positions on the next ridgeline, thus gaining the British a substantial local advantage. Lieutenant-General Sir Henry Rawlinson's IV Corps was assigned to make the actual attack. Rawlinson himself suggested making a very limited attack, covering only a few hundred yards, and to repeat the attack, with new objectives, a few days later. This would maintain better control over the troops and allow shells to be concentrated on fewer German trenches. Arguments over breaking through or conducting limited attacks would be recycled for the rest of the war, with Haig often preferring the most optimistic option but this time Rawlinson was probably too pessimistic: any element of surprise would be gone by the time the second attack went in and only advancing 300 yards was almost certainly a waste of all the resources that would be used in the first stage of the offensive. Since the BEF only had enough shells for one major attack in early 1915 (a fact that Rawlinson may not have known), it made sense to go for the bigger stakes.

The first question was how much artillery preparation there would be. Tests had shown that barbed-wire entanglements similar to those the Germans established could be demolished in 35 minutes. Since the wire had to be cut for an attack to be successful, such a bombardment was seen as the minimum requirement. It seemed likely that the German breastworks could be demolished in roughly the same amount of time (although there was no way to tell how thick the German breastworks were without attacking and capturing some), and this assumption thus became the basis for the whole fire-plan. The bombardment would be heavy; the BEF left only a defensive minimum of artillery on the rest of the front and concentrated its guns at Neuve Chapelle. The 18-pounders would cut the wire while all the heavier pieces (from 4.5-inch howitzers up to the 9.2-inch behemoths) would pound the German lines. The BEF decided upon a hurricane bombardment rather than a prolonged one, mainly because the German defences were thin enough that a hurricane bombardment would be enough to destroy them – at this stage of the war the debate on whether it was better to destroy the German defences (and defenders) or simply neutralise them had hardly begun. A few long-range guns were allocated for counter-battery fire, but this was not deemed a priority since the German machine guns were considered the main threat.

There were plenty of new features in planning a trench-warfare attack. Air reconnaissance had to replace ground reconnaissance, with aerial photos providing a key source of information. (At this stage the BEF lacked balloons.) The relatively flat terrain meant that ground observers in church steeples or other observation posts could not see enough to guide the artillery. The 'clock circle' was an innovation for the air observers, enabling them to signal something like '12 o'clock, 200 yards' for rounds that went 200 yards too far due north. The use of observers allowed the guns to be 'registered' on their targets: a new term for firing ranging rounds and then falling silent until the attack. To preserve some element of surprise, registration was done over several weeks, disguised amid the normal daily firing. Recognising how important communications would be, extra cable was installed so that telephones would be as far forwards as battalion headquarters. There was also a timetable for the artillery, telling each battery what target it would engage at what time. And there was even what later became known as a curtain barrage, intended in this instance not to act as covering fire for the advancing troops but as a barrier (the direct translation of barrage from French) to German reinforcements. Later such barriers would be used to cover both the flanks and the rear of an objective.

The battle started on 10 March and began well for the British. Two witnesses show how impressive the bombardment appeared:

The village, the neighbouring trenches and the whole German position selected for attack were blotted from sight under a pall of smoke and dust. The earth shook and the air was filled with the thunderous roar of the exploding shells. To the watching thousands the sight was a terrible one: amidst the clouds of smoke and dust they could see human bodies with earth and rock, portions of houses, and fragments of trench hurtling through the air.[3]

The purely physical effect on us was one of extreme exhilaration. We could have laughed and cried with excitement. We thought that the bombardment was winning the war before our eyes. Incredible that the men in the German front line could have escaped. We felt that we were going to pour through the gap.[4]

Used to recognising the build-up for an offensive, the Germans had been caught napping; the short bombardment gave the BEF operational as well as tactical surprise, so there were hardly any German reserves in the area. The centre and right of the attack made good progress, but the left was held up by German fire – the trenches on that side had been missed because those 6-inch howitzer batteries that had arrived just before the attack had not adequately registered the target. The rudimentary artillery communications did allow a second barrage and the German positions were eventually taken. Overall, communications to the forward infantry soon broke down and the advancing troops grew confused and could not get reports of continuing enemy resistance back to the forward telephones. This confusion allowed the Germans to occupy some recently completed strong-points (probably the basis for another defensive line); since these had not been noticed by the air observers and were invisible from the British front line, it was hard to adjust support fire to deal with them. Barely one German reserve battalion (plus the remnants of the front-line troops) held up the two attacking divisions. When British reserves did get forwards, it was almost impossible to coordinate their actions with the supporting artillery fire and at least one other British attack in the afternoon was sped up because British shells were hitting their own men – it was better to attack than to suffer the shelling and try to attack later. Renewed attacks on 11 and 12 March met more German reserves (as had been predicted before the battle, the British needed to break through quickly or they would not break through at all) and gained negligible ground in exchange for rising casualty lists. Battalions tried to coordinate their attacks, but 1/Worcesters refused one plan, commenting: 'No, it is mere waste of life; the trenches had not been touched by artillery . . . A frontal attack will not get near them . . . impossible to go 20 yards much less . . . 200 yards.'[5] With reserves thrown into the battle as soon as they arrived, the German counter-attacks suffered as heavily as the British had done. Late on 12 March Rawlinson and Haig decided not to continue the attack. A clue to future doctrine was shown in the changing perception of counter-battery work: in the original fire-plan eight heavy guns were assigned to counter-battery work but by the end of the battle only seven were *not* firing on the German guns. Part of this was due to the changing nature of the battle – the German machine guns were not a problem if the British were not attacking, while the German guns would be a problem if the Germans counter-attacked – but it demonstrated the importance of counter-battery work.

There was much to learn. Air observation had proved to have limits; inexperienced photo interpreters had missed the German reserve positions and a flooded trench was shelled because it was obvious even though it was clearly unoccupied. Communications were crucial to switching fire on to new targets but information from the front lines dried up as soon as the infantry went 'over the top'. The BEF assessed the results very positively – trenches could theoretically be broken in only 35 minutes and there was now a template on how to attack and win the war in 1915. This conclusion ignored the possibility that the Germans might assess the battle with equal thoroughness and make changes to their own system, such as thickening their defences with additional barbed wire and improving their parapets. On 9 May British battalions crashed into intact German defences with predictable results and the attack was broken off in one day. In some ways the rest of the war would be a race between the defenders and the attackers' artillery: since barbed-wire had to be cut before an attack, barbed-wire entanglements required a lengthy bombardment. If the attacker was spending days cutting wire, the defender had time to move up reserves, and that in turn forced the attacker to batter the defences, which further lengthened the preliminary bombardment. Only tanks (which could crush wire), weak defences or poor morale appeared to be able to change the grim equation.

With the technology available in 1915, the BEF decided to rely on using a prolonged preparatory bombardment to prepare for an assault. At Neuve Chapelle the goal had been to destroy the German defences although what was accomplished was neutralising the Germans (through a high-density but short bombardment), but some argued that this was merely fortuitous. For the attack at Festubert on 20 May the BEF ordered a 60-hour preliminary bombardment and there was no argument about adopting a different method of attack. Another method, proposed after Neuve Chapelle but quickly discarded, was the use of limited attacks – initially taking a few trenches and then punishing the Germans when they counter-attacked – thus trying to fight an efficient war of attrition. In the early spring of 1915 it was far from clear that the Great War would be a war of attrition and there was only a single datum point to establish a discourse on potential British doctrine for attacking entrenchments. Since the obvious tactical flaws at Neuve Chapelle seemed as if they could be ironed out without ditching the underlying strategic premise, it should not be a surprise that the BEF continued trying to break through and win the war sooner rather than later. The final problem was that in mid-1915 the Dardanelles Campaign was absorbing too many resources for the BEF to launch either attritional attacks or breakthrough operations and the British front was relatively quiet until September and the Battle of Loos.

The Germans were not sitting still. Austrian weakness dragged German attention to the Eastern Front, but they believed they needed to show strength in the West and pin down Allied reserves. Thus they used chlorine gas (released from cylinders, and thus technically not a violation of international law which specifically forbade asphyxiating gas projectiles) at Ypres on 22 April, and a reasonable amount of artillery but relatively few infantry – which was the resource they were trying to conserve for the Eastern Front. The attack gained some ground and also disrupted Allied plans so that the Allied attacks had to be delayed a bit, while the Germans launched their attack at Gorlice-Tarnow.

Indecision before the Storm: Przemysl to Gorlice-Tarnow

German experiments with gas in early 1915 proved abortive due to the extreme cold but the German Eighth and Tenth Armies continued to hammer Russian forces deployed near the Masurian Lakes. Struggling through the driving January snow and faced with desperate counter-attacks, the Germans brought their battering train within range of Ossoviets but failed to break through the outer enceinte. In contrast, the Russians fared rather better against the Austro-Hungarian fortress at Przemysl, encircling it and forcing a surrender (including all the fortress's stocks of artillery and ammunition) on 22 March. The assault on Przemysl required super-heavy guns to be transferred from the naval arsenal at Kronstadt and these did not arrive until January. To assist in this process, STAVKA organised the artillery reserve on each of the three Fronts into separate heavy artillery *Divizions*. These were intended to be the 'heavy artillery fists' for Front commanders to use to smash through the enemy's front line.[6] To supplement Russia's meagre supply of heavy guns, from 1915 through to 1917 the Western Allies supplied both artillery pieces and instructors to the Russians (no fewer than 442 heavy guns were despatched), though the Russians usually preferred French liaison officers to their less well prepared and often linguistically challenged British equivalents. The Russians had the same ammunition supply problems as the other Great Powers but there is little evidence that this gave the Germans a decisive advantage before 1917. Rerberg even asserted, after the battle of Gorlice, that 'not once in my nine months of service as a chief of staff, was there a shortage of shell'. The Russians produced 2 million shells between January and April 1915 but this was only approximately 20 per cent of demands. The problem was that the Russian production shortfall was magnified by successive echelons of command hoarding shells: staff at each headquarters were convinced that they were a better judge of where such resources should be allocated than their profligate subordinates. A great deal was stored in the fortresses, much of it concealed so that it would not be found by inspectors.[7]

Unlike those in the West, Eastern armies did not have the resources to create layers of defence in every vulnerable sector. Where sufficient intelligence emerged to warn of an attack, there might be time to make stealthy preparations but for most of the war both sides focused on creating a strong first position; with far fewer railways (and, in the case of the Russians, poorly organised rolling stock), they simply hoped to be able to send in sufficient reserves on foot before the enemy made too extensive a breakthrough. When one corps, in the Gorlice sector, asked if they could build a reserve position, they were told that if they could spare the labour for such a project then they clearly had too many men![8] As a result, the Russian defences around Gorlice were relatively poor even by Eastern Front standards; the ground was deemed unsuitable for digging, the requisite tools were often scarce and the men were reluctant to dig in ground already filled with corpses from the previous year's fighting. Even though the area was of strategic importance (it flanked the Carpathian passes), the Russian infantry reserves in the area had been swapped for cavalry that lacked sufficient supporting artillery. The Russian doctrine was to keep the reserves close to the front-line defences so that they were ready for offensive operations, but this only exposed them to the accurate and devastating fire of the German heavy batteries and the dreaded *minenwerfer*.

Falkenhayn was keen to relieve pressure on his Austrian allies and despatched von Mackensen to command the army that he had created by reorganising the basic German infantry division into a 'triangular' structure of three three-battalion regiments. Conrad had requested a small-scale effort in the sector but Falkenhayn, recognising an opportunity to unhinge the entire front line and roll the Russians out of Polish Galicia, radically increased the numbers of troops suggested by the Austrian High Command.

August von Mackensen, the elegant hussar general, was an inspired choice as the commander of the Eleventh Army, as he worked extremely well with the Austrians and, unlike his less diplomatic colleagues, respected some of the arcane protocols that enabled the Austro-Hungarian army to function. Hans von Seeckt was assigned as his Chief of Staff and together they formed one of the most impressive command teams of the Great War. The impact of the new leadership was immediate. Plans were prepared and disseminated and protocols designed to enhance operational security. German troops conducting reconnaissance patrols in the sector were ordered to wear Austrian uniforms to prevent the Russians from realising that fresh units were arriving. Even with this precaution, reports of the presence of German units started reaching STAVKA by 26 April but there is little evidence that the Russians saw these signs as clear evidence of an imminent offensive; Radko-Dmitriev, commanding the Russian Third Army, was confidently informed that 'there is nothing in Third Army's situation to suggest any danger'.

At 21.00 hrs on 1 May the preparatory bombardment, described by Oberst Alfred Ziethen as *störungsfeuer* (harassing fire), began with key sections of the defences being battered while the troops moved forwards to their start lines. Mackensen focused on taking key strong-points on high ground before making the final assault and saw no reason to rely on unproven techniques against positions as formidable as Mount Zamczysko and the cemetery at Gorlice, the former assigned to General Kneussl's Bavarian mountain troops and the latter to the XXXXI Reserve Korps. After 2 hours the bombardment was halted and teams of engineers went forwards to cut wire and ascertain if any of the breaches in the forested terrain were practicable. After an hour of frenzied activity the engineers withdrew and the bombardment recommenced for another 2 hours; this remorseless process continued until 06.00 hrs on 2 May when 4 hours of heavy preparatory bombardment commenced. This shattered the already battered defences and cut all communications with both flanking units and almost every key headquarters. The system was remarkably efficient but von Seeckt's methodical approach was hugely facilitated by the Russians placing many of their key defensive positions on forward slopes.[9]

The final phase saw a savage *minenwerfer* bombardment of the front line; the hurricane of fire caused a general panic and allowed the German infantry assault to sweep through the shallow defensive system and penetrate 8 miles. One Russian officer described the experience in biblical terms:

> It seemed to me that the 'Second Coming' had arrived! The havoc of the guns was so terrible that all our advanced trenches were razed to the ground. Earth, men and ammunition, all formed a sort of 'kasha' [porridge]. The heavy artillery explosives battered our lines. Then the German attacks began. Austrians and Germans mixed together, advanced column after column. It was an easy task to repulse the first, the second; but the number of their columns did not cease . . .[10]

Multiple-layered defensive systems only existed where potential strong-points had been identified and reinforced, and therefore the Russians were often forced to fall back over open country and were often caught by the barrages intended to create chaos in the rear areas; it is estimated that the Russians lost a third of their men to gunfire during the breakthrough phase alone. Units that managed to hold their sector were quickly encircled and thousands were taken prisoner. As the defensive system collapsed, the Russian artillery failed to cover itself in glory, pulling back as soon as its positions were threatened and leaving the infantry to struggle unassisted against coordinated German attacks supported by an innovative artillery support fire-plan orchestrated by von Seeckt.[11]

Building on his experiments on the Western Front, von Seeckt's basic concept was for the corps artillery planners to organise the preparatory bombardment under the overall control of an army *Artillerie Kommandeur* (the redoubtable Alfred Ziethen), then for the divisional assets, augmented by some heavier batteries, to exploit the breakthrough. Each corps was trusted to arrange for the most efficient use of its resources; General Kneussl allotted most of his assets to the officer responsible for taking the key objective in his sector, while XXXXI Reserve Corps centralised the corps assets in a *groupment* that could react to developments. As in the preparatory bombardment, pauses were stipulated for all fire-plans so that the pioneers could clear obstacles and confirm the extent of the damage inflicted on the enemy defences.

Much of the battle-plan was based upon methods that had proven effective on other fronts. The bombardment pauses were intended to reduce the barrel-wear created by prolonged firing and the infantry tactics were no different from those of the Western Front – with similarly heavy casualties.

Original features included every battery keeping an ammunition reserve of 100 shells per gun for the second phase, locating the artillery staffs alongside their divisional equivalents, the use of field batteries that stayed with the infantry for close support in each succeeding attack, the close co-operation between the air force and the artillery (a collaboration that was hugely facilitated by the detailed target distribution sketches of the area that the Austrians had provided for the offensive), and the bright and sunny weather on 2 May.

Herman von François, commanding XLI Reserve Corps, recorded his impressions of the final phase of the bombardment in his report on the battle:

> Six o'clock! The 12cm gun on hill 696 fires the signal shot, and all batteries, from field cannon to heavy mortars, fire a round at the Russian positions. Then follows rolling and growling, crashing and braying; 700 guns open their fiery jaws and belch forth steel and iron which cleaves the air hissing and whizzing. Over there the projectiles bore their way into the soil and hurl clods of earth, wood splinters and parts of [wire] entanglements into the air. On the other side of the Russian lines smoke and flames issue from buildings and villages. Now and then one can see Russians fleeing from trenches and support lines, but our shrapnel falls amongst them, dealing death. Heavy railroad artillery kept the enemy's routes of approach under fire – north of Gorlice a heavy column of fire flares up house-high, black masses of smoke rise, deep into the clouds – an unforgettable touching spectacle.[12]

The Russian artillery response was even less effective during the retreat. The scarcity of ammunition reserves and the devastation caused by the German fire-plan were compounded by the woefully inadequate plans for cooperation with the infantry, but even with the artillery withdrawing prematurely they still lost 200 guns in six days of fighting. Radko–Dmitriev requested additional ammunition but STAVKA could supply barely half of the shells he demanded; as one disbelieving staff officer acidly observed during the retreat, 'unless you have been throwing away your shell-boxes, there must be enough'.[13] According to Mackensen and Seeckt, most of the German casualties came from machine gunners missed by the preparatory bombardment who reached their guns before the advancing infantry could swarm over their positions.

Even though the first attacks were a success and the breach was formidable, the Russians fought doggedly, desperately throwing their fragile cavalry divisions into the line to stem the German tide, and as a result a full-scale breakthrough was not achieved until 5 May. As the Eleventh Army, now described by some as the 'Mackensen Phalanx' or the 'Mackensen Wedge', forged towards Przemysl, the Third and Fourth Austrian Armies joined in the pursuit and the Russian Third Army literally 'bled to death' fighting to defend the River San.[14]

After Gorlice-Tarnow, Mackensen turned his phalanx against Lublin and Cholm and exploited his advantage in artillery, using the heavy guns as a methodical battering ram to smash his way through the Russian defensive system. As General Nicholas Golovine bitterly observed after the war:

The heavy artillery would take up positions in places which were entirely – or almost entirely – beyond the range of the Russian field artillery, and the heavy guns would start to shower their shells on the Russian trenches, doing it methodically, as was characteristic of the Germans. That hammering would go on until nothing of the trenches remained, and their defenders would be destroyed.[15]

As soon as the infantry had secured the enemy position, the artillery moved forwards and the whole process was repeated. Mackensen's new system was successful but inevitably used huge quantities of ammunition and advanced incredibly slowly, enabling the Russians to maintain their gradually shortening line as it steadily retreated eastwards. As Hindenburg noted, 'the Russian Bear had escaped our clutches, bleeding no doubt from more than one wound, but still not stricken to death'. Army Group Mackensen's brutal but effective approach has sometimes been confused with the famous 'creeping barrage' but the basic manoeuvre was operational and not tactical and was not based on the close coordination with the infantry assault that a true creeping barrage required.

The breakthrough at Gorlice-Tarnow and the loss of Poland in the summer of 1915 had brutally exposed Russia's inability to supply her armies with sufficient ammunition during an evolving battle. Like the military staffs of the other powers, STAVKA had assumed that having what appeared to be a healthy reserve of shells at a given moment was as effective as being able to sustain reliable production rates and then efficiently issuing those shells to front-line units. Creating the industrial capacity to supply the army continuously (the goal was roughly five times the estimated

requirement of 1914) would take time and money and the Russian government chose instead to import the shells they needed from Western firms,
which often struggled to understand the byzantine business practices
favoured by their Russian allies. Moreover, British and French factories
were already producing priority orders for their own armies but unhesitat-
ingly accepted advance orders in order to capitalise on future increases in
production. As a result the Russians only received a fraction of what they
paid for from their limited gold reserves while doubling their national debt.
Vickers came in for some particularly scathing criticism from the Russian
Artillery Department, Grand Duke Sergei snarling after yet another order
was delayed that 'they have unconscionably lied to us . . . it has been one
long, wicked piece of deception'.[16]

Depite this foreign duplicity, for most of the war the total stocks of shells
available to the Russians were broadly similar to their opponents. It was the
lack of an adequate defensive doctrine to reduce the damage caused by any
local enemy superiority in artillery and a ruinously inefficient supply
system that created the impression of a vast German shell reserve that was
blamed for every reverse. The artillery blamed the infantry for requesting
wasteful fire-missions, showing patrician disdain for any request from a
mere reserve division. Most perplexingly, both STAVKA and the artillery
commanders seemed unable to track and locate their own shell reserves.
Much of the ammunition was stored in fortresses and the Germans were
stunned to find 2 million shells when they captured Novogeorgievsk and
Kovno.

The shell shortage disguised a litany of errors and crises in the Russian
army. The infantry and artillery loathed each other; the Germans even
remarked on how difficult it was to capture a Russian gun from a second-
line division as they rarely stayed behind to cover the retreat of their 'lesser'
colleagues. As Norman Stone memorably comments, this was 'a clear indi-
cation that the artillery was leaving the *cattle* in the lurch', though it is worth
noting that the infantry lacked NCOs and it is difficult to see how they could
have collaborated as closely as the armed forces of other powers. There were
even reports of the artillery being used on their own men: at Opatów in June
1915 the gunners were ordered to fire on troops attempting to surrender.[17]

Eastern Promise: The Allied Landings at Gallipoli[18]
While the field commanders in France and Flanders struggled with the
complexities of trench warfare, the so-called Easterners sought strategic
alternatives, suggesting a range of proposals designed to dissipate the

resources of the Central Powers. While there appears to be consensus among historians that the war had to be won on the Western Front, there were a number of strategic opportunities in the East – opportunities that the Germans often proved far more astute in exploiting.

The Easterners seized on Turkey's declaration of war as a chance to rapidly knock out one of Germany's weaker allies and impress the neutrals. The key players (including Lord Kitchener, 'Jackie' Fisher and Winston Churchill) put forward various strategic options, but confusion and miscommunication on how to achieve the main objective led to considerable disorientation and an overambitious attempt to force the Dardanelles that fell foul of Turkish mines and heavy artillery. A mixture of coastal guns supported by 150mm howitzers drove off minesweepers and their lighter escorts.[19] One of the minesweeper captains had a nervous breakdown but a commander on HMS *Albion* recognised the inherent dangers of such work, noting in his diary that 'it must be very nerve-wracking being up there sweeping at night expecting the batteries to open fire at any minute'.[20]

Like the disastrous opposed landing at Tanga in 1914,[21] British joint planning for the landings at Gallipoli (the Turks name the campaign after Çanakkale) proved inadequate for the task; things started to go wrong even before they sighted the coast of Anatolia. Imperial units were generally poorly equipped with field artillery, the British force in Mesopotamia had around a third of the guns of a similar unit on the Western Front and Hamilton's Mediterranean Expeditionary Force was little better off (even by June 1915 the MEF had only two divisions' worth of guns supporting five divisions). Veteran mountain artillery batteries were available but they tended to be of lighter calibre and lacked high-explosive shells.[22] As Brigadier-General Simpson Baikie of the Operations Staff at GHQ later remarked: 'The whole story of the artillery at Cape Helles may be summed up in [these] few words: insufficiency of guns, ammunition and howitzers for the operations undertaken; no high explosive ever available for field guns; no spare parts or spare guns ever available, lack of aeroplanes, and no guns of heavy calibre available to compete with the hostile heavy guns.'[23] An additional month's delay was caused by poor initial loading, which required much of the invasion equipment to be re-stowed at Alexandria. The difficulties of making a successful landing appeared insurmountable and even the highly competent Sir William Birdwood saw the combination of established defences and artillery as potentially ruinous, but assumed that 'all would be well' once the troops were ashore. This focus on getting the troops on to the beaches instead of encouraging rapid exploitation on to the high ground, dominating the peninsula, proved to be a fatal error.

Sir Ian Hamilton, in overall command of the expedition, was reluctant to interfere with the commanders directing the landings, while those who came ashore, as Tim Travers notes in his criticism of Aylmer Hunter-Weston, tended to direct their attention to tactical challenges instead of operational opportunities. Naval gunfire support was more effective at Helles due to the clearer terrain and the opportunities for flanking observation, but these advantages were not available at Anzac Cove, the New Zealand War Diary laconically observing that 'we had obtained no gun support from the Navy while the enemy made free use of artillery'. Getting field guns and howitzers inland was an enormous problem. There were few tugboats to get them ashore and then few horses, so it was difficult to get artillery into position to support attacks and even moving mountain guns forwards took considerable effort.[24] The few guns that could be deployed forwards were highly effective but their observers lacked decent maps and good observation positions, so the Turkish gunners had a crucial advantage over the Allied troops struggling below. Birdwood, commanding the Anzacs, noted how 'the very first shot from one of our mountain guns had an electrifying effect on our troops, who felt they could now hold their own'.[25] The terrain was even deemed unsuitable by some artillery officers and a number of batteries were fatally delayed in getting ashore or were even sent back when it was apparent that no suitable positions were available. The infantry were understandably irritated and demoralised by this chaotic staff work – particularly as the Navy found it difficult to eliminate the Turkish batteries deluging Anzac Cove with shrapnel. Luckily the Turks had their own problems coordinating their infantry and artillery and even though Mustapha Kemal, commander of 19 Division and the future founder of the Republic of Turkey, showed exemplary leadership in his attacks on the beachhead, his artillery appeared happy enough to shell boats in the open but mysteriously failed to shell the Anzacs once they reached the beach.

In May, once the Allies were established and the artillery started to move inland, the combination of improved mapping, better observation, greater quantities of munitions and more effective fire-planning started to exact a toll on the Turkish defenders. The Allies initially had only 26 artillery pieces available for the First Battle of Krithia and only 78 at the Third Battle, and most of these were 18-pounders and therefore incapable of damaging more than small sections of the Turkish defensive system.[26] Even with this small force, the effects were visually impressive but some sources suggest that the Allied planners failed to coordinate their infantry and artillery effectively. Liman von Sanders complained to his superiors about the British having 'unlimited supplies of ammunition' and Hans Kannengiesser, commanding the Turkish XVI Corps, was stunned by the increase in the destructive power of the Allied batteries: 'Even later, in August 1917, in the battles of Flanders, I did not have the same over-whelming impression of concentrated shelling as during this period.'[27]

At the tactical level few Allied officers understood that they were poorly equipped compared to their colleagues on the Western Front and most appear to have thought the artillery preparations before their attacks were adequate, without understanding the vastly different operational circum-stances at Gallipoli and the weaknesses of the artillery they had been allocated. The Turks, with even fewer guns and limited supplies of ammu-nition, suffered heavy casualties attacking across the chaotic rocky terrain of the peninsula without adequate artillery support. The steep-sided hills, lacerated with a network of deep gullies and ravines, were a machine gunner's paradise and, as both sides discovered, only substantial artillery support guaranteed success.[28]

Once the Allies were established inland, artillery pieces and munitions slowly began to flow and by June it was the Turkish forces that were having difficulties transporting their materiel, much of it being carried by mules down the rugged peninsula because bold submarine commanders were sinking the Turkish coastal shipping in the Sea of Marmara. This was only the last in a string of problems for the Turks, who produced almost none of their heavy ammunition requirement; the Serbs certainly were not going to allow the enemy to ship shells, and neutral Romania allowed only very restricted quantities to be shipped. This limited the amount of support that could be given to attacks and prevented effective counter-battery operations.[29]

As the campaign unfolded, Hamilton, like Rawlinson on the Western Front, became increasingly convinced that to 'bite and hold' was the only way to wear the enemy down. 'The old battle tactics have clean vanished ... The only thing is by cunning or surprise, or skill, or tremendous expen-diture of high explosives, or great expenditure of good troops, to win some small tactical position which the enemy may be bound (for operational reasons) to attack.' At the Third Battle of Krithia Hamilton ordered a Chinese Barrage to trick the defending batteries to unmask and commence a premature counter-preparatory barrage – giving the Royal Artillery an opportunity to identify the concealed batteries and bring them under fire.[30]

His Chief of Staff, Walter Braithwaite, also learned rapidly and urged his colleagues to follow the French practice of lifting the supporting artillery barrage just before the infantry reached their objectives (though the French inexplicably failed to follow their own doctrine at the Third Battle of Krithia and took heavy casualties). Some commanders learned rather more slowly, Hunter-Weston in particular insisting on lifting the barrage supporting his June attack 2 minutes early due to concerns about inaccuracy. Friendly fire has always been an unpleasant way to become a casualty but in the Great War reducing the risk of 'blue on blue' often gave the enemy time to reach their machine guns and thus inflict far greater casualties. Where the French used their formidable 75s to support British attacks in July, the difference was obvious, one artillery major noting (with a professional's appreciation of the difficulty involved), 'they simply poured [shrapnel] on to the hostile trenches [and] our infantry had an easy task that day'. Another observer of the same attack recorded in his diary that the Turkish trench was devastated and 'carpeted with the dead bodies of Turks horribly mangled and dismembered by our shell fire'.[31]

The Australian Light Horse attack on 7 August, which involved naval gunfire support and artillery batteries switching targets during the operation, turned into a bloody fiasco. The timetable for the attack slipped when one of the flanking gullies proved impassable and the Turks were able to concentrate their fire on the Australians; in addition, according to some sources, the Turks had several minutes to recover before the attack went in. Much post-war acrimony has focused on this event but Tim Travers plausibly argues that the overall preparatory bombardment had already been largely ineffective and the attack was probably prolonged beyond the point where success was possible. With the wire intact and the enemy machine-gun positions undamaged, continuing to launch attacks was arguably illogical and it is not surprising that some bitterness persists about this episode.[32]

The attempt to dislodge the Turks by establishing a new base of operations at Suvla Bay failed owing to an absence of strategic direction. Key objectives overlooking the Anzac sector were not given priority and the lessons of the earlier landings led to less artillery being provided instead of solutions being found. Braithwaite told Stopford (commanding IX Corps) that the need for draught animals meant that only limited numbers of guns could be landed in the first phase. Stopford and his chief of staff were understandably cautious about advancing without guns and the inexperience of some of their units also hampered the process of fighting inland and seizing the heights. Even when the artillery was available, communication problems persisted; as units fought their way inland, towards Kavak Tepe and Tekke Tepe, contradictory orders arrived and confusion as to the availability of artillery exacerbated the growing disarray. By the time 53 Division was committed to the battle on 10 August the problems had still not been solved and one witness of the carnage snarled 'whoever ordered [the attack] should have been shot'.[33] In the final series of attacks late alterations to the fire-plan led to the New Zealanders assaulting Hill 60 without support, and rumours circulated that the British units had priority. Even when the artillery was available, the batteries did not have the technical ability, the air support or the key observation posts required to support the infantry effectively and little could be done to eliminate the key strong-points or to interdict Turkish reserves. Where naval guns could make a difference, von Sanders merely ordered his men to pull back into the interior or to establish positions closer to the Allies, positions where the primitive maps made indirect fire from ships problematic.

The Turks had similar ammunition supply problems and their lack of heavy artillery made it difficult for them to eliminate defenders in well established positions. The batteries they did have available could be redeployed to face Allied attacks and the Turks were perfectly happy to manhandle heavy guns through the difficult terrain. The Turks held the key observation positions throughout the battle but it took time for them to master the technical requirements of artillery operations and their inexperience enabled the Allies to dig in and establish the grim stalemate that prevented either side obtaining a clear victory. Technical inexperience also meant that the Turkish gunners found it difficult to support their infantry during Allied assaults, thus giving the Allied machine-gunners lethal opportunities.[34]

After the misery and chaos of the failed assaults, in which the available artillery on both sides often proved unable to support the infantry, and the resulting stalemate, where the shelling of each other's positions became a process of attrition, the evacuation was a masterpiece of planning. Rumours of the arrival of heavy guns certainly influenced the Allied decision but the strategic opportunity had clearly been lost and withdrawal, even with the likely result of heavy casualties and a catastrophic loss of prestige, appeared to be the only option. The Turks recognised that an evacuation was likely but were unable to discern the exact date so failed to disrupt the process with a general assault or artillery fire. With his men stricken after days of sleet, blizzard and frost, Liman von Sanders was reluctant to risk an attack until he had accurate intelligence and, after an elaborate Allied deception campaign, his gunners only commenced firing on the beaches around Anzac Cove 1½ hours after the last man had departed on 20 December. The subsequent withdrawal from Helles, on 7 January, could have turned into a disaster but the Turks seemed relieved that the Allies were leaving and their final attack was less than enthusiastic. Only a few worn-out guns were left behind and the initial estimate of artillery losses of over 60 per cent proved wildly exaggerated. Thanks to Birdwood's superb planning staff, the recovered guns were soon disseminated to units in Egypt, Salonika and the Western Front.[35]

The Second Battle of Artois

Victory on the Marne, with the German heavy artillery lagging behind the infantry, was regrettably presented at the *guerre a l'outrance* enthusiasts' GQG as a vindication of many of their pre-war assumptions. However, there were enough officers who were horrified by the unnecessarily high casualties to push for reform. By April 1915, as a result of the limitations created by the lack of long-range heavy artillery, the idea of a 'methodical battle', based on a succession of attacks, was advanced, utilising improved liaison, counter-battery fire, the elimination of key sections of the defences (such as machine-gun posts) and interdiction of the movement of reserves from both the flank and rear. Even though the core concepts appeared eminently sensible, GQG's main objective remained restoring the sort of manoeuvre warfare where the old principles could thrive, and therefore the succeeding attacks were assumed to occur in the same sector as the first.

The weaknesses in the methodical battle concept appeared as soon as it was tested at Champagne in April and at Arras in May. The improved German front-line and communication trenches survived the preparatory bombardment, which lifted far too early, giving the Germans plenty of time to man their defences. Even where the French managed to reach the German front line, they were unable to communicate these successes to their own artillery and request support against determined counter-attacks. At Arras effective artillery support would have been impossible anyway as the French 75s lacked the range to reach their own forward elements on the heights.

The problem with making a succession of shallow penetrations without long-range artillery is that each phase of the attack cannot eliminate the defenders' artillery, and poor communication with the attacker's own artillery reduces his ability to break up enemy counter-attacks. Where the salient driven into the front line was narrow, the enemy could concentrate their own, essentially untouched, artillery from several sectors and subject the attackers to flanking fire; this situation was made far worse when the delays between attacks gave the enemy time to recover and redeploy his reserves. Attacking on a broader front merely meant inadequate numbers of guns supporting the main assault and being outgunned wherever the Germans decided to concentrate.

French analysts understood that dealing with the German artillery was 'one of the first obligations of our artillery' but their initial analysis, in April 1915, focused on counter-battery fire during the assault and not during the preparatory phase. Supporting artillery should 'counter-battery and silence the hostile batteries, whose positions should have been previously discovered, or those positions should be searched for by every possible means as the battle proceeds'. The problem was that the artillery resources were insufficient to allow the defences to be destroyed at the same time as deluging suspected enemy artillery positions. The only viable solution was to wait until the enemy guns were committed and then engage them decisively.[36]

The flawed methodical approach of 1915 was primarily created not by an underlying weakness in doctrine but by the lack of adequate artillery support. Long before the Germans considered new ways of breaking the deadlock, the French began to seek alternatives to leaving the initiative (and French territory) to the enemy and merely waiting for heavier guns. Captain André Laffargue, recovering from a wound received in Flanders in May 1915, explored the problem in a remarkable pamphlet entitled *The Attack in Trench Warfare: Impressions and Reflections of a Company Commander*. Laffargue noted that 'the character of this [methodical] attack is that it is not progressive. We cannot nibble away, piece by piece, at the whole series of redoubtable defences; they must be gobbled in one blow, with one resolute stroke.' He then expanded on his analysis and concluded that small units of highly trained and well equipped assault troops, working closely with dedicated artillery support, could penetrate the enemy's defensive system. The pamphlet was distributed but failed to make an impression on GQG, even when Foch despatched the author to join the General Staff with a glowing reference; on arrival, Laffargue was assigned to menial staff work. The Germans were far more impressed with it, and as soon as captured copies were disseminated, they served to confirm the validity of their own experiments in infiltration tactics.[37]

At Artois in May 1915 the French attacked a 15-kilometre section of the front line with five corps. Beyond each division's three *groupes* of 75s, the French deployed 400 heavy guns and a number of heavy trench mortar batteries (*Artillerie de Tranchée*), using an array of improvised systems.[38] The few advances were limited due to a combination of poor weather and inadequate ammunition and were soon lost to vigorous German counter-attacks supported by almost three times the number of heavy guns, most of which were capable of rapid fire. The French barrages were made up of 75s with scattered heavy batteries, while the German barrages were fired by coordinated batteries of heavy guns.

GQG made a detailed study of the battle and its report, submitted in July 1915, concluded:

> The attempts made both by us and the Germans show that by applying the necessary means in heavy artillery, the rupture of the enemy's lines will be certain . . . The defences are torn up; the only elements which sometimes resist are well placed casemates and cave shelters, which the Germans generally use. [The problem was that] when the assault was made, the machine guns, which had been shel-tered in cellars during the bombardment, again appeared.

One solution appeared to be to conduct an assault on a broad front, with adequate artillery support, in the hope of overwhelming those sectors where the defenders survived and chose to make a stand.[39] As the French felt that they had continue to conduct assaults with inadequate resources, they needed to develop more sophisticated tactics. In June 1915 the French began to experiment with stratagems designed to surprise the Germans. In what would later become known as the 'Chinese Barrage', future French artillery fire-plans were to include irregular pauses in the bombardment as it was 'essential to keep the enemy in a state of uncertainty as to the real time of the attack, so that he may prematurely man his trenches and expose himself to later bursts of fire'.[40] The artillery also improved its co-ordination with the air force (the initial instruction of 2 May 1915 was radically updated on 12 August) in the hope of improving counter-battery efficacy.

While the Germans were beginning to consider defensive tactics that would lead to 'defence in depth', the French were initially constrained by an emotional need to defend every foot of French territory but bitter losses in 1914 and 1915 gradually forced GQG to recognise the need to deploy flexibly. A note written in June 1915 suggested that the French should concentrate their reserves in 'stronghold' positions along the front line; this, however, created targets that the Germans quickly identified and obligingly pounded on a regular basis. From July 1915 front-line corps were ordered to hold a large proportion of their reserves ready for manoeuvre as 'the battle has only begun when the enemy passes the first line . . . counter-attack should be immediate for sector reserves and very prompt for army reserves; otherwise the enemy becomes installed on the position that he has conquered'. Regrettably the French found it easier to create strongholds that the Germans could identify than to pull their sector reserves back from the front line. As a result the French forward positions remained over-manned when compared to the German defensive system.[41]

Impressed by the German success at Gorlice-Tarnow, the French made a detailed study of the battle, also carefully examining successes in smaller-scale operations for evidence of how the enemy had utilised their artillery. The spectacular introduction of the hurricane bombardment, liberally mixed with asphyxiating gas shell, made an enormous impression on French planners, particularly the way in which the Germans used gas to isolate the front line from the reserves. The problem was that these successful attacks had been made against weaker Allied defences and, as the French were soon to learn, directly applying the lessons learned in the East and from minor successes in the Argonne (June/July 1915) would be far less effective against the rapidly evolving German defensive system.

The French 'offensive' school assumed that more artillery, a broader front and a longer bombardment would solve the main problems that had emerged in the early part of the war but their influence was being gradually undermined by a new generation of officers with genuine battlefield experience. Pétain had been one of the first to emerge, having commanded XXXIII Corps at Arras with particular distinction. Unlike many other commanders, Pétain insisted on each battery practising pre-registered fire and close infantry–artillery liaison and allowing the minimum possible delay between the preparatory bombardment lifting and the infantry assault. In addition, he supported the introduction of naval gunnery techniques to the heavy artillery, including the use of both meteorological data and accurate calibration, and he focused their fire against the strengthened emplacements that the 75s could not normally penetrate. These reforms were based on grim experience; in May 1915 Pétain's corps had failed to break through at Vimy, though this was partly due to the XXXIII Corps' reserves taking 6½ hours to move from their start positions, out of range of the German counter-preparation, and into action.[42]

The Price of Irredentism: The Italians Enter the War

The Italians declared war against Austria–Hungary on 25 May. However, it would be several weeks before they would finish mobilising and start attacking and it would take even longer for their industrial base to begin supplying the ammunition their armies desperately needed to compete with Austria–Hungary's veteran armies. Italy's declaration of war surprised her own general staff and created a grim new opportunity for modern artillery to demonstrate its effectiveness. Operationally constrained by the Tyrol, the Italians sought to secure the Austrian Littoral along the Isonzo, including the Adriatic port of Trieste and the Istrian Peninsula – the area that nationalists saw as the *Italia Irredenta* (the natural border of Italy). Unfortunately these aspirations required the inexperienced Italian army to fight across some of the most difficult terrain in Europe against a skilled and determined opponent, and as a result the battlefield casualties were unprecedented.

Italy was poorly prepared for war, with a fraction of the resources of the Central Powers and an underdeveloped industrial base. Relations between different ranks, arms and services were poor and, although the artillery regulations were relatively sophisticated,[43] senior officers appeared to make little attempt to study the lessons learned by either side in the expanding Great War. High illiteracy rates undermined the NCO cadre that Italy needed to ensure training and morale, and limited both innovation and expansion in the artillery. Most damagingly, low stocks of ammunition and slow mobilisation meant that Austro-Hungary had valuable time in which to secure her frontiers. The problems were exacerbated by the petulant character of General Luigi Cadorna, the recently appointed Italian Chief of the General Staff, an officer who had spent much of his time preparing for war with France. His belief in the efficacy of the frontal assault and immunity to advice from any quarter made him the stereotype of a First World War general.[44]

Austria's disasters in the Balkans and on the Russian Front were assumed to have created an opportunity for Italy to thrust across the Isonzo river through Gorizia towards Trieste, striking a blow at the heartland of the Austro-Hungarian Empire. The Austro-Hungarians were known to be pitifully weak along the Isonzo valley and Russian pressure was expected to pin down Austrian forces in the east. But the dramatic victory at Gorlice-Tarnow transformed the strategic situation and a number of veteran units were rapidly transferred to the Littoral in time to face Cadorna's first offensive across the Isonzo.

The *k.u.k. Armee* was still weak in both the quality and quantity of its artillery and tactical methods, having yet to entirely absorb the lessons of the fighting in 1914. Most importantly, while Austro-Hungarian munitions production was expanding, it was struggling to keep up with the ever-increasing demands for ammunition, so stocks were low. Italy and Austro-Hungary had similar divisional structures but the Italians were initially far weaker in both heavy and mountain artillery; even after months of preparation, only 112 of Italy's 2,000 guns were heavy weapons, and doctrine assumed guns and not howitzers would handle counter-battery fire.[45] Shell production was also a problem, with only 14,000 rounds being produced a day, and the Italians would soon find themselves relying on their infantry to break through.

In the First Battle of the Isonzo most of the initial assaults ran into determined resistance but specialist *Alpini* were able to secure the locally dominant Mount Krn and Cadorna's men rolled forwards until the Austro-Hungarians managed to consolidate their defences and adapt their experiences on the Eastern Front to alpine conditions. Relieved by the Italian failure to break through, the Austrians were particularly stunned by Cadorna's inability to seize the initiative in the still weakly held Tyrol. Krafft von Dellmensingen noted the 'great caution' shown by the Italians: 'they approach the positions slowly, behind which they can place their artillery, and then immediately after they entrench underground. From a tactical point of view it is not an inept procedure but strategically they behave in an unconsidered manner. The opportune moment [. . .] passed . . .'.[46]

General Svetozar Boroević, commanding the Austro-Hungarian Fifth Army, understood the importance of holding the key positions along the Isonzo and ensured that his men used every topographical advantage to hold their positions and issued standing orders for units to counter-attack at the earliest opportunity. Counter-attacks meant higher casualties but could roll back an attack if the Italians did not coordinate their infantry and artillery. The Italians soon discovered that carefully sited machine guns and concealed artillery, firing indirectly from *kaverne* blasted into the mountainside by construction units, were able to concentrate fire on the front ranks struggling up the mountainside; the terrain often canalised the attacking infantry into spearheads, creating near-perfect targets. A strategic prominence like Hill 383, near Plava, could be held by relatively few troops and only the Austrian ammunition supply limited the number of Italians that could be slaughtered by the hail of fire. If ammunition ran out, then a few desperate units found that throwing rocks could also be effective against decimated attackers.[47] The Italians understood that they had a problem but their staff system was inherently dysfunctional and thus they had trouble finding solutions.

Italian artillery did not coordinate closely with their infantry and most of the shelling in the first battle was scattered across suspected Austro-Hungarian positions.[48] Likely observation points received the most attention and the FOO position on Mount Santo (Sveta Gora), a famous medieval monastery overlooking Gorizia, was devastated in a full day's bombardment. On the South Tyrol front the Tre Sassi Fort, covering the Val Badia, was blasted with over 200 shells in early July, rapidly collapsing the roof, but an enterprising Austrian officer ordered lights to be lit in the fort at night and the bombardment continued for an entire month!

Cadorna made no attempt to monitor and improve communications between the artillery and the infantry, and it is difficult to escape the impression that he believed that heavier and heavier bombardments followed by ever more vigorous frontal assaults could triumph against determined troops. Where the corpses could not be buried, they were scattered with quicklime, and both sides doggedly focused on preparing for the next phase of the campaign. The Austro-Hungarians extended their network of infantry and artillery *kavernen* while the Italians brought up more ammunition and replacements. Both sides recognised that the struggle had become one of grim attrition.

Cadorna increased the number of guns and stocks of ammunition for each of the battles on the Isonzo and the Fifth Army started to lose more men as the heavier artillery pieces pummelled their positions. On Mount St Michele, in the Carso region, the shelling reached unprecedented levels. One soldier noted 'the gigantic, hard-pounding hammering of thousands of shells, which no words on God's earth can express', while another grimly prepared himself 'to die bravely as a Christian', writing, just before he was killed, 'It's all over. An unprecedented slaughter. A horrifying bloodbath. Blood flows everywhere, and the dead and pieces of corpses lie in circles, so that . . .'.[49] But increasing the number of guns did not ensure the success of the assault; Italian infantry still advanced in dense columns and the rapid losses of both officers and standard bearers soon stalled the attacks.

Where breakthroughs did occur, the Austro-Hungarians sometimes succeeded in clearing the Italians from their hard-won prizes with determined attacks led by local reserves. The defenders soon learned that it was better to attack quickly with small numbers of men armed with knives and battle-clubs so that they were ready for the close-quarter battles that followed. Where successes occurred, it showed what Italian artillery could do, particularly when they had the ammunition to shell rear areas:[50] if Austrian reserves moved over obvious routes they would be shelled and the counter-attacks would usually fail. While the Italian artillery *groupes* were finding it difficult to support attacks and to assist the infantry against the menace of snipers (the hated *cecchini*), they were proving increasingly adept at hitting the areas behind the Fifth Army's front line and were beginning to be used to support smaller-scale harassment raids. Observation positions in the mountains enabled any units in the open to be targeted and in one case a Croatian battalion was shattered while trying to return to the line after a rest. Italian artillery was also effective in defence. One Hungarian *Honvéd* division was blown apart in an over-enthusiastic counter-attack into the Italian start-line because the Italians had pre-planned defensive barrages.[51]

Trench mortars were found to be useful for supporting limited attacks in the mountainous terrain and under continuous pressure both defensive systems gradually improved. While the Austro-Hungarians drilled and blasted more *kavernen* into the mountainsides and improved the water supply, with pumping stations to keep the defenders supplied, the Italians began to expand their own supply system, building what would become the *Via Ferrata* – a remarkable network of cables, ladders and bridges designed to improve the movement of supplies and ammunition into the front line.[52]

By the Third Battle of the Isonzo, in October, Cadorna had tripled the number of heavy batteries and amassed a reserve of a million shells. He thought using old fortress guns and some French super-heavy howitzers could shatter the *kavernen* and break the Austrian artillery, but the preparations were obvious to Austrian observers and intelligence analysts, enabling the defenders to make final preparations and reallocate their meagre stocks of artillery ammunition. The bombardment lasted 70 hours but, for reasons that are still unexplained, there was a 2-hour gap before the Italians began the assault – more than enough time for the Austrian commanders to plug every gap created by the bombardment. Rudimentary body armour and helmets were no protection and the surviving Austrian artillery batteries tore into the assault columns. The Italian *fanti* died in droves.[53]

The year ended with the Italians having made only marginal gains for huge losses. While they had increased their artillery reserves enormously, this material advantage had been countered by Austro-Hungarian defensive innovations and a vigorous, if costly, doctrine of immediate counter-attack.

Crisis in Galicia and Poland

After the breakthrough at Gorlice-Tarnow the Germans drove the Russians out of Galicia, freeing the Austrian province and somewhat restoring the reputation of the Dual Monarchy – although it was obvious that the Germans were the real strength of the Central Powers and the Austrians were merely supporting actors. Since it would take weeks if not months to move troops from Poland to the Western Front, the Germans made the best of their limited resources and continued the attack in a series of sequential operations, driving south from East Prussia into Poland, and taking several fortresses (with immense quantities of guns and shells) and Warsaw. They also drove northeast into what is now Lithuania, capturing a number of important cities more through Russian incompetence than through superior operational finesse or strength. They cleared the rest of Poland with an attack northeast from Galicia. By the end of the summer the Russians had lost around a million men, a number of fortresses, thousands of guns and immense prestige. Meanwhile, the British and French had been doing little. British resources were still going to the Dardanelles, and their Western Front was in a lull; it was obvious that the BEF lacked enough guns and shells to make a meaningful attack. The French were also gathering their strength; they only had two divisions at Gallipoli but they were sending some munitions to the Serbs and also debating whether to land troops in Greece to reinforce their Serbian ally and create a meaningful front against the Austrians. Instead, Joffre and the 'Westerners' won the day, and the French stockpiled resources for an autumn offensive. It would be launched in Champagne.

New Tactics in the West: Pétain

The Champagne–Artois offensive of September 1915 gave Pétain an opportunity to evaluate the evolving battlefield and the viability of the outdated tactics favoured by GQG. The French deployed 872 heavy guns (and 1,175 75s), firing for three days, against a front of 35 kilometres in Champagne and 400 heavy guns, firing for six days, against the 15 kilometres of front near Artois. The French also deployed 500 trench mortars to deluge the front line. It was assumed that 'fires of adjustment' would still take several days to pound the German defences, and almost all batteries were pushed as far forwards as possible. As Pétain noted, 'We had taken the precaution to push our heavy guns well to the front, otherwise we would not have been able to counter-battery the hostile artillery on the day of the attack.' The limited hitting power of his obsolete heavy pieces also influenced the section of front line that he attacked: 'on account of the inability of artillery to reduce effectively natural strong-points we had selected a zone of attack that did not include any [villages]'.[54]

The use of smoke and gas (including asphyxiating projectiles) clearly made an impact on the Germans and some gains were made and prisoners taken. However, the German defences (with a fully developed second line and supplementary positions) were far more sophisticated than the French fire-plan had allowed and a breakthrough proved impossible. The French air force, deployed in unprecedented numbers and supported by tethered observation balloons, also made a difference and improved air liaison with the artillery enabled considerable progress in the early phases of the battle but this positive influence rapidly declined as soon as French troops reached the second line and encountered powerful counter-attacks. A GQG note of 5 December acknowledged the new reality, the 'warfare of positions which the enemy has organised in our front during the last ten months has changed in character'.[55] Inevitably, although some progress in tactical innovation was being made, the impact of German improvements meant that far too many men were being lost for minimal gains. Lucas notes that ordinary French soldiers were already losing confidence in their officers and remarks on their growing cynicism in 1915: 'this indicates the danger of starting or of allowing the circulation of rumours (of imminent success), of which we are not absolutely sure. The soldier is taken in by them once, but never twice; and, essentially distrustful by nature, he soon believes only what he sees.'[56]

Pétain studied the battle in detail and recognised that the Western Front had become a 'war of siege'. Against the German defence in depth, only large quantities of artillery with adequate ammunition and centralised planning could enable even limited objectives to be secured. Artillery preparation had to be improved and the strong-points that protected key objectives had to be subjected to decisive fire. Like Rawlinson, Pétain began to believe that the German propensity for immediate counter-attacks could be used against them. Until new artillery was available, the German second line was far beyond the point where Allied artillery could decisively intervene in the battle and therefore the only way to defeat the enemy reserves was to launch a series of linked offensives which forced the Germans to counter-attack into sectors where the French artillery was still effective. The problem was in laying the foundations for a successful series of operations without indicating the objectives by moving substantial reserves and conducting a lengthy bombardment.

Castelnau and Foch both supported abandoning the *coup de main*; indeed, Foch supported many of Laffargue's proposals and advocated improved use of air power for artillery observation: 'Mastery of the air appears to be the only way to give the artillery that effectiveness without which our infantry, even after a successful assault, runs into danger. The Air Force should be asked to make a special effort in this direction, and only regard bombing operations as a subsidiary role.'[57] Previous artillery production programmes were paying off: more medium artillery became available in 1915, enabling artillery commanders to use their guns more appropriately. The new 155mm howitzers were allotted to destroying strong-points, while the 75s would provide close support. Army commanders were also allocated stronger artillery reserves and attempts were made to improve training and standards of infantry–artillery coordination, such as disseminated daily reports to all units in the Second Army's sector listing the latest information on the position and activities of any confirmed targets in their area. Guided by the appointment of a dedicated artillery training officer (Lieutenant-Colonel St Claire-Delville), Pétain's tactical innovations were increasingly seen as a model for how corps artillery could be organised, and improved planning and liaison with the infantry began to lead to both more effective close support by the divisional artillery and to a far more efficient use of ammunition.[58]

The Champagne offensive also saw the introduction of the first creeping barrage (*le barrage roulant*). General Robert Nivelle, the dapper and charismatic commander of III Corps, had noted that the traditional preparatory fire phase often lifted before the infantry were close enough to make the final assault and gave the Germans ample warning that large numbers of targets were moving across no-man's-land. Nivelle's solution was to use the fast-firing 75s to lay down a continuous and advancing line of steel rain that would advance just ahead (80 to 100 metres) of the infantry assault. Infantry commanders were informed of the precise speed of the barrage and could try to coordinate their plans with the complicated but predictable advance of the barrage.

Without much in the way of active encouragement by GQG, Second Army's relative success in the offensives led to its methods influencing the new training documents being circulated to all armies. Training centres at Châlons, Amiens and Toul disseminated both the new operational methods and fresh instructions on the use of heavy artillery (20 November 1915), updated artillery officers on the new corps artillery intelligence units and improved techniques for both indirect and counter-battery fire.[59] The problem was that any successes by the French Army were still assumed by GQG to be the result of their superior strength of character and nothing to do with the introduction of new technologies or innovative approaches to operations.

Improvements to defensive systems were also discussed and although the French were slow to apply some of the bitter lessons learned in 1915, key officers clearly understood the principles. GQG noted after the autumn battles that 'the second position should be so placed as to escape the action of the hostile artillery against the first position (5 or 6 kilometres behind the first position) . . . It was to be dissimulated as far as possible from direct and aerial observation, by making full use of woods and counter-slopes . . . The [defensive systems] already constructed [should] be modified or completed accordingly.'[60] Some lessons proved difficult to learn and the French persisted in concentrating their artillery against the attacking infantry during an enemy assault and not the artillery; French fire-planners still assumed that they would have time to identify and destroy counter-battery targets during the enemy's preparatory bombardment. The German advantage in combining quick-fire artillery and an effective counter-battery doctrine was thus maintained longer than was necessary, giving the Germans a priceless advantage if they ever decided to launch an offensive in the West.

Rehearsal for the Somme: The Battle of Loos

The British high command was divided about their role in the autumn offensive; the French had been keener about it than the British, and Sir John French had been especially reluctant.[61] The French wanted a British attack to coordinate with theirs, although they realised that the British lacked the resources for as strong an attack; around 20 per cent of French guns were heavies, while the British only had 5 per cent. Sir John French was reluctant to attack at all (ironically proposing just some artillery fire to distract the Germans), but Joffre went to London and Lord Kitchener decided the BEF had to participate for diplomatic reasons and because Russia was in such dire straights: 'Unfortunately we have to make war as we must, and not as we should like to'.

Over the summer the British had resisted French pressure to attack, citing their artillery shortages, instead taking over sections of the line (thus releasing French troops into reserve) and stockpiling most of the few munitions that arrived. (The New Army divisions that were arriving needed time to finish training, while the Territorial divisions needed to upgrade their elderly artillery for modern pieces.) The Germans used the time to start building not just a second trench behind the front line, but a whole second position. That way, even if the Allies captured several trenches they would not break through but would have to bring their artillery up and start a fresh bombardment – and to do that, they would have to rebuild the roads. All this would buy the Germans time to bring up reserves so that a tactical defeat would not have strategic repercussions. Often the Germans also put the second position on a reverse slope so it would be out of sight of Allied ground observers.

The British agreement to attack pretty much decided the sector: Loos was close to the French–British boundary and a British attack there would cover the flank of the French operations. The terrain was a problem for the BEF, as the Germans held most of the hills and slag-heaps in the otherwise flat mining country. Because the Germans had higher observation posts, the British guns had to be sited further back to avoid German counter-battery fire, thus reducing the damage they could do in the depths of the German position. The Germans were also fortifying the villages, and that (combined with the obvious work on a second position) led to discussions about tactics for the attack. The BEF would not have enough heavy artillery to break through, so should it launch a shallower attack? That proposal was turned down (it would not put nearly as much pressure on the Germans, nor would it placate the French) and instead the BEF would rely on chlorine gas to replace artillery. One option that was not discussed was narrowing the attack to what the artillery could support, but a lesson learned in earlier battles was that a narrow attack meant the infantry would take flanking fire.

A wide attack (two British corps would be attacking, with support from another one and a three-division corps in reserve) meant that command-and-control (C2) systems would be even more important, and the BEF had been developing its C2 methods during 1915. For the artillery, the 'Artillery Adviser' (a brigadier at each corps headquarters, without any staff) was retitled the Brigadier-General Royal Artillery, and given a small staff. But it was not entirely clear what his role was, whether he really commanded the artillery or how he would work with the existing staff and commanders, and some of the existing artillery advisers were not effective in their changed role. The result at Loos was a hodge-podge of echelons (one corps put its artillery under the BGRA, another had groups and sub-groups in various sectors) for the artillery that did not help anyone. The field guns were generally under divisional command because they would be cutting the German barbed wire under infantry inspection, but all other bombardment artillery would be under the BGRA. The First Army retained control of counter-battery artillery and of the heaviest pieces.

Two factors meant the C2 problems would have relatively little impact on the battle. First, the amount of time available to plan the bombardment allowed enough conferences to settle most problems. Secondly, the shortage of guns meant that no commander could have made much difference. There were more guns and shells than ever before, but at the same time the frontage was wider and the Germans had more trenches and strong-points to bombard. Smart things were done, such as deliberately targeting German HQs, observation posts, telephone exchanges and communications routes. These were the right targets, but there simply too few shells – and thanks to the quality problems that the new munitions plants were having, roughly a third of the shells available were duds. The decision to try for a breakthrough caused other problems: the BEF had to shell the German second position at least a little (the wire had to be gapped) but only the long-range guns could reach the target. In 1915 the BEF was still working out air observation, and while the 'clock code' was used, there was also a great deal of ad hoc work, and an observer would customarily work with a particular battery. While this worked to a degree, it was necessarily limited because observers and batteries alike each had problems working with someone else. Anticipating some accuracy problems the BEF stretched the bombardment into four 12-hour periods over four days; this would allow as much observed fire as possible, even if the Germans would be able to make some repairs at night. Problems with both ground and air observation, caused by the dust that was kicked up from the chalky soil and the fact that there was no correcting for daily meteorological changes, all reduced the accuracy of the British shelling. Adding that to the shortage of shells (allowing only two 4.5-inch and one heavier howitzer round per yard of German trench) meant the bombardment would do little damage.

Conventional artillery support was recognised as being inadequate and gas was supposed to provide an alternative. However, gas did not do everything that artillery did: while it might kill Germans, and reduce their effectiveness when they had to wear masks, it did not cut barbed wire, nor destroy either HQs or the telephone exchanges. It was obvious that the gas would be dependent on the weather, and that led to awkward twin-track planning. If the weather cooperated, there would be a wide attack with the artillery spread to cover it. A contrary wind would mean a narrower infantry attack, with denser artillery support as some guns from the flanks were given alternative targets to support the smaller attack. As it turned out, the wind was mixed, a distinct help in some sectors but neutral in others and probably hindering the British infantry elsewhere. (There was not really enough gas available but by the time that fact was clear the BEF was committed to the attack.)

One thing the gas would do was obscure German troops; the cloud would cover the British attack, and smoke was added to this. Everyone knew that there would be German resistance, and the 'poor bloody infantry' would need all the help they could get. So a covering barrage was planned, to hit the front German trench and then 'lift' to other targets (other German trenches and strong-points) at set intervals. This would help, but if the British infantry could not keep up, or if the German infantry fought from positions outside the trenches, the British shells would do no good. Since the British were planning on a breakthrough, there was planning on how to handle it: the barrage would only last 80 minutes and at that point the field artillery would switch to divisional control and could advance on pre-planned routes once it received orders to proceed.

During 20–24 September the British bombarded; it turned out that the wire-cutting was patchy (probably because the German positions were on reverse slopes and the British guns had to be well back), and the few shells that could be spared for bombardment and wire-cutting on the German second position were virtually ineffective. The bombardment had so few shells that the Germans thought it was a feint, and that probably contributed to their tactical reserves being too far back on 25 September when the attack began. Results of the attack were very mixed, ranging from heavy casualties and negligible gains to breaking through the entire German front position. But British communications broke down, and there was no way to sustain the momentum. British reserves were too far back to make much difference (and there would be a fierce fight between Sir John French and Sir Douglas Haig over whose fault that was; it would end with Haig being given command of the BEF) and an ill-organised and unsupported attack on 26 September resulted in slaughter. German artillery was active and heavy, indicating problems with British counter-battery fire. First, there was inadequate reconnaissance; second there were too few British guns to destroy many German guns ahead of time. Instead, British plans relied on neutralising German guns after they fired. Unsurprisingly the Germans lost few guns and reinforcements meant their artillery quickly grew in strength during the battle. (The Germans did have some problems; where British guns had advanced, the Germans had trouble locating them and neutralising them. The German observation network and command system had similar problems to those of the BEF during the battle.) Unfortunately those advanced British batteries hit their own troops a fair amount on 26 September, pointing to problems in liaison between infantry and artillery; the British command system could handle the first phase in an assault on a defensive position trench but was too rigid for even small advances beyond the first line. Part of the problem was having to rely on telephones and runners but there was also the need to experience a problem before attempting to solve it. In addition, there were real difficulties in the British planning. The reserve corps had made no adequate artillery plan and when the battle dragged on intermittently for two weeks no British attack had the support it needed to succeed. Planning was rushed (and sometimes incoherent), there was poor air reconnaissance and poor communications; and the Germans won the counter-battery struggle, giving them a priceless advantage. While the battle ended with British gains, the Germans had successfully counter-attacked and retaken much of the key ground so the 50,000 British casualties seemed to have been for little gain. Kitchener reminded his colleagues that the BEF had to attack to maintain pressure on the Germans 'even though by doing so we may suffer very heavy losses'.

The BEF sorted through the results of Loos, and made several changes. First, it would never again rely on cloud gas to cover an attack on a specific day. Either the attack would have flexible dates or gas shells would be used. Counter-battery fire would no longer just be responsive, and 'prepared to reply' when the Germans opened fire. Part of the artillery staff would keep lists of Active Hostile Batteries so that there could be a preliminary bombardment of the German artillery as well as the German trenches. But perhaps the biggest change between 1915 and 1916 was the scale of resources. Shells would finally be ample (although quality would remain an issue) and there would be enough guns to fire them. However, that was the future.

The Field of the Blackbirds: The Defeat of Serbia

By the autumn of 1915 the Central Powers' drive into Russia had slowed but Allied pressure (from the Loos and Champagne attacks) was weak enough to enable Germany to gather some reserves. Looking around, Falkenhayn decided to deal with Serbia.[62] (The Serbs, having taken heavy losses in 1914 and then suffered a typhus epidemic over the winter, had been quiet for most of 1915.) Diplomacy – the Germans promised a slice of Serbia – brought Bulgaria into the war and her forces would outflank the

Serbs' northern defences. The campaign began on 6 October, and was a race against time because British and French forces had landed at Salonika, to protect the rail line into southern Serbia.

The Serb northern defences comprised a thin line backed by reserves; they could not be strong everywhere, especially with reserves being shifted to face Bulgaria. The Germans made the main attack, once again led by von Mackensen, and intended to use guns rather than men, deploying every-thing including the 42cm 'Big Berthas'. There were some problems finding gun positions, since there were wide marshes along the rivers, and the Serb bank typically overlooked the Austrian one. The Germans had air superi-ority and they picked the focus of their operations carefully and rapidly concentrated overwhelming force. With a vast superiority in medium and heavy guns, the Germans easily smashed through the first line and crossed the rivers. The Serbs did not bother to counter-attack because they could see the German bridgeheads were protected by artillery. The advance was delayed when bad weather interfered with the building of pontoon bridges, but proved inexorable. The only thing that really slowed the Germans and Austrians was the wretched roads: autumn weather on the already poor Serb roads meant guns could only move a mile in 2 hours. Meanwhile, the Bulgarians had a second front going and their substantial numerical superiority meant they were able to push the Serbs back. Yet they never broke through and never outflanked the Serbs, neither separating the northern and southern Serb elements nor cutting across Serbia and surrounding all the Serb troops. They did capture a number of elderly border forts, with eye-catching numbers of mostly obsolete guns.

The Allied forces that had landed at Salonika moved north as fast as they could but had a number of problems. First, they could not rely on Greek neutrality and had to watch their own rear (they had hoped Greece would join the Allies, but King Constantine was pro-German and kept Greece neutral). Secondly, the port had limited capacity and it took too long for the Allies to assemble enough units to head into Serbia. Thirdly, the Bulgarians were already closer to the main railway. Bulgarian pressure meant the Serbs could not simply retreat south to Salonika, but had to head southwest across the mountain highlands of Kosovo and Albania in horrendous winter con-ditions. The army abandoned its equipment, discipline slipped and there were fearful losses from weather and local partisans. Still, around 150,000 men survived to be evacuated from the coast to Corfu, where they would be nursed back to health, reorganised and re-equipped, and sent to Salonika – ultimately to rejoin the war.

Once it was clear the Serbs were heading away from Salonika, the British and French fell back. The Bulgarians advanced to watch over the port but the Germans and Austrians decided they were happy with the outcome of the campaign and pulled most of their troops out. They had several reasons: first the Germans were happy for the British and French to divert ten divisions from the Western Front, secondly the Austrians needed troops to crush Montenegro (which they did by January 1916) and nobody could be sure what the Greeks would do if the Central Powers invaded. So the Bulgarians (with a small stiffening of Germans) were left to watch over Salonika, a theatre that became a backwater for years.

Conclusion

Despite the bitter fighting and the introduction of new tactics and technologies, neither side had broken the deadlock on the Western Front. In the East the Germans appeared to have developed a brutally effective formula capable of dealing with the initially primitive Russian defensive system. Unsuccessful against Germany but usually capable of defeating the Austrians, the Russians were continuing to mobilise manpower and trying to reorganise their industrial power. The British were still building up their new armies on the Western Front and had found the traditional strategy of operating against peripheral strategic targets, with distinctly meagre equipment, problematic at Gallipoli and in Mesopotamia. The Russians were facing the Turks in the Caucasus and neither side had much artillery that could operate effectively in the mountains. The Bulgarians had attained most of their territorial goals and were happy to sit outside Salonika, while the Austrians were too weak to do more than react to the offensives launched by Russia and Italy. Germany was the only country that could take the initiative and attack. Her plans for 1916 were designed to do just that.

Chapter Three

1916

Over the winter of 1915/16 both sides reflected on the previous year and made plans for the coming year. The Allies recognised their superiority in numbers and resources, and intended to make that count by all attacking at once. France, Britain, Italy and Russia would all attack in mid-summer; the Central Powers would lack the reserves to respond everywhere and the Allies hoped that the line would crack somewhere (other fronts, mainly British operations against the Ottomans, would be treated as secondary and receive fewer resources). Allied industry would have had time to produce far more guns and shells, and new weapons for trench warfare were arriving, such as trench mortars for the British and heavy howitzers for the French. Just days after taking command in France, Sir Douglas Haig expressed optimism about driving the Germans back as early as April due to the 'unlimited ammunition' that would be available. Italy, with a smaller industrial base and a year less to mobilise, would lag behind in the production of both guns and shells.

The Central Powers acknowledged their long-term weakness, but assessed they had a temporary edge: Russia had been badly battered in 1915, and the crushing of Serbia had freed up Austrian units, so they had some options. Needing to move quickly, they seized the initiative. The Germans (mainly through the personal preferences of the Chief of the General Staff, Erich von Falkenhayn) thought that further attacks on Russia would be pointless since the Russians could simply retreat eastwards. Attacking Italy would be equally useless; her defeat would neither break the Allies' strategic capability nor hamper their resolve. That left the Western Front, and Falkenhayn had a choice between attacking the British or the French. He judged that Britain could not be crippled on land but would require defeat by sea, while he thought French morale was already staggering under the dual impact of heavy losses and their disappointments at the negligible strategic results derived from their attacks in 1915.

Although Falkenhayn knew that he needed to attack, he intended to try something a little different: an attack that embraced attrition. Rather than trying to break through the enemy line, or seizing a strategic objective, he simply sought to kill as many Frenchmen as possible – an *errmat-tungsstrategie*. To do it, he intended to rely heavily on artillery, substituting firepower for manpower. The attack would be launched in February at Verdun, and it would drive French strategy for the year – but the intense German pressure would also pull Allied strategy along with it. The British and Russians would have to adjust and help out the French; in the end the Germans failed to take Verdun, but they retained the initiative.

The Austrians attempted their own, smaller, version. With Russia weakened, Conrad turned on his personal enemy, Italy. The *strafexpedition*, an alpine offensive in April–May, embarrassed the Italians by gaining ground (despite the Italians having had adequate warning) but was a strategic loss because Conrad had weakened the Eastern Front to attack Italy. And the Russians were far from finished, as Brusilov's June offensive would demonstrate. This failure would persuade the Romanians to finally enter the war and created a political crisis that both brought Hindenburg and Ludendorff to power in Germany and provided the Central Powers with one of their easiest victories.

Verdun: The Mill on the Meuse

The German plans for Verdun appear to have entirely abandoned the idea of a breakthrough, Falkenhayn himself describing such a full-scale assault as a 'doubtful operation . . . which is beyond our forces' and which might lead to German forces being trapped in untenable salients that could be pounded from both flanks. Verdun was chosen as the objective since it was perceived both as a base from which the French could launch a potentially decisive offensive and because it had acquired an almost mystical significance during the Franco-Prussian War. Ironically, the Germans underrated their own fascination for the fortress city. The ever-aggressive General Charles Mangin noted that 'Verdun has always exercised a singular fascination upon the German imagination, and its capture, which seemed relatively easy, could in itself be celebrated as a great victory in Germany and in neutral countries.'[1]

On the French side the success of German heavy artillery in 1914 had convinced GQG's theorists that fortresses were potential death-traps which might enable the enemy to isolate and capture large numbers of men. The capitulation of forts on the Eastern Front in 1915 appeared to further confirm the lessons of 1870 and Joffre had ordered the remaining forts to be stripped of their guns in late 1914 to reinforce the army artillery. The theory was that fortresses supported the defensive system but were too fragile to function as a strong-point upon which the entire system could succeed or fail. Placing valuable artillery in a position that the enemy could easily target seemed akin to placing too many eggs in one basket. General Herr protested that there was a difference between an isolated fortress and a fort in a defensive system[2] but his memoranda were ignored. Herr's problem was exacerbated by the relative inactivity seen in the Verdun sector since the Marne. With major assaults being planned elsewhere and the rumours of an attack assumed to presage a limited assault, GQG assigned Verdun territorial units and concentrated on offensive planning.

Oblivious to their unintended assistance from GQG, the Germans deployed vast quantities of equipment and ammunition and began to construct bomb-proof *stollen* (shelters) for the assault troops being moved into the line. Infantry units were given strict instructions not to push out 'parallels of departure' or Russian saps that might give away the on-going preparations for the offensive.[3] Artillery units were moved forwards and carefully concealed. Most batteries were under orders to hold their fire until Operation *Gericht* had commenced so that the French would be surprised by the 306 field guns, 542 heavy guns and 152 *minenwerfe*r directly behind the assault units and the 400 additional guns supporting the offensive on the flank. Entirely fooled by the German deception plan, the French artillery was outnumbered by a ratio of 4:1 and French military intelligence had identified only 70 gun emplacements before the battle. Most dangerously, they totally missed the larger guns assigned to smash the forts, including the 420mm and 380mm heavy howitzers; the latter could drop 40 shells a day on almost any target in the Verdun sector.[4]

In General Schnabel's fire-plan, the 210mm batteries were assigned to pulverise the front line then place a curtain barrage to block any potential counter-attack as the leading assault units consolidated their hard-won objectives. Strong-points would be reduced by both the heavy guns and *minenwerfers* and the 150mm batteries would then be assigned to both counter-battery missions and to interdict the supply network and rear areas. 'No line is to remain unbounded and no possibilities of supply unmolested, nowhere should the enemy feel safe.' The 150mm batteries assigned to counter-battery work would use zone-fire, deluging entire areas instead of trying to hit individual targets, adjusting rapidly with the aid of air observers, instead of relying on more precise methods of adjustment. This required substantially more ammunition but the use of asphyxiating and lachrymatory agents delivered by gas shell successfully enabled the German gunners to neutralise the French batteries. The lighter guns would move forwards as soon as the assault began so that the heavy guns could be shifted to new positions capable of covering the new front line. The Germans stocked 2.5 million rounds alongside the batteries, and intended to fire the bulk of them in only 9½ hours on a 22-kilometre stretch of front before an infantry attack only 7 kilometres wide. It would be an unprecedented demonstration of the power of modern artillery.

The bombardment was delayed by poor weather but finally began on 21 February. It was initially general, with batteries concentrating on key objectives only after the French defensive communication system was judged to have been sufficiently disrupted. In the final stages of the fire-plan, patrols were filtered into the gaps between the main target zones to assess the remaining defences. A horrified French air observer saw no evidence of a gap in the carnage and reported that 'there are gun batteries everywhere. They follow each other non-stop; the flames from their shells form an unbroken sheet.'[5] Another described the fire as 'a storm, a hurricane, a tempest growing ever stronger, where it is raining nothing but paving stones'.[6] Fire jumped to the second line and continued on into the rear areas and out on to the flanks as the infantry advanced and the Germans surged forwards, only to halt as soon as they reached their primary objectives. They had been instructed not to push beyond these locations and new units moved forwards methodically to assault the second line; the General Staff had seen the effect of artillery barrages on attacks that were unsupported by counter-batteries and were wary of repeating what they saw as Gallic over-enthusiasm. 'The mission of infantry units is generally as follows: to seize a part of the hostile fortified system on a front and to a depth which has been delimited in advance; and then to hold it against intense artillery fire, and resist hostile counter attacks.' A note written by a staff officer in the same division (the 20th Bavarian Brigade) summarised the official view on initiative:

> It is possible that the enemy situation may be such as to permit the attack to be continued beyond the line that has been designated, and to capture certain points which the subordinate may consider of secondary importance. Do not forget that our artillery will not be in condition, if progress is made beyond the designated line, to immediately execute a new preparation and to quickly support the operation . . . The decision made by a subordinate commander to extend the

attack beyond the objective is a very serious one and should be the exception. Furthermore, the responsibility of the leader is affected, if a position which has been taken be retaken by the enemy, even though the adversary thus gains only a moral success.[7]

The highly regulated approach to securing the first line of objectives (although this theoretically abandoned any chance of a *coup de main*) enabled the Germans to exploit along the flanks of the initial penetration of the defensive system. German units that secured the initial objectives instinctively sought out opportunities to assist other units still struggling on their flanks. The French defensive system was severely ruptured but the combination of inflexible assault timetables and the leadership and defensive innovation displayed by the redoubtable if doomed Colonel Driant, in the section of the line dominated by the Bois-de-Caures, bought the French enough time to stabilise the front line before the Germans could realise how close they had come to a breakthrough. Driant's simple but effective tactic was to scatter his men among the shell-holes so that the German lifting barrage, designed to 'lift' just before the assault infantry swarmed over the defences, fell on his empty trench line and not on the men of his beleaguered command.

During the first stage of the Verdun offensive General Fayolle noted:

> The Boches have captured the front-line trench and the support trench. How do they do it: all their attacks succeed . . . they knock over everything with a horrifying bombardment after concentrating superior means. Thereby they suppress the trenches, the supporting defences and the machine guns. But how do they cross the barrage? Probably their infantry infiltrate, and since there is no one left in the fire trenches they get in, and when they are there to get them out we need to have the same artillery superiority.[8]

The effect of the German heavy bombardment, involving a rate of fire that the French simply could not match, soon earned the mordant nickname *trommelfeuer* (drumfire). An officer of the 243rd Infantry was stunned by the destruction: 'by three o'clock in the afternoon, the section of the wood which we occupied which, in the morning, was completely covered in bushes, looked like the timber-yard of a sawmill; a little later, I had lost most of my men.' Kronprinz Wilhelm was delighted by the apparent destruction but was quick to note the relatively low casualties inflicted during the bombardment:

The enemy, surprised by the annihilating volume of our fire, only shelled a few villages at random. At 5 p.m. our barrage jumped on to his second line, and the skirmishers and shock troops of all corps left their trenches. The material effect of our bombardment had been, as we discovered later, rather below our expectations, as the hostile defences in the wooded country were in many cases too well concealed; the moral effect was immense.[9]

Mangin was rather less impressed with their initial moves in the battle:

The offensive of 21st February was both terrible and stingy at the same time; it was staged on too narrow a front, which while it widened out slightly, again contracted, in spite of the great array of artillery with which it was provided, and the limitless use of infantry in deep formations, it advanced only with great effort and did not know how to profit by the gaps which were in front of it on certain days. When it was decided to extend it to the left bank of the Meuse, it was too late; the defence had got a new hold on itself and had been organised.[10]

As Mangin had noted, the first assaults were focused on the right bank of the Meuse and ignored the defensive positions on the left bank; for planning purposes, it was assumed that the counter-battery artillery would deal with any batteries flanking the main assault. Considering that the German plan was intended to maximise French casualties by retaining complete air and artillery dominance of the battlefield, the decision to leave the French batteries on the left bank almost completely unmolested by infantry seems to have been a major error in the planning for the first phase of the operation. As successive assaults went in, the obsolete but cunningly emplaced 155mm batteries on the left bank shrugged off the increasingly desperate attempts to silence them and poured fire into General von Zwehl's *VII Korps* every time they recommenced their advance. In spite of a spirited defence and an overly methodical fire-plan, the Germans still drove deep. Their overwhelming superiority in both guns and tactics enabled them to consolidate most of their initial objectives but as soon as the French threw in reserves, they launched vigorous counter-attacks and casualties on both sides began to mount. What Mangin bitterly described as the age of 'mechanical' battle had begun.

After the under-garrisoned and ill-armed Fort Douaumont fell, isolated by a near-constant barrage that gradually drove the supporting units to positions from where they were unable to cover the entrances to the fort, the Germans commenced a series of remorseless assaults on positions on both banks of the Meuse. Stunned by the initial reverses, Joffre sacked all the officers he saw as responsible for the débâcle and assigned Pétain to command the sector. Colonel Driant's tactical success with dispersed defences in the Bois-de-Caures during the first day of fighting was extended into a broader operational concept based upon 'an advanced line of resistance' consisting of forward outposts and observation positions backed up by 'a principal line of resistance' where localised reserves could gather and retake any lost positions with the assistance of attached artillery units. The concept of the easily identified defensive line was being abandoned in the face of increasing firepower. Counter-battery and curtain barrages by the heavy artillery units delayed the enemy while creeping barrages supported counter-attacks.[11]

Pétain, ably assisted by the slippery but brilliant Nivelle and the implacable Mangin, stabilised the Verdun sector by creating a *position de barrage* behind the front line, then using the old forts as armoured bastions in a defensive system that served as a protective zone in which the reserves could gather and launch counter-attacks. Unsurprisingly the artillery was seen as the key to this enhanced system and Pétain demanded additional artillery.[12] The continuing carnage forced Joffre to confront the consequences of years of mismanagement at GQG. The French artillery was still outclassed and outranged by the Germans, giving Kronprinz Wilhelm a priceless advantage in a battle where artillery was the key to victory. The evidence was conclusive enough to convince Joffre, who demanded that 960 medium and 440 heavy guns should be produced as quickly as possible.[13] Even with better weapons, French supplies were being brought along a narrow-gauge railway and the one forlorn, wreckage-strewn road into the salient and Army Group Centre could not hope to equal the near-continuous German barrage even if they wanted to. An American, working as a volunteer ambulance driver, asked about the rumble of thunder he heard as they approached the city and wondered if there was a storm coming. The driver shook his head in despair. 'If it were thunder the noise would stop occasionally. The noise is constant. It's Verdun.'[14]

Pétain and his staff drafted a new artillery programme and it was disseminated in May 1916. The roles assigned to each type of artillery and their proportions were adjusted in recognition of the new realities revealed by the battles around Verdun. Divisions gained additional medium howitzers while all the 155mm howitzers and heavier, bunker-busting mortars went into the corps and army artillery *groupes*. Once again it was the Second Army's training pamphlet that was circulated to the entire army as accepted doctrine, outlining advances in support, counter-preparation, communications, liaison, counter-battery techniques and the rapid concentration of fire from dispersed batteries.[15] Pétain also set up a Centre of Artillery Studies to coordinate research into new technologies, techniques and doctrines and to disseminate the most effective approaches to artillery operations. The new programme changed production schedules and increased the French artillery regiments from 115 to 247: a radical increase in dedicated manpower at the very point at which the French were beginning to run out of fresh reserves.[16]

Pétain took a personal interest in the activities of his hard-pressed gunners and often started meetings by asking corps liaison officers 'What have your batteries being doing? We'll discuss other points later.' Coordination was to be their new watchword and they were instructed to 'give the infantry the impression that [the artillery] is supporting them and that it is not dominated'. Such a policy increased artillery casualties but heartened the infantry, who were increasingly seeing the artillerymen as rear-area troops who had found a way to avoid genuine combat. One of the key innovations was the artillery offensive, a series of coordinated artillery raids on rear areas designed to disrupt movement and cause casualties. The Germans quickly noted the effectiveness of such tactics, observing that the French 'began the flanking fire on the ravines and roads north of Douaumont that was to cause us such severe casualties'.[17]

Even antiquated guns could make an impression if properly sited and, as noted above, the obsolete 155s placed to flank any German assault on the right bank of the Meuse inflicted horrific casualties during *VII Korps'* attempts to breach that sector during March. The French guns were concealed among the fortress lines on the Bois Bourrus ridge and there was nothing that General von Zwehl's gunners could do to prevent the French from slaughtering his men. The wounded streaming back to their start lines were described as 'a vision of hell' by one commander while another officer shouted 'What . . . battalion? Is there such a thing!'[18]

The next series of attacks focused on the left bank of the Meuse, centring on the grim slopes of the all-too-appropriately-named hill, Le Morte Homme. The terrain gave the attacking infantry considerable cover but the complex topography also favoured aggressive counter-attacks and the entire region was soon covered with blackened craters – one airman described the Verdun sector as appearing like 'the humid skin of a monstrous toad'. The German preparatory bombardments were horrifying and one description of an attack on Côte 304 creates a strong impression of both the improvements to artillery preparation being made by the Germans and the stubborn tenacity of their Gallic opponents:

> The pounding was continuous and terrifying. We had never experienced its like during the whole campaign. The earth around us quaked, and we were lifted and tossed about. Shells of all calibres kept raining on our sector. The trench no longer existed; it had been filled up with earth. We were crouching in shell-holes, where the mud thrown up by each new explosion covered us more and more. The air was unbreathable. Our blinded, wounded, crawling and shouting soldiers kept falling on top of us and died while splashing us with their blood. It really was a living hell. How could one ever survive such moments? We were deafened, dizzy and sick at heart. It is hard to imagine the torture we endured: our parched throats burned, we were thirsty, and the bombardment seemed endless . . .[19]

Pétain's new system was based upon building up a detailed record of all enemy artillery missions and battery locations and then centrally co-ordinating his forces to maximise his own guns' disruption and destruction.[20] Petain ensured that units spent only a few days in the front line before being relieved, the *noria* system, and this combination of firepower and a realistic understanding of what the infantry could withstand gave the French the edge they needed.[21] The army buckled but it did not collapse, even after the Germans launched eight frontal attacks on the defensive system around the heroic stronghold of Fort Vaux, finally taking its exhausted and parched garrison on 7 June. Undaunted, the Germans experimented with creating artillery corridors for assaults and the French found these extremely frustrating as it was difficult to predict the objective and resist the concentration of firepower. As Pétain noted, 'In effect, ignorant of the points threatened by attack, the defenders are obliged to be strong everywhere and to place in the front line increased numbers of personnel who must be replaced often.'[22] While the new tactic was successful in increasing French casualties, it could not win the battle without forming part of a wider operational plan; it proved to be yet another example of the Germans' inability to use their advanced tactics to achieve strategic objectives. In contrast, they ignored French logistics and throughout the battle ammunition and reinforcements flowed up the road from Bar-le–Duc to Verdun, endless lines of soldiers and 2,000 tonnes of ammunition a day moving towards 'the everlasting rumble of the guns'. For reasons that are still difficult to understand, neither the German artillery batteries nor the *Luftstreitkräfte* made a concerted effort to cut this vital artery and thus doomed both sides to a level of attrition that drained the fighting power of both armies.

Pétain, 'the master of scientific tactics', was promoted to command Army Group Centre in June and Robert Nivelle took over the defence of Verdun, 'the kingdom of the guns'. A new German offensive, led by the elite Alpenkorps and supported by a three-day bombardment that utilised large quantities of phosgene (a new asphyxiating gas), understandably described by Mangin as 'the most important and most massive attack that Verdun had to withstand', greeted Nivelle's appointment but the French artillery had reorganised and restructured since February. The precise German timetable of fire-missions and assaults that had worked so effectively in February fell apart in the face of a devastating series of counter-barrages that enabled French counter-attacks to retake all the key points. Another offensive in July ran straight into Mangin's veteran gunners and was pushed back to its start line by a series of savage counter-attacks. Verdun had become an open ulcer that threatened to swallow Germans as fast as it slaughtered Frenchmen. The German phase of the battle had ground to a halt and now the French could demonstrate what they had learned in the first six months of fighting.

It would take time to fully reorganise the French army to suit Pétain's vision of total war but most of the key concepts would be in place when their primary creator was placed in supreme command. The proof came when Nivelle and Mangin finally launched a successful attack to retake Fort Douaumont, after a number of costly but instructive failures, over-whelming the battered fortress with relentless fire from super-heavy guns – including two 400mm pieces which Joffre brusquely dismissed as being 'chiefly for the diversion of the public and the press'.[23] Nivelle dedicated enormous resources to the assault and a number of innovations helped the advancing French infantry. Every unit was thoroughly briefed on their objectives, a creeping barrage was used to keep the defenders under cover until the assault was on top of them and all communication wires were laid in 6-ft deep trenches to ensure continuous communications. The barrage moved 100 yards every 4 minutes, the 75s firing a hail of shrapnel only 70 yards ahead of the advancing infantry and the 400 heavy guns methodically pulverising the line with high explosive another 80 yards further forwards.

The supremely confident Mangin, described by one observer as literally licking his lips in anticipation,[24] even briefed Allied journalists on the morning of the attack:

> My 75s will engage the Boche trenches and I have an abundance of large calibre shells to smash every shelter . . . At H-hour, in two hours, the infantry will leave their own trenches and take the trenches before them; preceding them, at a distance of 70 or 80 metres, will be a blanket of 75 shells . . . When the creeping barrage catches up with it, the heavies will shift targets and hammer the reserves . . . We will continue towards the [German] reserves using the same method and they will be beaten by our troops . . . It will be an affair of at most a few hours . . .[25]

One officer saw the lines of guns being deployed and understandably snarled at the belated arrival of France's full military potential: 'If only we had been thus provided at the beginning of the war, we should not now be fighting in France.'[26]

Mangin ordered a continuous preparatory bombardment to prevent the Germans from improving their defences, a process he gleefully described as 'not burying the hatchet' and the Germans assumed that the French intended a series of localised attacks.[27] One French unit even withdrew to avoid being hit by any shorts from their own side during the massive barrage and some audacious Mecklenburgers on the other side of no-man's-land had the audacity to dash over and take cover in the abandoned French front line![28] The larger guns focused on Douaumont itself and as the 400mm shells began to smash into the fort's already shattered carapace, the German garrison withdrew to the interior – then, after the water was exhausted, all but a few men abandoned the fortress entirely.

The bombardment started on 15 December and lasted three days; when the French guns at last fell silent the Germans emerged from their *stollen* and dashed to their assigned positions just as their own guns commenced counter-preparatory fire. To the amazement of the front-line infantry, there were no enemy troops in sight – but then Nivelle's reserve of heavy guns commenced counter-battery fire against the freshly unmasked German batteries. The French 155mm guns pounded the German positions for an additional 36 hours, silencing or destroying 68 of the 158 batteries, before the creeping barrage began its relentless progress towards the main French objectives. The stunned Germans were completely overwhelmed as the French emerged from the morning mist and poured across the shell-scarred landscape, seizing positions that both sides had bitterly contested for months. In the foggy chaos Mangin and his staff soon lost contact with the assault regiments – a foretaste of disasters to come – but the key objectives were taken. French casualties were higher than hoped but the defenders suffered an even greater mauling and the Verdun sector was finally deemed to be secure.[29]

Joffre's influence faded during the battle for Verdun. His aggressive pre-war doctrine had simply collapsed in a battle where superior artillery played the decisive role. Heavier guns, indirect fire and greater range gave the Germans a valuable advantage but their strategic errors allowed the French to survive, a victory of sorts. With Papa Joffre politely kicked upstairs, the Young Turks were dispersed to field commands and the artillery was finally able to take full advantage of the increasing numbers of heavy pieces being supplied.[30] Planning began to focus around the artillery instead of the *furia francese*. The problem with such revolutions is that they occasionally lead to grand assumptions about the utility of the technical innovations forged during the collapse of the old system and tend to forget that the enemy has an even greater reason to monitor such changes.

The Battle of the Somme: Bitter Lessons

The German attack at Verdun had disrupted the Allies' planned offensives, but the British had long been preparing for an attack on the Somme. The sector had not been chosen for any particular tactical opportunity but simply because it was where the British and French lines met. One lesson of 1915 was that narrow-front attacks suffered disproportionately from flanking fire, and thus the wider the attack the better if it could be adequately supported, so combining the French and British attacks made sense. But with the continuous *roulement* of units at Verdun drawing in more and more French troops, the Somme inevitably became a mainly British operation.

Haig had contemplated launching preliminary assaults in different sectors to inflict losses on the Germans and draw down their reserves before the main attack on the Somme, but thorough staff-work had shown that the British artillery could not be moved between sectors fast enough (and would need too much time to bombard in the second sector) to actually make progress; the Germans would therefore have sufficient time to rebuild their units. So Haig discarded the notion of preliminary attacks and settled for making the offensive on the Somme as powerful as possible.[31]

Haig had far more resources than ever before and a variety of new weapons that promised to increase the chances of the offensive breaking the deadlock. British industry had finally produced a range of useful trench mortars: the 4-inch Stokes mortar could fire gas and smoke rounds (a 3-inch version that fired high explosive rounds would gradually be assigned to infantry brigades); a 2-inch medium version (nicknamed the 'toffee apple' because it fired a 40lb bomb on the 2-inch stalk) was short-ranged but had a sensitive fuse that made it effective in cutting barbed wire; while the 9.45-inch heavy trench mortar fired massive bombs that could easily collapse dugouts, trapping their occupants.[32] The 2-inch and 9.45-inch models were integrated into the preliminary bombardment, freeing some longer-ranged artillery for other targets. In addition, there were far more guns and shells than in 1915, as production finally took off under Lloyd George's energetic direction. Some new models were deployed, including 8-inch howitzers improvised out of old 6-inch gun barrels and lacking modern recoil systems, but also thoroughly modern 12-inch howitzers. Some 3,000 field and heavy guns were deployed, along with 1,400 trench mortars. Over a million rounds were fired in the preliminary bombardment and more shells were available in the supply dumps. Quality would remain a problem through 1916, and roughly a quarter of the shells were duds, while different batches of shells were actually differently shaped, leading to different ballistics. Some 18-pounders also broke down because their recoil springs were made with poor-quality steel and snapped far faster than expected.

The command and control system had also advanced from Loos, but would prove to have some problems. Each corps in the BEF now had a Commander, Heavy Artillery (CHA) and a Brigadier-General, Royal Artillery (BGRA). The BGRA was supposed to be in charge despite not (yet) being titled as General Officer Commanding Royal Artillery, and his role was to coordinate divisional and corps artillery in accordance with the commander's overall plan. The CHA was in charge of just the heavies, mainly focused on trench bombardment, but Heavy Artillery Groups (HAGs) were organised for different functions, either bombardment or counter-battery fire. For the first time there was an army-wide artillery order, with C.E.D. Budworth at Fourth Army laying down priorities and the corps artillerymen implementing it.

Despite the chain of command for the artillery, its commanders were distinctly subordinate to the army and corps commanders, and it was those men who laid out the parameters for the preliminary bombardment. Haig wanted to attack with as much surprise as possible, so the German reserves would be weaker; he initially wanted a hurricane bombardment as short as two days. Rawlinson, commanding the Fourth Army, wanted a longer bombardment, five days or more. Only by showing that a hurricane bombardment was impossible (the BEF did not have enough guns to fire the shells needed to sufficiently pound the upgraded German defences in only two days)[33] did Rawlinson win his point – and he responded to Haig's desire to degrade German morale by saying that the prolonged bombardment would deny them rest, food and water and would be more effective. Ultimately, the decision to have a five-day bombardment was the result of the dense barbed-wire entanglements: the wire simply had to be cut for the infantry to have a fighting chance. The progress of the cutting process had to be closely monitored, so this objective became a fixed point for the planning. The final plan required five days of bombardment with the 18-pounders and 2-inch trench mortars cutting the German wire, while heavy howitzers and heavy trench mortars pounded the German trenches. Only a few guns were allocated to counter-battery work – mostly the medium guns that had enough range to reach the German batteries.

Unfortunately, another of Haig's decisions would cause major problems: he wanted to break through the German lines and unleash the cavalry for a strategic victory. Rawlinson had been far more cautious, and wanted only to capture the Germans' first position (the first series of trenches; there were three separate positions) before advancing the artillery and attacking again using the French approach. Haig was trying to win the war quickly, while Rawlinson sought to solve the tactical problems. With Haig in command, he set the objectives: the Fourth Army had to try to take both the first and second positions. Artillery fire would thus be spread over twice as many targets, and much of the second position was out of range of the 18-pounders, so little of the second line's barbed wire would be cut. (The medium guns had that as yet another responsibility beyond counter-battery and harassing fire, although to the Germans it seemed there were many medium and heavy guns.) Haig may have been hoping that German morale was already low or that the Germans would have few troops in the second position, or he may not have realised the real implications of his ambitions for the offensive.

The bombardment started on 24 June.[34] The field artillery duly fired on the German wire (a process that was supposed to continue 'until the Officers Commanding the attacking units are satisfied that the obstacles to their advance have been adequately destroyed', but it had to be within the allotted time) and also practised conducting creeping barrages at different times each day, to deceive the Germans about the real Zero Hour (the creeping barrage itself caused the Germans problems in identifying Zero Hour, as it was intended to). The wire cutting was quite successful (although the attack would be launched regardless; a tactical problem in a battalion or brigade sector was not going to be allowed to hold up an eight-division attack that also had to be coordinated with the French) and the succession of false barrages probably caused the German infantry to fire their SOS flares, getting the German artillery firing and revealing some positions.[35] The heavy artillery pounded the German positions, especially the villages and trenches. A German corporal near Thiepval wrote: 'One's head is like a madman's. The tongue sticks to the mouth in terror. Continual bombardment and nothing to eat or drink and little sleep for five days and nights. How much longer can this go on?'[36] The German artillery pulled away from the villages, trading cover for concealment; this was a trend that would increase into 1918, with guns and infantry seeking open countryside away from an identifiable landmark that was easy to shell. Each British infantry division had a Heavy Artillery Group (HAG) to control the heavies bombarding its sector and the two HQs were located together for better coordination. With a 3:1 superiority in the air, the Allies had their artillery observation planes (and balloons) working without interruption and also drove away the German observation aircraft. Having balloons just sitting on the horizon was demoralising for the German troops, who knew that artillery observers could watch for the slightest movement in the rolling hills or calmly observe fire on any target in sight.[37] The Germans could not miss the Franco-British build-up but Falkenhayn chose to continue the German attacks at Verdun, so there were few reserves to send; he sent some labour troops (who built rear defences and artillery positions) and a few batteries, some of captured guns. Though modest, these reinforcements may have been more than the Allied counter-battery fire destroyed, and the German artillery was still active on the eve of the attack. British counter-battery efforts mainly focused on neutralising German guns rather than destroying them; at this time that was probably a reasonable decision. (The Germans did pull their OPs out of the front line after taking losses as they discovered that OPs were equally effective a few hundred yards to the rear.)

While the bombardment did a solid job in cutting the German wire, and nightly harassing fire interrupted supplies, there were relatively few casualties among front-line units, perhaps only 10 per cent of the forces in the defensive system. The British had not expected to kill every German;

while Rawlinson had openly stated that the infantry would only need to march forward and occupy their objectives, this was a morale-boosting speech and should not be taken literally. (The Germans did think the 'overwhelming artillery' contributed to the 'immense confidence' of the British infantry.[38]) The provision of covering fire, in the form of a creeping barrage, is proof enough that the planners knew that Germans would survive and have to be suppressed. The idea had been around in the BEF since mid-1915, and a lifting barrage had been used at Loos; now all the attacking troops would be covered by a barrage, but it was still experimental enough that each corps (and some divisions within corps) had slight variations.

On 1 July the Allied attack was relatively successful in the centre (the French left and British right) but far less successful on the flanks. The British right did well where the Germans were weaker and had not put as much effort into their trenches. Due to German batteries being emplaced on reverse slopes, British interdiction barrages, designed to disrupt the movement of reserves and communications, and counter-battery efforts had mixed results. The latter fire missions were much more successful where ridges did not block key German gun positions from view – such as around Mametz and Montauban. Also the creeping barrage was better in this sector, and the infantry used somewhat better tactics.[39] Major Alan Brooke (Lord Alanbrooke after the Second World War) prepared the 18th (Eastern) Division's fire-plan and adapted a French template for the creeping barrage, though some officers had suggested that a lifting barrage was preferable as it would not throw up as much dust and debris.[40] Even with good tactics and a good barrage, the 18th Division suffered 30 per cent casualties in taking its objectives – there was no cheap way to succeed on the Somme. In the British centre and left the Germans were largely successful, partly because their artillery was in better condition (the Germans identified certain locations, such as the Schwaben Redoubt, that would have yielded observation over their battery positions as key points to hold), partly because the British had less imaginative tactics, partly because there were more German troops available, and partly because fickle fortune played a role. The Germans would later note that they had been lucky, though in retrospect they lacked guns (especially heavies) and shells. The guns that they did have were worked hard. Major von Mellenthin of Field Artillery Regiment 6 wrote:

We had our hands full. The barrels steamed, no one could touch them. The gunners had to open and close the breeches with pieces of wood.

> We cooled the barrels with wet sandbags and poured water through them if we could. . . . Just remember that we were firing 2–3,000 rounds per battery per day.[41]

Shaken by the heavy casualties and their lack of success on 1 July, the British shifted their main weight to the right, reinforcing the successful units and planning to seize more ground before swinging northeast and outflanking the German lines further north. In theory this would create a solid base for a breakthrough attack. The Germans were startled by the initial advances and had to feed reinforcements in piecemeal, without planning, organisation or solid positions to hold. Aside from a major British night attack on 14 July, there were few major (or successful) attacks until mid-September. British attacks by as little as one battalion gained negligible ground and damage to the Germans was mainly from artillery fire. (Small attacks would often have inadequate artillery, just their divisional guns and the corps guns, and might not even have a creeping barrage if the division HQ was particularly overworked.) XIV *Reserve Korps* produced an interesting analysis of Allied artillery: while guns firing high explosive and shrapnel inflicted the most casualties (presumably because of the volume of shells and because their high velocity meant they arrived before the Germans could duck), the heavy (9.45-inch) trench mortars and 6-inch howitzers did the most damage to defences. The trench mortars had an enormous bursting charge (90lb of high explosive) but were limited by their very short range (only 2,400 yards), but that the 6-inch howitzers were given credit over the 8-inch and 9.2-inch versions was presumably because the smaller pieces were far more common and had more ammunition. While these attacks kept the pressure on the Germans, they often hit the same places time after time because they were too weak to take the objectives. Just why such small attacks were permitted by Haig and Rawlinson, when they had been iden-tified as ineffective in 1915, is a mystery, but it irritated the French who launched some independent attacks of their own - with the same problems and the same results. The French, though, were also losing men at Verdun and Joffre halted these pointless attacks until the British offered to launch a serious attack. While Allied losses were high, the Germans still had to feed in major resources; in July and August the Germans would fire 11 million shells and replace 1,600 field guns and 760 heavies.[42] (Guns were being worn out by over-use and under-maintenance; the Germans would later realise they needed to assign repair shops to each army.) The

Germans rotated infantry divisions, which caused command and control problems for the artillery as divisions were broken up: the guns could not be spared. Because the Germans subordinated heavy artillery to divisions, rotating divisions meant that the heavy artillery (and the immobile guns that stayed in a sector) had far too many commanders and lost effectiveness. Moving the guns, meanwhile, meant reorganising communications and having to assign labour units to bury telephone cables. German commanders thought about organising a separate heavy artillery HQ, but their tradition was unity of command and adopting such an HQ was haphazard.

Except where the attacks were too small, the British bombardments were heavy enough as there was no shortage of guns or shells. There was a shift in the 'planning rule of thumb' for attacks: instead of so many yards per howitzer, it became X shells per yard of German trench, with the number varying according to the strength of the German defences and the size of the shells. (Thus two 4.5-inch shells might replace one 6-incher.) This did not represent a shell actually hitting every inch of trench, but that number of shells allocated to bash the German trenches. The German First Army ruefully reflected: 'The power of concentrated artillery fire is so great that losses of ground will be inevitable even in the finest positions.' Max von Gallwitz, commanding the Second Army, recognised the grinding losses, in bodies and spirit, of his troops: 'It is true that the loss of one piece of ground after another does not amount to much in itself, but the repetition serves to strengthen the enemy and weaken us.'[43] Thus the strength of their defence shifted from the infantry holding the front lines to a mix of forward infantry, long-range machine-gun fire, defensive artillery fire and counter-attacking infantry. They reduced the front-line garrisons, hoped their defensive barrages would be able to 'nip the enemy's attack in the bud', and launched more and more counter-attacks to regain ground. Nipping attacks in the bud was rare but the Germans soon changed their artillery tactics. They concentrated their guns more, narrowing (but deepening) their defensive barrage zones, trying annihilating fire before an attack but barrage fire during it (to block British reserves advancing so that German counter-attackers would have an easier time of it), and largely ignoring counter-battery fire. (During an attack the priority was stopping the attack; for their own attacks the Germans would engage counter-battery fire to suppress the British guns, using gas against both batteries and observation posts; they earmarked most of their gas for counter-battery missions.) As Fraser-Tytler described it:

the Hun appears to have reinforced his artillery greatly and fairly pours in shell; weeping gas and poison gas unite with the most appalling stench from the heaps of dead to form a combination very trying to the temper, especially when one is struggling to speak down a line which is being cut to pieces every ten minutes either by shell-fire or by the frantic digging of the infantry . . . The only balm is being able to see one's own shells really doing execution.[44]

By September the Germans were rotating a division a day into the Somme. Most only lasted a fortnight, mainly because there were almost as many German counter-attacks as Allied attacks, but morale was dropping because the units lacked time to really recuperate and integrate replacements. When Hindenburg and Ludendorff came to power they assessed what was happening on the Western Front; there were too many counter-attacks and poor infantry–artillery coordination.[45] Coordination would be a problem for all combatants, but the Germans tried some different steps and made some different choices. When they rotated a division in, they tried to get the chief of staff and senior artillery and engineer officers in a few days early to learn the sector; they tried to keep an artillery commander in a sector for at least four weeks (although this divorced the infantry and artillery in a division); and they tried to co-locate the divisional commander, the divisional artillery commander and the sector's heavy artillery commander. The Germans put most artillery (except long-range guns, which they lacked at first so that harassing and interdicting fire was paltry) under the command of the division holding the front; divisions even split artillery up among the infantry regiments so the men on the spot could have the resources they needed. The artillery group commander would also be far forwards, with an observation post to personally direct fire. They tried to persuade the infantry to accept more counter-battery and counter-preparation fire and fewer defensive barrages, which wasted shells (and tired the gunners), when the British infantry was not in the open. Counter-battery fire was mainly destructive rather than neutralising, and depended on the availability of ammunition and good observation; the Germans did not have shells to waste on neutralising fire, and also put the counter-battery role under the infantry commander – the man in charge of a sector was in charge of the artillery in that sector, whatever it was doing. *Minenwerfers* were integrated with the artillery groups, and where possible there was a separate communications network for the artillery, offering some redundancy to communications. Hindenburg and Ludendorff also overhauled the artillery system, bringing in more maps, better communications (for instance tying air and balloon observers more closely together), producing maps of active Allied batteries, improving the repair system and providing a stock of spare guns to tide units over during repairs.

By mid-September the British had regrouped and decided to prepare a major attack, this time supported by the new 'tanks'. A good bombardment was fired ('all at once a thousand-voiced throaty scream came at us from the sky, and a long chain of flashing impacts announced that the *Trommelfeuer* had returned'),[46] but the covering barrage was problematic, precisely because of the tanks. Tank developers had mentioned the tanks' extreme vulnerability to shellfire (German or British) and the idea came up to leave 100-yard wide lanes in the barrage so the tanks would at least be safe from British fire. Despite the best of intentions it was a bad idea: a third of the tanks broke down before the starting line and, since they had been earmarked for the toughest sectors of the German line, the infantry would be attacking those areas without any covering fire. By this point the barrage was both denser (fewer yards for each gun to cover, and more shells), moved more slowly (so the infantry could keep up), and started in front of the German front trench because they had learned to sneak into no-man's-land before an attack. The lanes probably increased the losses (which were 40–50 per cent for most divisions), but the bombardment and barrage were good enough and the Germans lost a good bit of ground as well as suffering heavy casualties. Fraser-Tytler rejoiced as 'the Huns that escaped the Infantry ran into our barrage and ceased to exist'.[47] (A German home-front account noted: 'The unprecedented English artillery fire on the Somme is filling the hospitals more than ever, all those on the Rhine being over-filled, so that the wounded are being transported straight from the Western Front to the Tempelhofer Hospital in Berlin.'[48]) German guns knocked out several tanks, however, and they were certainly not anti-tank guns. They were ordinary field guns, deployed reasonably far forwards: the Germans liked to have guns about 3,000 yards behind the front lines so that they could fire 2–3,000 yards into enemy rear areas. It put the guns at risk if there was a breakthrough, but the artillery existed to take part in the battle, not to save its own skins. (*XI Army Korps* noted that guns must 'remain in position to the last. When all the gun ammunition has been fired the guns must be defended by means of rifles and hand grenades until an infantry counter-attack can bring relief.'[49]) If the infantry were at risk, the gunners (British and German alike) would stay at their guns regardless of incoming fire; if there was no attack happening then they were allowed to take cover. The infantry on both sides also liked supporting fire, even if it was accomplishing little. The British treated SOS flares as a demand for fire, while the German infantry would protest if defensive barrages slackened even if they were not working; wearing down gunners and guns meant nothing to an infantryman who felt his life to be at risk. To save shells, at one point the Germans limited fire to three-minute bursts, but the British noticed this tactic and took advantage of the lull after the initial burst of fire.

The BEF learned that tanks were 'entirely accessory' to the normal (i.e. infantry–artillery) attack methods and must not be allowed to dictate tactics (so there would never again be lanes in the barrage), and the Germans learned that they needed to move some machine guns back and fire them at long range instead of losing them to the preliminary barrage. Since Haig wanted to exploit the victory (he again thought German morale was cracking), there would be another round of attacks and of tactical developments. While the Germans were using long-range machine guns, the British added indirect machine-gun fire to the creeping barrage, which now had multiple bands of fire, including 6-inch howitzers, 4.5-inch howitzers, machine guns and 18-pounders. There might even be gas or smoke from 4-inch Stokes mortars on to particular strong-points within range. From the German perspective:

> A sea of iron crashed down on all the front and support lines of the area. The noise was terrible. Impact after impact. The whole of no-man's-land was a seething cauldron. The work of destruction grew and grew. Chaos! It was impossible to imagine that anyone could live through it. Square metre after square metre was ploughed up. . . . It was like a crushing machine, mechanical, without feelings; snuffing out the last resistance with a thousand hammers.[50]

As the weather worsened it could take 10 to 12 hours to move an 18-pounder to a new position. Muddier ground reduced the damage caused by high explosive and reduced accuracy as each shift in position affected the aim. Gloomy weather also worsened observation, whether from the ground or the air – and by now the Germans had built up their air strength and gradually reduced the Allied advantage. Despite the British firing four times as many shells, advances were painful. By October the Germans had suspended major operations at Verdun, and could reinforce the Somme; they could also relieve some of the most exhausted batteries. (Ammunition fired in September was roughly twice that fired in August, but was not limitless; there was a shortage of sulphuric acid for explosives.) That was some help, but one reinforcing unit noted 'there was nothing to see but ploughed-up torn-apart earth, brown mud, and the sites of former battery positions which had been so thoroughly shot-up as to be nothing but a dismal mash of iron, timber, and earth'.[51] The British slogged onwards, with the worsening weather affecting tactics: the infantry were hampered and slowed, and it became harder and harder to bring shells up to the guns. Haig and Rawlinson pressed on obstinately, repeatedly attacking but not necessarily gaining much. Fraser-Tytler recorded one attack in mid-October:

Just before Zero Hour everybody comes up to Switch Trench. It makes a splendid grandstand; as the batteries have already all the endless lift and alterations of range, we at the OP are simply spectators. I have seen many of these zero hours, and they get more stupendous each time. Often there is a lull during the last five minutes; then at the appointed second the whole world seems to explode. It is impossible to exaggerate what Hunland looks like on these occasions, erupting as it were in one vast volcano! Then the endless Hun SOS rockets ascend and down comes a Hun counter-barrage, followed by a period in which there is nothing to be seen except whirls of flame-stabbed smoke, incendiary shells bursting, and more rockets.[52]

By early November there was little point in continuing the attacks; there would be no breakthrough and, as the region became increasingly cold and muddy, losses were wholly disproportionate to gains. After protests by a courageous corps commander, Haig ended the offensive on 19 November.

The BEF would learn several things from the Somme offensive. Major-General Noel 'Curley' Birch, the Major-General Royal Artillery at GHQ, drew four lessons from the campaign. First, the artillery plan had to come from army level in order to coordinate matters. Secondly, there needed to be as much counter-battery fire as possible. Thirdly, the British needed more accuracy; although the Germans certainly felt the British were hitting their targets, Birch wanted them hit sooner so that more shells could be fired at other targets. Fourthly, the Royal Artillery needed better intelligence. Haig had instituted a 'lessons learned' organisation to improve the BEF between campaigns, and for 1917 the BEF would have new manuals (with a new doctrine) that would not only include what artillery should do but how to coordinate infantry and artillery – some of these ideas were modelled on French practices.[53] But Birch's emphasis on counter-battery fire would be the main difference between 1916 and 1917: not only would there be more experience of what to do, there would be a new organisation (headed by a Counter-Battery Staff Officer, or CBSO) and new technologies in the shape of sound-ranging and flash-spotting.

The Germans would also change things, paying attention to Verdun as well.[54] They emphasised depth and flexibility in defence, with far fewer defenders (and defences) forward, careful use of key terrain features and more barbed wire.[55] Artillery would focus on counter-battery fire when there was no attack imminent; that would slow the enemy's preparations and delay the attack. When an attack was expected, counter-preparation would be fired on the enemy front-line trenches; that should catch the infantry forming up, and if reserves were already forwards they would also be hit. Only if an attack was under way would barrages be fired, and they were still subject to change if a 'living target' was observed: shellfire could not stop all attacks (or attackers), and hitting men was more important than potentially blocking an approach route.

The Germans also continued to counter-attack, differentiating between immediate counter-attacks (*gegenstoss*) and deliberate ones (*gegenangriff*), but seeking to regain positions that were important rather than simply regaining the line where the front had happened to settle in 1914. Where a counter-attack was thought impossible artillery could be used to make recently vacated positions untenable.[56] General von Bülow had begun to lose heart: 'the battle in progress entails the loss of so many men for no purpose in the defence . . . I am forced to prescribe that the methodical counter-attack will never be made; except those of minor importance and which are only of an absolutely minor character'.[57] The German tradition of initiative at low levels ran into the timetabling problem common in the Great War when infantry ran into their own *feuerwalz*; they could not both exploit the opening and stay out of the curtain of fire.

The Germans decentralised most of their artillery to division rather than corps level; while this improved the response to the infantry in battle, it meant problems in concentrating fire across divisional boundaries. It also made rotation of units more difficult, as a divisional artillery staff had to stay in a sector when the infantry were burned out. However, even though Falkenhayn demanded 'immediate' counter-attacks,[58] in defence the Germans only needed to disrupt the British infantry–artillery attack – they did not need to do all the things the attacker did.

The Somme: The French Experience

With the carnage at Verdun, the French were initially able to assign only the Sixth Army to the planned offensive on the Somme, although by the end of the battle they had made a far more substantial contribution than is often assumed by British historians.[59] Most of the units on the right flank of the British assault had recent experience at Verdun and were familiar with many of the latest innovations in artillery tactics. Even without surprise, the Allies expected to effect a rupture in the Somme sector by wearing down German reserves and creating an opportunity to break through the defensive system. General Marie-Émile Fayolle, previously professor of artillery tactics at the *École de Guerre*, was one of the supporters of the new methodical approach,[60] but suspected that a battle of attrition on the Somme would merely lead to another 200,000 casualties.[61] His patience bore fruit in the relatively impressive gains made by the French divisions assigned to the battle on the first day. 'Some officers seem to fear that the method [methodically fighting from objective to objective] may break the dash of the infantry. In reality, what breaks the dash of the infantry is the presence of intact wire and or the opening up of flanking machine guns. That is why the purpose to be accomplished is to destroy them before each attack. Not a slow preparation, but one to which all time necessary is devoted to make sure that it is certain, then rapid execution; such is the formula for the attack.'[62]

The French fire-plan for the assault on 1 July was organised to batter the first position, enable initial registration on the second and support the infantry with 'an impressive and precisely regulated [creeping] barrage'. The objectives were selected on the basis of their influence on the next phase of the battle rather than the British approach of making a general advance, and 'the artillery preparations determined what the infantry could achieve'.[63] The German lines south of the Somme were closer, easier to observe and relatively weakly held, and this gave the French a crucial advantage over the British gunners. Trench artillery was used to eliminate key positions in the first line and the huge guns of the *Artillerie Lourde à Grande Puissance* were targeted on German positions deep within the defensive system. The Germans were horrified by the destruction and the *crapouillots* of the *artillerie de tranchée*, organised in grand batteries, proved far more effective than their sceptics expected.[64] Counter-battery plans continued to use the French system of corps-level analysis, with air and forward observers updating trench maps and reporting on the locations of enemy batteries.[65]

The French committed 1,200 heavy guns and 1,200 mortars to the assault in September – probably the maximum that could be targeted on the assigned objectives. From this point onwards the French concentrated on technical improvements to their guns and further improvements to artillery planning and liaison. As with the British, gaining dominance of the air was seen as an essential precursor for success, while improved gas projectiles promised to shorten the bombardment and ensure that the defending batteries were neutralised and the enemy reserves unable to intervene in the battle. The French recognised that lengthy bombardments gave the Germans vital time to prepare and an increasing number of commanders were alert to any technology – such as the tank – that could shatter the deadlock and ensure that the attack retained enough momentum to achieve its objectives.[66]

The French were unimpressed by the initial performance of the British on the Somme, Joffre noting that 'the British suffered from the fact that their artillerymen were less successful than ours and their infantry less experienced'. Joffre recognised that the Germans had not expected a French attack in the Somme sector but credited the success of the initial offensive to 'the excellent work of the artillery'. French officers, including Foch, believed that the British had not grasped either how to concentrate fire effectively (it was 'dispersed and wasted'), or how to conserve men until the Battle of Morval in September,[67] while Fayolle, rather less generously, dismissed the British failures as the result of using 'infantile' tactics. Liaison between the two forces was close where the French artillery was available to assist the British infantry but this did not stop misunderstandings from occurring and certainly did not prevent both sides blaming the other if mistakes led to casualties – creating bitterness that obscured the more successful aspects of their collaboration.[68]

The attacks in September faced more difficult objectives and the French soon discovered that a methodical battle that went awry in the first phase made succeeding attacks more difficult as German reinforcements fought doggedly to prevent the assault units from supporting each other. When the plan succeeded, German counter-attacks were relatively easy to repulse.[69]

Although the French were operationally far more successful than the British during the first phase of the offensive,[70] their tactical dependence on the methodical artillery fire-plan was seen by some as undermining the instinctive élan of the infantry. A report submitted by a division fresh from the carnage of Verdun noted: 'It is the infantry that conquers ground and holds it. Even when the artillery has laid a perfect preparation, if the infantry does not function then nothing is accomplished.' The terrible power of modern weaponry had shattered the theory of the *offensive à l'outrance* but surviving the modern horrors of war still required an equally impressive form of bravery and final victory continued to depend on the morale and élan of the front-line infantry soldier. In August Fayolle, usually famed for his caution, noted acidly:

> There has been noticeable lately, in a number of infantry officers, a deplorable mentality which, if it persists, will tend to rob the infantry of all of its offensive power [and] make of it nothing more than a passive agency for the occupation of terrain that the artillery has previously cleared of all obstacles and even of all the enemy . . . [The infantry] often demand complete destruction . . . The cannon prepares attacks by opening the way, by overthrowing the material obstacles which oppose the infantry, but only the latter can exploit these destructions by progressing into the enemy's lines [and] exploiting local conditions to the utmost. In a word, the infantry must fight and fighting consists of will and intelligence . . .[71]

Fire-planning appears to have achieved the status of a truly scientific approach to warfare, with a level of predictability that arguably only existed when Vauban himself conducted sieges. The infantry, although re-organised into assault teams of light machine-gunners, grenadiers and riflemen,[72] wedded to the mathematical fire-plan, often stuck like glue to the rolling barrage set for each successive objective and the process of making an assault became increasingly formalised. German reports from the Somme noted that the first French infantrymen aimed to enter their defensive system just as the creeping barrage passed over the trenches. A number of officers recognised the weakness in this approach and supported the infantry's need to adapt to changes on the battlefield. Mangin was among those who was dubious of the efficacy of planning for everything, noting after the war about the lessons of 1916 that 'the establishment of various plans that regulated everybody's part in the attack was still con-sidered necessary, as if it were a question of taking a position which had been leisurely organised . . . Methods can be learned, but only practice develops the sense of improvisation, when such sense is not inbred.' A contemporary divisional report made the point even more succinctly: 'the automatic attack, where every detail up to the final culmination has been arranged for beforehand, is a utopia.'[73] The French focus on liaison enabled them to plan methodically but now appeared to be undermining their ability to seize opportunities on the battlefield. With classical ambiguity the GQG note of 27 August 1916 contradicted itself by requiring officers to show dash and initiative but sternly reminded them to be mindful of the artillery fire-plan: 'exploitation of success is not accomplished by the infantry alone'.

The French artillery made a number of technical improvements in late 1916. Counter-battery methods were improving and heavier quick-firing guns were becoming available.[74] Fire-plans now included targets deep within the enemy defensive system and GQG reminded planners that 'the objective assigned to an attack constitutes a minimum line which must be reached with certainty, but beyond which progress may and should be made'. In December 1916 improved plans for the operational displacement of artillery were introduced so that the attack could proceed in successive stages without giving the Germans time to consolidate their defences or commit reserves; progress was assumed to depend on enemy resistance but both the communication and liaison system still required radical improvements before genuine tactical flexibility could be reintroduced to the battlefield. Communications in defence were rightly seen as having equal importance since a prolonged bombardment often destroyed telephone wires, obscured visual signals and slaughtered runners.

Counter-battery precision substantially improved during 1916, and the *Service du Renseignements d'Artillerie* was created to collate and disseminate intelligence on the locations of enemy batteries. Von Bülow, who commanded the Second Army in the July battles, was particularly impressed, noting after the Somme that 'it is striking to observe that the guns of our enemies also seem to have far less dispersion than our own. Our enemies also seem to understand map-firing much better than we do. In fact, in weather that precludes any direct observation and which requires considerable corrections of the moment, they succeed in making precision fire upon objectives of very limited dimensions.' Some modern historians have tended to denigrate the ability of the French army to take the lead in technical matters, but the Germans could not afford to underestimate their opponents so casually, and studied emerging French and British tactics and technologies with great interest. The success of French and British artillery in breaking up counter-attacks was duly noted and the artillery was given an increased role in the defensive system. The German *Regulations for the Defence in Position Warfare* of late 1916 noted:

In the conduct of the battle, the defence should not give up the initiative. By its activity, particularly the activity of the artillery, and by the

A German pre-war 15cm howitzer (1902 sFH) battery deployed for action. Note the distinctive artillery *Kugelhelm* ('ball helmet'). *(Pen & Sword Collection)*

(*Above*) 14th Battery, Royal Australian Field Artillery, near Ypres, 1917. To cover an attack with a creeping barrage, these 18-pounder guns would fire two to four shells (22lb per round, including cartridge and propellant) per minute, for 50 minutes of each hour (the guns needed to cool and have the sights checked) for up to 6 hours. Each fuse had to be set by hand, and the elevation had to be adjusted as the gun and air temperatures changed, and depending on the batch of propellant involved. (*IWM photo E920*)

(*Opposite, top*) A British quick-firing (QF) 18-pounder. With a calibre of 84mm, this was the British equivalent of the French 75mm and the German 77mm field guns. The 18-pounder was designed for mobility and robustness across all the climates of the Empire. Thus it had a pole trail instead of a box trail, which saved weight but shortened range. It also used a spring instead of a pneumatic recuperator.

(*Opposite, below*) Dump of empty 18-pounder shell cases near Fricourt, September 1916. Since these were made of brass, they were recycled up to four times, which is why they were collected in dumps. During 1916 the BEF fired several million 18-pounder rounds, so these cases represent only a tiny fraction of the total. (*IWM photo Q1471*)

T M Ratcliffe, 2010

A British quick-firing 4.5-inch howitzer battery deployed in woodland. (*Pen & Sword Collection*)

This factory scene shows one of the sorting sheds, possibly at the Royal Shell Filling Factory at Woolwich, with women workers checking the lifting plugs fitted to completed high explosive shells. The plugs were removed and replaced with fuses when the shells reached the battery. (*Author's Collection*)

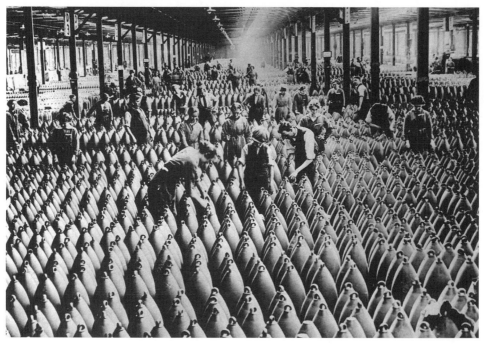

A British 4.7-inch medium gun in action on the Somme. Note how calm the horses are, considering the battery is firing directly over them as they withdraw! *(Pen & Sword Collection)*

(*Above*) British soldiers removing the camouflage from a British Mark V 12-inch railway gun, 'Peeping Tom'. Note the cable outriggers used for steadying the gun when firing. (*Pen & Sword Collection*)

(*Opposite, top*) Digging a gun emplacement, 21 August 1918. Even with the growing Allied superiority both in artillery and in the air, it was still important to dig in. Camouflage was also important: the gun immediately behind the men, and the shells to the right rear, are under netting. (*IWM photo Q8238*)

(*Opposite, below*) Repairing worn-out 60-pounder guns at the ordnance workshop at Lovie, 22 August 1917. A major concern in 1917 was the wear that artillery pieces were suffering from firing thousands and thousands of rounds. Each round fired wears a tiny amount of the barrel away, and eventually muzzle velocity and accuracy decrease. The problem of wear across the BEF's whole stock of artillery was so severe that it affected operational choices, because the BEF could not use large quantities of artillery to take limited objectives in attritional battles. (*IWM photo Q2769*)

55th Siege Battery, Royal Australian Garrison Artillery, Voormezeele, 15 September 1917. The 9.2-inch howitzer was an excellent weapon with good range and shell power. However, it was not very mobile; the large box at the right was part of the weapon's frame that helped hold it in place. Every time the howitzer was moved it had to be emptied of around 9 tons of earth, disassembled, moved, reassembled, and refilled. In 1918 the rough rule of thumb was that these howitzers were of no use if the front moved more than 3,000 yards per day, as the time taken in moving the weapons far outweighed their time in action. These gunners, near the Ypres Salient, are presumably firing a night harassing mission. They are masked against German gas. Gas was commonly used at night because sleeping soldiers were more likely to breathe enough gas to incapacitate or kill them before they could be woken by an alarm. (*IWM photo E693*)

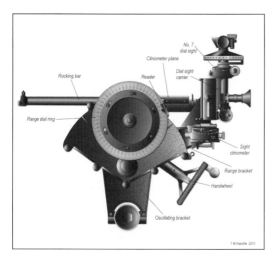

(*Left*) Carrier no. 7 dial sight (used to ascertain direction) and rocking bar sight (elevation) as fitted on the 9.2-inch howitzer. With the assistance of a forward observation officer or accurate maps, the mechanism illustrated enables the artillery piece to be accurately positioned in relation to both the rest of the battery and the intended target. This allows the howitzer to conduct 'indirect' fire missions (at a target that is not within direct line of sight), by reference to a known object (the director or aiming point) that is within sight (as opposed to 'direct' fire).

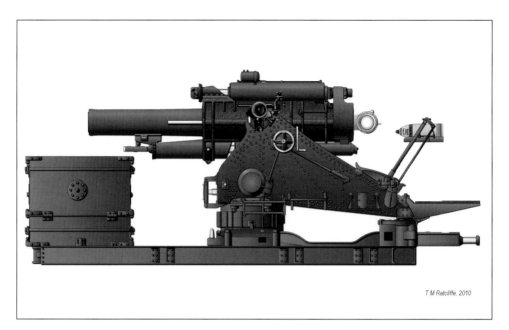

T M Ratcliffe, 2010

The British 9.2-inch howitzer was designed just before the war as a siege weapon. Robust and reliable, it had a good combination of shell weight and range, although during the war new designs of shells and longer barrels increased range. As a siege weapon, its lack of a wheeled carriage was not a problem. The design was scaled up for the 12-inch and 15-inch howitzers, mainly by increasing the number of recuperators. The arrangement of buffers and recuperators is shown below.

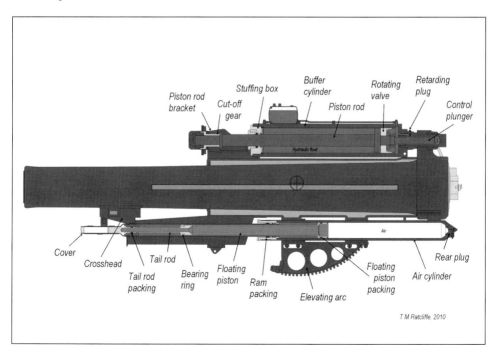

T M Ratcliffe, 2010

Barbed wire in front of the Hindenburg Line near Bellicourt, 4 October 1918. This photo was taken six days after the British broke through the Hindenburg Line, and the depth and density of the belts of barbed wire are clear. The senior artillery officer in the sector noted that the artillery had not done enough against the barbed wire to clear the way for an attack, and had it not been for the much lower morale of the German infantry the British would not have won the battle. (*IWM photo Q9382*)

A 9.2-inch battery deployed in a chalk pit. Both guns are shown in the process of being stripped for maintenance (almost certainly conducting routine testing and inspection of gun carriage recoil and recuperation performance), with the barrels set at full recoil. Heavy howitzers were loaded with the barrel set at horizontal before being elevated into a firing position (see p. 116). Note the use of a disruptive camouflage pattern, and that the howitzer in the foreground has been nicknamed 'Persuader' by its crew. (*Author's Collection*)

A German observation post near Bazentin-le-Petit, November 1916. Part of the counter-battery effort was shelling German observation posts. While casualties would be few, the German artillery would be disrupted. Depending on the sector of the front, observation posts would be in trees, in buildings (often reinforced with concrete) or simply on high ground. (*IWM photo Q4469*)

A knocked-out tank being used for cover on the Somme in 1916. Note the primitive tank corps helmets. (*Pen & Sword Collection*)

(*Above*) Heavy machine guns firing tracer ammunition at night. This kind of fireworks display would often be followed by Very flares indicating a request for an artillery SOS fire mission. (*Pen & Sword Collection*)

(*Below*) This German pillbox eloquently demonstrates the difficulty the artillery had in hitting concrete strongpoints with indirect fire. (*Pen & Sword Collection*)

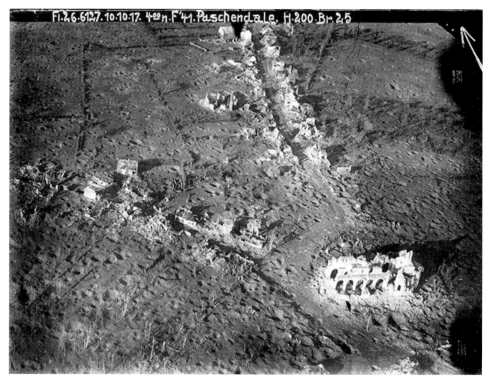

(*Above*) The remnants of the town of Passchendaele on 10 October 1917, after the Battle of Poelcappelle (9 October) but before the main assault on 12 October (First Passchendaele). After the battle only the stumps of the church nave and vague markings of what were once streets and houses in the shell-scarred landscape remained. (*Pen & Sword Collection*)

(*Below*) A dense creeping barrage near Meteren, 18 August 1918. The 9th (Scottish) Division made a limited attack on 18 August after heavy artillery preparation and under a dense creeping barrage. The clouds are partly from smoke shell (25 per cent of the barrage) and partly from the dusty ground. (*IWM photo Q6990*)

German stormtroopers dragging a 7.62cm *Infanteriegeschütz* L16 in action – a battery of six of these was attached to most stormtrooper battalions in 1918. (*Pen & Sword Collection*)

(*Opposite, top*) A German 77mm gun, carefully dug in so it could fire in indirect fire mode, served by artillerymen in gas masks. (*Pen & Sword Collection*)

(*Opposite, below*) New Zealand artillerymen loading limbers with ammunition near Albert, September 1916. Every shell that was fired in the First World War was handled many times on its way to the front, requiring a tremendous amount of labour. Loading the limbers was one of the last stages, before the limbers went forward to the gun positions, where the shells were unloaded close to the guns. The white crosses on the end of each round are cloth handles that were secured by light metal clips; they simply made it easier to pull the rounds out of the limbers and generally made them easier to handle. (*IWM photo Q1249*)

A Royal Garrison Artillery sergeant copying down instructions for SOS lines near Monchy-le-Preux, 18 March 1918. The quantity of data the sergeant has to record indicates some of the technological advances the artillery made during the war. In addition to this information, recent meteorological information would have to be considered, and each gun's individual wear would have to be factored in as well. In defensive fire this was paradoxically somewhat less important than in an attack, because defensive fire that came to friendly troops at least did so while they were in cover. However, accuracy in bombarding and counter-battery fire was extremely important. (*IWM photo Q10895*)

mobility of its forces, it should check the advancing power of the attacker, force him to thicken his first lines, break up his plans, harass his troops in their assembly positions, prevent movement and inflict on him the maximum losses . . . It is of exceptional importance to overcome the hostile artillery . . . by conducting well adjusted fire for destruction against a definite objective until that objective has been annihilated.[75]

The French were equally interested in studying and emulating the defensive improvements they had encountered on the Somme. They surmised that negating an attacker's artillery preparation required moving the reserves much further back and out of the conventional linear system and into bunkers, underground tunnels and strong-points. In all cases the new positions were to be carefully camouflaged. Where necessary, the infantry were to utilise available shell-holes so that the true defensive system was deepened and the enemy bombardment would be less effective. The French recognised that any isolated strong-points could be bombarded by heavy guns and then outflanked by enemy assault parties; thus, although the French infantry continued to contemplate digging trenches with Gallic disdain, their new defensive systems were planned with both adequate support from machine-gun nests and forward observation posts and they were echeloned in depth. Most importantly, devising an effective counter-preparation could reduce the devastation created by the barrage and enable the defending artillery to both tear apart the attacking infantry and support counter-attacks. The main lesson of the battle of Verdun, noted by GQG as early as April 1916, had been that 'the artillery has been able to reduce the material means of the defence and to wear down its morale, but it has not been able to destroy it'.

Surprise had played a key role at Verdun but the continuing preponderance of obsolete artillery pieces demanded prolonged bombardment. Tactical utility still had to take precedence over strategic surprise until the French artillery acquired the tools they needed to achieve their objectives before the German reserves were committed but some commanders – Foch in particular – were beginning to understand how a sequence of limited operations, based upon objectives the artillery could adequately cover, might lead to a strategic fracturing of the German defensive system. Success was assumed to emerge out of the 'methodical artillery struggle'.[76] While French planners still struggled with the problem of matching technology to aspirations, the gunners focused on finding the best way to support the infantry without access to substantial numbers of modern heavy guns; the main objective of the artillery remained the precise destruction of enemy assets and defensive positions but gradual improvements in neutral-isation being demonstrated by the enemy batteries were carefully monitored. Gas shells appeared to present an important alternative to precise targeting of enemy batteries and strongholds but combining them into the main fire-plan still presented problems. The French even began studying captured documents on tactical methods, although they often found it difficult to admit where the information had originated from when it was disseminated.[77]

The Brusilov Offensive

After the disastrous engagements of 1915, when the German artillery had convincingly demonstrated its superiority in artillery planning and close support, STAVKA was understandably reluctant to risk further reverses until the Russians had built up substantial reserves. As usual, the pressure of events on other fronts soon frustrated any attempts to thoroughly retrain and re-equip the artillery. In March, as Verdun began, the Russians came under increasing pressure as the Allies demanded an offensive to divert German reserves. Reluctantly, given the season, the Russians launched Smirnov's Second Army against Eichorn's Tenth Army in the marshy area around Lake Narotch (just over 50 miles east of Vilnius). Even with an advantage of 5:1 in infantry and the largest artillery preparation the Russians had yet attempted, the attack was easily spotted and faltered in the face of withering counter-preparatory fire and the quagmire created by an unusually early spring thaw. The artillery batteries were poorly directed (partly due to fog) and much of their fire-plan merely spattered mud in every direction. The attack was driven back after savage fighting and the Germans regained all of their initial positions. The Russian planners were also hopelessly outclassed by their German opposite numbers, including the remarkable individual who had been assigned to control *XL Korps'* thirty batteries.

Lieutenant-Colonel Georg Bruchmüller was an artillery officer with an undistinguished pre-war career; he had quietly retired after receiving a medical discharge in 1913. After languishing in a minor post in a fortress in 1914 he was briefly assigned as a corps artillery staff officer then as a divisional *Artillerie Kommandeur* (ARKO). As reports of the Russians massing for an assault came in, Bruchmüller suggested abandoning the traditional divisional artillery system and instead proposed using massed, centrally controlled fire directed by the corps artillery commander to break up enemy attacks as soon as their plan became apparent. His direct superior, Borkenhagen, was unimpressed but Bruchmüller took the plan to *XL Korps'* chief of staff, Emil Hell, and convinced him to test his theory on the Russians. Bruchmüller's method proved startlingly effective and the Russian infantry and artillery paid a heavy price for their ineffective preparatory barrage as the Germans focused their own fire on the sectors where the Russians were massing instead of reacting to individual attacks. To support the counter-attacks, Bruchmüller used a variant of the creeping barrage and this tactic drove the Russians back in disarray. Hell was immediately transferred to the staff of an army group, and Bruchmüller was assigned to his delighted patron's staff.

As the battle of Verdun intensified, STAVKA remained keen to assist their Allies. Alexsei Brusilov came from a long line of professional soldiers but stood out from his colleagues in the cavalry due to his interest in the academic study of war, his enthusiasm for both field exercises and training and his roguish sense of humour. Artillery was one of his main areas of interest before the war and he continuously stressed the importance of close coordination between the artillery, cavalry and machine guns in his first battles as the commander of the Eighth Army. 'An artillery commander must direct his fire in much the same manner as a conductor directs an orchestra and his role is of the greatest importance.' As the Russians retreated after Gorlice-Tarnow, Brusilov's men suffered heavy casualties from effective German fire-plans and he quickly recognised that the German approach – using firepower to smash though the lines and create temporary flanks that could be rolled up by breakthrough units – would be impossible for the less technically adept Russian army.[78]

Russian studies concluded that 400 heavy rounds or a substantial number of light rounds (perhaps 2,500) would be required to blast a 50-metre gap in the weakest sections of a German defensive system.[79] Trying to dash through such a gap would result in heavy casualties, but trying to radically widen the assault would require the creation of a fire-plan for thousands of guns. French officers gave advice on the tactics that had proved successful in Champagne in 1915 and Brusilov quickly recognised how the French approach might be applied to the problem of breaking through the enemy's defensive system, particularly if these methods could be used against Austro-Hungarians who had no experience of the new tactics. With reserves concealed close to the front line and approach trenches sapped forwards to provide cover, the artillery bombardment could be made as short and as intense as possible (using *trommelfeuer*) and still keep the German and Austrian troops under cover until it was too late. The difference was that Brusilov's men would be attacking on a front of some 450 kilometres.[80] It was an audacious solution, and the other Front commanders were less convinced. Dismayed by the failures in the spring, Evert dismissively suggested that 'without superiority in heavy artillery, there is no chance of success'.[81]

Theoretically, given that he was intending to attack established defences, Brusilov's command was weaker than the four Austro-Hungarian armies that he intended to maul. Even with superior artillery techniques, numbers remained the main factor in a successful attack and the South-West Front fielded no more guns than their opponents. Preparation and surprise would have to supplement Brusilov's meagre assets. French-style *places d'armee* (*platsdarmy* to the Russians) were constructed along the front line to enable the reserves to shelter during the final phase of the preparation and the Russians started methodically sapping forwards to within 100 metres of the complacent Austro-Hungarians.[82] Earth ramparts were even erected to conceal some of the preparations. Aerial photographs and intelligence provided rich detail on the enemy's defensive positions and the Russian army commanders were able to make detailed plans for the assault, with both the infantry and the artillery using accurate models of the Austrian positions to create their final assault and fire-plans.[83]

Brusilov intended to give the impression of a general offensive but each of his four army commanders was to select a section into which they would pour their main assault units, made up of roughly two corps. Ninth Army, its fire-plan prepared by the talented Lieutenant-Colonel V.F. Kirey, attacked a 14-kilometre sector, with the main breakthrough focused on the central 3.5 kilometres. Kirey disseminated detailed maps to his batteries with lists of assigned tasks for each phase, deploying his guns only 3 kilometres from the front line to ensure close support, and thus creating opportunities for interlocking fields of fire and easing the usual coordination problems. In his final orders he reminded his gunners that 'for every drop of artilleryman's sweat spared, the infantry would weep tears of blood'.[84] Registration was to be conducted prior to the main barrage, carefully arranged to appear as if was little more than sniping or Chinese barrages designed to unnerve the defenders throughout the sector, with selected batteries moved forwards into pre-prepared positions to support the exploitation phase.[85] Light guns were allocated to the divisions, assigned the role of blasting gaps in the wire and then eliminating the machine guns, but all the heavy guns were ordered to focus on the communication trenches in the first phase to confuse the Austro-Hungarians as to where the real attacks were going in.

The Austro-Hungarian artillery had substantial ammunition reserves but had been weakened by the transfer of heavy batteries to the Italian Front.[86] Their defensive theory, based upon the successes of the previous years, was to keep their support batteries close to the first line and commit them early to break up Russian attacks, assigning reserves as the main axis of the enemy operation became apparent.[87] The problem was that the Russian preparations, observed warily by the Austrians (and compared with German reports of recent French operations), were far too extensive for commanders to do more than reallocate a few reserves and launch selective spoiling attacks in the hope of disrupting the forces concentrating against them. Whatever assets the Austrians had, there was little chance of them being where they were most needed. Commanders had asked to fire off some of the accumulated shells as counter-preparation, but the Austrian High Command seemed to think that waiting until the Russians attacked would enable the artillery to repeat its earlier successes. Linsingen, an army group commander, was told 'the use of munitions for aimless firing and registration has been restricted but not that for important tasks'. As the Russians gathered for one of the largest operations in history, it is difficult to see what more 'important task' there could have been than disrupting their preparations.[88]

Following a complex fire-plan (see below), after 12 minutes of hurricane fire against their primary targets the infantry would advance under a final creeping barrage, a technique based on the approach used by Bruchmüller at Lake Narotch. As the four waves surged over the first line, seizing or destroying their assigned objectives, the artillery would refocus on counter-battery fire against the guns in the first line and then begin pounding the next line of trenches. The light guns were redeployed close to the attacking units the night before the attack, leaving behind one gun per battery to continue the deception and surrounded by carefully created false battery positions. In contrast the heavy guns stayed in their pre-assault positions but focused on hammering the second line once the infantry had seized the first positions.

Bedevilled by delays and last-minute concerns from other commanders, Brusilov unleashed the South-West Front on 4 June 1916. The main bombardment commenced at 04.00 hrs and continued for 3 hours before halting for an hour so that engineers could gather intelligence on the

damage to the enemy's defences. The Russians continued the bombardment for another 3 hours, then sent out more patrols. When the guns fell
silent at noon, the Austrians commenced their usual counter-preparatory
bombardment but no infantry emerged to be destroyed by the storm of fire
that fell into no-man's-land. The higher level commanders were puzzled
by the apparent width of the offensive and the peculiar approach to
conducting a full-scale bombardment. Ludendorff shrugged and casually
dismissed the initial reports as evidence of a gargantuan 'demonstration' by
the Russians, failing to realise what was waiting behind the 'colossal smoke
and dust clouds, which hindered observation'. Local commanders soon
grew tired of ordering their men to deploy every time there was a gap in the
bombardment and many units retired to their shelters and waited for
orders. The British liaison officer, Major-General Alfred Knox, watched
the Russians work with obvious approval, noting that 'fire was continued
all day methodically with careful observation of each shot. After dark the
volume of fire slackened and was chiefly directed upon the passages cut
through the enemy's wire during the day to prevent all possibility of
repair.'[89]

The real assault commenced at 18.00 hrs and although some of the
attacks were driven off, the Russian Eighth Army burst through several key
points in the shattered defences. As the Austrian Second Army reeled backwards, the front line started to collapse and the Russian Eleventh Army was
freed to join the pursuit; many of the Austrian guns only fired a few rounds
before falling back. The Russian Ninth Army had slightly less success with
its own initial bombardment, but its commanders had chosen their ground
carefully as the topography was technically unsuitable for the artillery of
both sides and observers noted that the artillery operated with 'unprecedentedly good timing and thoughtful preparation'.[90] When conditions
were suitable, the pre-planned staggered bombardment caused heavy casualties, the numbers undoubtedly increased by Letschitski procuring a few
heavy fortress guns which proved more than a match for the Austrian
Seventh Army's bunkers.[91] The Austrians fell back rapidly but Letschitski
fatally combined caution with recklessness in his pursuit of the Austrian
infantry, giving the enemy time to reorganise their artillery for defence but
not giving his own gunners time to plan and implement a fresh fire-plan.
Inevitably they were badly mauled before the Austrians pulled back to a new
defensive line. The Russian Seventh Army was less keen on Brusilov's
operational concept and had less success than the others.[92]

The Austrians were utterly bewildered by the attack; they were simply unprepared for this level of sophistication from the Russians.[93] Stunned by the vast extent of the line being attacked, their generals could not identify any of the strategic objectives for the operation, the divisional commanders lost contact with their brigades and the brigade commanders could not coordinate their units effectively. Experience against the Russian Seventh Army in December 1915 and the success at Lake Naroch had convinced the Austrians to rely on using a combination of concentrated infantry and artillery firepower to blunt what were expected to be clumsy assaults by untrained and poorly led troops. As a result the Austrians built their defensive lines close together, with bunkers to shelter the men from artillery raids, and their heavy *sturmabwehrartillerie* was placed close enough to the front line to be engaged by the Russians' light guns. Where the guns were deployed at a distance from the front lines, the communications system collapsed and the few remaining reserve medium and heavy batteries were unable to make a significant contribution to the defensive battle.[94]

The carefully constructed and comfortable bunkers, filled (according to the Russians) with surprisingly large amounts of lingerie,[95] turned out to be death-traps, and were easily bypassed by the first wave of Russians, then destroyed or forced to surrender by units tasked to deal with the rapidly isolated shelters. Much of the front line consisted of only one trench line and a few strong-points. The Austrians also neglected to develop any contingency plan for conducting either an active defence or a fighting retreat, magnifying the potential impact of any breakthrough; a situation made worse by the sudden 'illness' reported by several senior commanders as their reason for failing to adapt to the stresses of the campaign. It is important to note that Kaledin's Eighth Army was the only army that outnumbered the defenders facing its assault and it was assigned more powerful artillery reserves than other units, deploying 114 heavy and medium guns to supplement its 206 field guns.

Operations continued on 6 June with the Russian Seventh Army troops exploiting their breakthrough and forcing the Austrian Seventh Army to retreat while the Eighth Army moved to face Olyka after sapping to with 50 yards of the new Austrian positions and unleashing 'a firestorm of unprecedented intensity' that concealed the final assault under a vast yellow dust cloud. The succession of hammer blows continued with the Russians succeeding whenever they could place their artillery effectively and only failing when their enemies succeeded in identifying the main Russian objective and concentrated their batteries. Kaledin's advance only began to slow after the Russians had surged past the main Austrian depot at Lutsk and he realised that he was running out of shells. Historians argue over whether he should have ordered his men to consolidate their new defensive line after four days' fighting, but there is little doubt that his reserves were exhausted and any further assaults would have been made with minimal artillery support.

Where the Austrian artillery had time to recover, it proved effective against the Russian assaults and quickly pinned them down. The more skilful Russian commanders retained some respect for Austrian gunnery and either pursued relentlessly, giving the Austrians little time to recover, or waited until they could initiate a fresh preparatory bombardment to batter hastily built defences and cut communications with the heavier batteries sited well behind the lines before sending in wave after wave of infantry to overwhelm the defenders.

STAVKA's inability to get the other Fronts to capitalise on the South-West Front's success left Brusilov with exhausted troops and limited ammunition reserves. The only option was to continue the general offensive before the German redeployed their reserves and the opportunity to crush the Austrians evaporated. Conrad was unaware that Brusilov lacked support from the other Fronts, and was horrified by the savage fighting that had shattered the line between Kovel and Czernovitz; he bitterly observed that 'numbers of men and munitions alone decide the power'. Far worse than the military defeat, the Germans had been forced to despatch both troops and experienced commanders to stem the tide. Austria's decline into the junior partner of the Central Powers was now assured.

Further operations proved problematic for both sides. The Germans had immediately transferred a powerful corps, Group Marwitz, to the Kovel sector and this was available as a reserve before the Russians finally re-commenced their offensive. Marwitz's men, shocked both by the steadfastness of their new opponents and by the quality of their artillery support, made little headway in their initial counter-attacks. To some German observers the Austrians appeared to have lost their nerve entirely and increasingly acidic observations flowed between the various headquarters as the new situation gradually unfolded. The Russians were little better off. The few supporting attacks did not use Brusilov's tactics and hopelessly uncoordinated assaults (supported by unregistered artillery) failed dismally against German-held defences. Lengthening supply lines meant the forward artillery was sometimes low on shells and, most importantly, the South-West Front was now so low on infantry that attacks lacked the reserves to break through and pursue the Austrians before they retreated to new positions.

The lack of support from the other Fronts and the arrival of German troops left Brusilov with little choice but to revert to making a series of direct assaults on a limited frontage, where he believed that further break-throughs were the only way to keep the offensive moving forwards. The Germans and Austrians, although they argued about how the sector should be coordinated at higher levels, were thus able to concentrate their own reserves and make the most of the heavy artillery they could transfer from other commands. Suffering heavy casualties, but still making break-throughs against the shakier Austrians, the Russians continued to make slow progress during early July, forestalling a hastily prepared counter-offensive and widening the salient around Lutsk. Some Austrian officers found it difficult to understand why Brusilov's men seemed so difficult to slow down. Rudolf Kundmann, Conrad's adjutant, observed, 'I don't understand how it is that we just cannot hold anymore. Have the Russians become so good?' One of the main reasons was the drop in morale, often noted among the infantry but now increasingly apparent within the usually reliable artillery units. The Austrian 46th Division lost 12,000 men during the July battles but only two guns. As one Russian officer noted during the offensive, 'although the artillerists know their business well, they did not now have the courage to do their duty by the infantry. Batteries made off to the rear much earlier and more rapidly than they should have done, and left the infantry to its fate.'[96]

The key was not the quality of the Russians, although Brusilov had improved coordination with the infantry; it was the declining quality of the Habsburg forces that was preventing the Austrians from establishing a stable front line. One Russian prisoner remarked to his interrogators: 'if the Austrian artillery doesn't inflict losses on us then we have an easy time of it . . . We think little of the Austrian infantry.' The only solution appeared to be assigning German staff officers to the Austrian army headquarters, including von Seeckt, and the mixing of German and Austrian units so that there were reliable local reserves available to counter-attack penetrations before they became breakthroughs. The only question was whether there was time to complete the essential elements of the reorganisation before the Russians broke the back of Austrian morale.

In late July Brusilov continued the offensive. Using a variation on the previous assault tactics, he utilised gas shells to neutralise the Austrian gunners before unleashing six armies to smash through the latest defensive system. The German units, quaintly nicknamed *korsettstangen* (corset stays), fell back whenever they were left isolated by their allies but now the bravery of the Austrian artillery crews was universally noted; they often stayed by their guns to cover the retreat of the infantry. The Russians were still making progress but the terrain was becoming more difficult and heavy rains turned the rivers into raging torrents.

Brusilov had lobbied to be assigned the Imperial Guards Army as a reserve but soon discovered that the reputation of this elite formation was not based on its combat effectiveness.[97] The army's artillery was particularly poorly served; Brusilov later described the army chief of artillery, the Duke of Mecklenburg-Schwerin, as 'a good man at heart but [with] only a very vague concept of the role of artillery, though the use of artillery had grown vastly in importance and there could be no more success without the meaningful support of artillery'.[98] Predictably, the Guards attacked the defences at Kovel with great courage but suffered unnecessarily high casualties. Their commander, Bezobrazov, appeared unable to understand the urgency of maintaining momentum and the arrival of German troops in his sector caused him to switch to the defensive instead of maintaining the initiative his colleagues had won in the initial phases of the offensive.

The lack of aircraft also undermined the artillery preparation and prevented the Guards from eliminating flanking enemy batteries. Like the German troops attacking at Verdun, the Russians found themselves under heavy fire from guns they could not silence and were left wallowing in the marshes as the wounded sank, screaming, into the bloodstained muck around them. Falkenhayn was very pleased with the progress of the battle and later noted 'the poor shooting of their artillery, compared with their achievements in the early days of the war, was unable to give sufficient preparation for the attacks, and the infantry, driven forwards in unwieldy mass formations, were usually unable to cross the zone of our machine-gun fire'.[99] Knox noted that fire-planning and close support seemed to have declined in quality with one Guards officer sarcastically remarking that 'it was a pity that we spared our guns so much'.[100] In fairness to the Guards, the other armies also made only limited gains, just enough to justify another series of assaults but not enough for Brusilov to recognise that he had almost reached the culmination point of his offensive.

In August, once it became clear that the other Fronts were unlikely to attack with the same ferocity, the unified Austro-German command launched a series of counter-offensives against Brusilov's exhausted men. These made limited gains and Brusilov continued his own operations in the hope of prompting a complete collapse of the Austrian line and Romania's entry into the war. The mud was making the artillery less effective but the

German superiority in both airpower and topographical data gave them a priceless advantage. The Russian Guards suffered catastrophic casualties advancing into an Austro-German firestorm when the artillery failed to commence the barrage on schedule, leaving them helplessly struggling to cut their way through wire defences as the enemy forward observers directed their own fire on to the bewildered masses struggling in the mud. The follow-up assault, using dismounted cavalry, fared only a little better than the first, even though the artillery fired on schedule and losses were far lighter. Knox noted after the battle that his Russian colleagues 'had no plans of the enemy's defences and only the vaguest idea of the positions of his batteries, for our airmen had been unable to venture over the enemy's lines on their inferior machines . . . We were ignorant of the shape and extent of the wood [in our sector that] the enemy occupied, for our maps were last corrected nineteen years ago.'[101]

The Austro-Germans used their advantage ruthlessly and the positions of enemy earthworks, bunkers and saps were used to identify the next sectors to be attacked. Brusilov's inability to broaden the focus of his offensive gave the enemy a valuable advantage in the final phase of the fighting. Wave after wave of assaults were torn to pieces by artillery fire, leaving corpses that Marwitz ordered to be left strewn across the battlefield to discourage further attacks in his sector. (According to Hindenburg, some commanders had to order large numbers of bodies to be removed, if only to regain clear fields of fire for their machine-gunners.) During the final 45 days of the offensive, between 1 August and 16 September, the Guards alone advanced seventeen times into a firestorm of high explosive, machine guns and massed rifle fire, shattering their morale and wiping out many of their officers. Brusilov was bitterly disappointed and unburdened himself to Knox (who had the advantage of not being involved in the byzantine intrigues around STAVKA): 'The Duke of Mecklenburg is a very nice man but he knows absolutely nothing. [The corps inspectors of artillery] are no use . . . The artillery was directed as it might have been after two days of war instead of after two years.' Even the Czar recognised that such 'hopeless attacks' needed to be halted.[102]

Fatal Delay: Romania Joins the Entente

The Romanians entered the war on 27 August 1916 just as Brusilov's offensive was losing momentum. Like the Italians, the Romanians had been friendly towards the Central Powers but had little interest in intervening until the Allies made an offer that made the inevitable sacrifices worthwhile.

To the politicians in Bucharest the strategic threat created by Bulgaria precluded entry into the war until the Germans had their hands full. Waiting for the situation to be perfect only complicated the negotiations and with the Austrians in retreat and the Bulgarians busy in a flare-up at Salonika, the Romanians jumped at the apparent opportunity to seize territory. Falkenhayn, recently removed as Chief of the General Staff, was despatched to the East to restore the front line and von Mackensen was assigned the task of mobilising the Bulgarians; the interlopers were not to be allowed to change the course of the war. The Russians were distinctly unhelpful. Brusilov hoped that the Romanians could maintain some pressure on the Germans while his Front regrouped and reorganised, but STAVKA was not interested, and the Romanians found themselves utterly outclassed as soon as the Germans were able to transfer sufficient reserves to counter-attack.

The Russian general Anton Denikin described the Romanian infantry as 'splendid' and the artillery as 'adequate' but was deeply unimpressed by the 'effeminate' officer corps and their woeful disregard for the developments that had occurred around them since 1914; worse, 'in matters of equipment and ammunition, their levity was almost criminal'. A few Romanian officers were highly trained professionals, as Charles Springfield discovered when he was introducing the Romanians to the 6-inch howitzer in 1917: 'I asked [Captain Nicolescu] one day how it was that he was so different to the average Roumanian officer . . . "It's a simple explanation really – I was attached for two years to the German artillery".' Many of the other officers were rather less inspiring. In one demonstration Springfield noted the absence of professional training: 'as far as I could see, no safety precautions at all were taken and the guns just fired into the blue. I've often wondered if there were any casualties, especially as one round dropped 4,000 yards short of the target thanks to the gun being fired in the loading position.'[103]

The Romanian advance into Hungary was breathtakingly amateur and they failed to consolidate their meagre advances. Having stripped their southern forces of trained personnel, neglected to update their fortresses and failed to allocate sufficient reserves to deal with an intervention by Bulgaria, the Romanians found themselves in an impossible position. General Mihail Aslan was given little time to inspect his new command and soon discovered that the apparently formidable list of forces at his disposal was little more than a collection of aspirations and assumptions. The garrison of Turtucaia was particularly poor. Most of the officers were reservists and the 'artillerymen' were infantry, untrained in even the most basic artillery techniques. Unsurprisingly, the commander's claim that the fortress would act as a 'Romanian Verdun' proved to be hollow and the garrison performed poorly against Mackensen's North Bulgarian Battle Group, understandably finding it difficult to stand firm when subjected to a heavy artillery bombardment that their own batteries were unable to counter.

The contrast between the two forces at Turtucaia is instructive. The artillery assigned to the North Bulgarian Battle Group included the latest self-propelled guns and was able to collate detailed intelligence on the Romanian positions while, in contrast, their inexperienced opponents spent much of the first day firing continuously at imaginary targets. Only heavy rain and the difficult terrain slowed the Bulgarian and German units surrounding the fortress, while the Romanian high command wilfully ignored Aslan's advice that the garrison should seize the opportunity to retreat. With relief made improbable by the Russian contempt for the Romanian planners, and the lack of adequately trained and equipped local reserves, the garrison was left to its own devices. A warning sign of the artillery's poor quality came in the shape of reports of artillerymen abandoning their guns after the Romanian 9th Infantry Division received a mauling at Sarsânlar on 5 September. That same evening the untrained garrison at Turtucaia performed rather better, fighting desperately to defend their gun emplacements, but the uneven German/Bulgarian fireplan gradually shattered the weaker infantry units, allowing the better-led Romanian commands to be surrounded and ruthlessly eliminated. Von Mackensen was not pleased with the quality of coordination between the artillery and infantry during the first day but it must be noted that monitors of Romania's Danube Flotilla had many units under heavy fire for much of the battle. On the second day the attackers were more successful, as much of the defending artillery had been neutralised and von Mackensen's Bulgarians (led by the aggressive General Pantalei Kiselov) faced the last of the Romanian reserves, which were operating with little or no artillery support. These soon found themselves under a 'hurricane of shells' and the city's defensive system collapsed entirely. The combat casualties, at around 7,000 each, were even but von Mackensen's troops also captured 40,000 Romanians and 151 guns – but only three generals.[104]

Russian attempts to assist the Romanians by attacking in the Carpathians failed due to the inexperience of the cavalry units that STAVKA managed to despatch to the front. Few were trained or equipped to deal with mountain warfare and the Central Powers had air superiority. The Germans skilfully positioned their artillery on reverse slopes and made the Russians pay dearly for every few hundred yards of mountainous terrain. The Romanian offensive in Transylvania fared little better, and when Falkenhayn's Ninth Army commenced its counter-attack the entire front buckled and Romania's brave but disorganised armies rolled backwards in disarray. Instead of being the decisive event in the East, Romania's intervention gave the Central Powers access to new resources and forced the Russians to divert 27 divisions to avert catastrophe. Combined with the heavy cost of the offensives during the summer, the Russians appeared poorly equipped to face the challenges in 1917.

One innovation suggested that STAVKA had learned from the summer's qualified success. In December 1916, after it had become apparent that artillery reserves had been poorly utilised in the Brusilov offensive, STAVKA created the specialist XLVIII Corps. This new corps would act as the main heavy artillery reserve under the direction of the commander-in-chief. The Germans failed to identify this new six-brigade unit even though several Front commanders bombarded STAVKA with complaints about transferring precious artillery reserves to the new corps. One of the main problems was the limited availability of educated officers after three years of war: 70 per cent had peasant backgrounds by the end of 1916 and hardly any had the professional training required to be an effective artillery officer. The Austro-Hungarians faced similar problems and the quality of the units of both armies suffered accordingly.

Grinding into the Mountainside: Italy on the Isonzo

On the Isonzo front, both sides suffered from the winter conditions, including ice storms and avalanches. Shelling and snipers forced both sides to work at night. The mountain troops on both sides grew more proficient at raiding and specialist weapons like flamethrowers made their first appearance. Boroević's outnumbered Fifth Army still lacked enough shells but constantly improving defences and superb intelligence gave him a priceless advantage.

For the Fifth Battle of the Isonzo the Italian artillery continued to rely on area fire and not a detailed fire-plan, even after new regulations were disseminated[105]: a 48-hour bombardment by over a thousand guns was simply more indiscriminate shellfire. Late snowfall and mist only compounded the coordination problems and the Italians were driven back with heavy losses. *Alpini* units, supported by their own mountain artillery, had more success. Both sides began to use mining in the high alpine passes to edge towards and under enemy positions, blasting holes in San Martino in 1916 and eventually honeycombing the Little Lagazuoi in the Dolomite Range.[106]

Conrad von Hötzendorf was eager to punish the Italians for breaking the Triple Alliance. He could not match the strong Italian forces on the Isonzo, so he decided to shift the battle westwards to the South Tyrol and ordered Colonel-General Archduke Eugen to prepare a suitable plan for April 1916. The Fifth Army yielded some of its reserves and fresh artillery soon followed. The Italian First Army was poorly deployed and Cadorna, easily distracted by a minor thrust on the Carso, became aware of Austrian preparations too late to affect the outcome. Eugen's infantry and artillery, supplemented by the units stripped from the Russian front, were well co-ordinated and made significant gains before they outpaced their already meagre supply system and Cadorna finally managed to stabilise the front line. The Archduke was pleased with his men and, although most of his reserves were withdrawn after Brusilov's attack, he gave a press interview to publicise the fact that the defenders had lost more men than the attackers. Eugen believed that better defences and closer infantry–artillery co-ordination gave the Austrians a huge advantage over the Italians:

[On the Isonzo] it was demonstrated what our [Trentino] offensive has now confirmed: that our men, but not the Italians, could stand the horrors of drumfire . . . Specifically, the close cooperation between our infantry and our artillery, and the batteries among one another has been the main source of our success. Our artillery-based defence has cost the enemy veritable hecatombs of dead . . . The Italian prisoners unanimously declared the effect of our artillery fire was frightful, simply unendurable. Under cover of this artillery fire, it was possible for our infantry, with […] slight losses, to tear from the enemy, position after position . . . The Italian artillery answered our fire only weakly – not, as captured magazines afterward showed, from lack of ammunition, but because they were holding back for our infantry attacks . . .'.[107]

The Sixth Battle of the Isonzo, in August, finally saw the Italians use a genuine artillery fire-plan. Colonel Pietro Badoglio, later a key figure in Mussolini's regime, was assigned to plan the offensive and he and his staff selected a range of key targets including command bunkers, known supply dumps and artillery batteries. To show his confidence in the plan, Badoglio opted to personally lead a brigade attacking Mount Sabotino. For once the Austrians misread the situation and the size of the offensive surprised them. With only four heavy batteries and fewer than 600 light and medium guns, the Fifth Army was heavy outgunned and ran ruinously low on ammunition. The artillery bombardment cut all communications to the positions on Mount Sabotino and the Italians were able to overwhelm the defenders and trap many of them in their formidable *kavernen*. This time, when the inevitable counter-attack came, the Italians had enough time to establish their own defensive system. A similar success was experienced on San Michele but here the Austrians ran out of ammunition and their counter-attacks were driven back with heavy casualties. Just as a breakthrough glimmered, Cadorna lost his nerve and the Italian artillery reverted to re-arranging the geography while the Austrians strengthened the new defensive line on the Plava and received urgently needed shells. Further Italian attacks were predictably beaten back after savage fighting. Russian prisoners of war were brought into the Fifth Army sector to help construct an expanded defensive system, and as the Italians dithered, fresh artillery arrived to further strengthen the position.

Once again Cadorna returned to planning how to batter his way through to the Carso and the Duke of Aosta's Third Army was instructed to prepare the latest assault. The fire-plan on this occasion required the artillery to soften up the front line, and to use heavy guns against the rear areas before intensifying the so-called 'annihilation barrage' just before dawn. The 9-hour bombardment was impressive but the Austrians held firm and their surviving gunners broke up the attacks. The bombardment of a key water pumping station that supplied the front line threatened to force the defenders to retreat but some Austrian naval flying boats destroyed the Italian long-range battery by bombing.[108]

The new Italian tactics worked when the Austrian artillery was weak or low on ammunition. The Italians, not understanding how important artillery was to the Austrian system, did not emphasise counter-battery fire. That, combined with the strong Austrian defences, meant that too many attacks were broken up before they could make any progress. Worse, poor concealment meant that the Austrians could shatter attacks even before they commenced.[109] Technical problems also hampered the Italians: their air force was still relatively weak, flash-spotting was difficult when the guns were in *kaverne* and sound-ranging was almost impossible in the mountains.[110]

The bombardment before the Eighth Battle (although involving an even more intense barrage that destroyed 41 of the Fifth Army's guns) made real progress because of the combination of dust and fog in the Carso sector during September. Austrian counter-battery and counter-assault fire inflicted heavy casualties but the Italians retained the advantage in both guns and ammunition. By the Ninth Battle the Italians were finally using curtain barrages to protect their hard-won advances, deluging the inevitable counter-attacks with gas and shrapnel before moving on to attack the Austrian second line. Only frenzied counter-attacks straight into the Italian advance prevented a major breakthrough. The Italians had learnt a great deal in 1916 but the Austrians were better at balancing resources and results. By comparison, the Italian success 'bore no relation to the mighty expenditure of men and materiel that it cost'.

Conclusion

The year 1916 is often identified as a turning-point in the Great War and the point at which the artillery attained a level of dominance that relegated the infantry into acting as 'standard bearers marking the zone of superiority established by the artillery'.[111] The French and British had pyrrhic victories at Verdun and on the Somme, and the Allies' materiel and technical advantages were finally beginning to make an impression on the battlefield – Britain alone produced 50 million shells in 1916, though moving such vast quantities of munitions created additional problems. Germany's superiority in artillery doctrine and equipment appeared to have melted away in 1916 but careful analysis of the Allied operations led to the development of new tactics and many of the advances the Allies assumed would bring them success in 1917 would be negated by the increasingly 'elastic' German defensive system.[112] Even the industrial might of the Entente (and her 'neutral' suppliers) would not suffice to break the deadlock: firing more shells wore out barrels, reducing accuracy, so the Allied advantage in materiel had to be combined with ever more sophisticated tactical and operational methods against an opponent also evolving.[113] In 1917 the Germans would develop new assault techniques of their own, combining Bruchmüller's artillery methods with infantry infiltration tactics. Hindenburg and Ludendorff exploited this qualitative advantage ruthlessly but they never capitalised on the strategic potential of these technical advances.

Chapter Four
1917

After the grim battles of 1916 there was less optimism about a decisive victory, although there was plenty of determination on all sides to 'see it through'. The German army had been heavily bled (and especially noticed the demise of their pre-war NCOs and junior officers) and they feared that the dreaded *materialschlact* (war of attrition) was now inescapable. In previous years the German high command had felt that quality would overcome the enemy's quantity but artillery and machine guns were indiscriminate killers and the Allies appeared undaunted. The 'Turnip Winter' also depressed morale, with German civilians starving in large numbers. German leadership had changed, with Hindenburg and Ludendorff now leading Germany's war effort. They wanted more munitions and established the Hindenburg Programme to double the output of artillery and machine guns; they wanted more manpower, so they pulled garrison troops forwards and tried to call up more men. To get more workers, the Auxiliary Service Law was passed to compel industrial service. Examining Germany's strategic prospects, they decided on a largely defensive approach: Russia was collapsing, and U-boats would be unleashed to knock Britain out before the US (which would declare war because of the U-boats) could make any difference. If the army avoided defeat, the Entente would collapse. To avoid further fighting on the Somme, the Germans built the *Siegfried Stellung* (Hindenburg Line) and then pulled back up to 40 kilometres and shortened the line by around 30 kilometres; they chose the most favourable terrain, largely on the basis of what would be out of sight of Allied artillery observers. The heavy fortifications would also deter Allied attacks, allowing the Germans to minimise the garrison and have more troops for elsewhere.

Many of Ludendorff's plans were strategically flawed. Convoys would stymie the U-boat scourge, while the Auxiliary Service Law only showed how little the German army understood politics, proving that it was impossible to compel enthusiasm. Germany was equally tactless towards its allies, and the rest of the Central Powers warily copied their ally's defensive posture and hoped that a German victory would leave some crumbs for them. Even the Hindenburg Programme showed how little the German army understood about industrial bottlenecks: propellant production could not be expanded, so the extra guns were far less useful, although they did replace most of the old and captured guns which were then used as 'position batteries' in defensive sectors.

But the Allies still had to attack, and remained determined to do so, even after the losses of 1916. The French were desperate for a quick victory and they picked General Robert Nivelle as their new commander-in-chief. He puffed up morale by promising victory, but defeat in April would puncture the balloon and the French *poilu* refused to commit to any large-scale attack until Pétain was put in charge, using casualty-minimising tactics that largely focused on artillery.

The British were also becoming increasingly casualty-averse. The new prime minister (David Lloyd George, whose wartime reputation hinged on his earlier performance as minister of munitions) wanted the French to fight more on the Western Front while Britain fought on the periphery. Whatever his strategy, Lloyd George was determined to win the war and his move to 10 Downing Street was proof that Britain was in it to win. However, the war correspondent Philip Gibbs, circulating freely behind British lines, recorded that 'the British army lost its spirit of optimism, and there was a sense of deadly depression'.[1] The BEF would fight alongside the French in the spring (at Vimy and Arras), and when the French were teetering they would fight separately (at Messines and Ypres) while still finding the resources for colonial campaigns. Fighting in Palestine made little headway but Turkey took a beating in Mesopotamia. The Allies were benefiting from increased munitions production (UK production of shells increased from 45 million shells to 76 million),[2] as well as from new designs of guns, fuses and gases and increased reliability from their fuses and shells.

Meanwhile, in the East the Russians tried an attack in late winter. It failed, from war weariness and Bolshevik subversion as much as from German firepower. Until the autumn, when the Germans scraped up half a dozen divisions and captured the politically significant city of Riga with new artillery and infantry tactics, the Russian Front was quiet. Russian railways could not move food, let alone raw materials, to the cities, and munitions output fell, contributing to failing morale.

Italy also proved itself stubbornly determined on victory. Continued attacks along the Isonzo finally gained ground and it seemed that Austria might collapse. The Germans diverted a handful of divisions and displayed their new assault tactics at Caporetto. The Italian line broke, with roughly a quarter of a million men taken prisoner, but still the Italians continued fighting.

The US declared war in April but made no significant contribution in 1917. American industry was already producing munitions, although its output would increase, and American manpower needed training – the 120,000-strong regular army was far too small to make a difference. Only a single American division was in the line by December.

The British Army: The Battles of Arras and Vimy Ridge

The Allied plans for 1917 saw separate but coordinated attacks. The British would attack at Arras (and also storm Vimy Ridge) to pin down German reserves and set up Nivelle's French attack.[3] The BEF would be using new methods based on the experience of 1916. Over the winter the BEF had revised its doctrinal manuals; artillery priorities were now 1. counter-battery 2. hitting the German infantry and 3. hammering the German defences. This roughly reversed the 1916 priorities and put more emphasis on the success of the initial attack rather than on a possible deeper penetration.

Counter-battery techniques had made major progress in 1916. In 1915 there had been optimistic hopes of 'silencing' all German batteries but the immediate problems caused by machine guns and barbed wire had pushed the counter-battery issues to the bottom of the list. In 1916 there were enough British bombardment resources that counter-battery could be tackled. In general the British began differentiating between neutralising fire (when there was an attack under way) and destructive fire (when the infantry were not in the open), and realised that howitzers were key for destruction and that guns were useful for neutralisation. New technologies also played a role, with flash-spotting (finding German batteries by tri-angulating their muzzle flashes) and sound-ranging (using newly invented microphones to listen for the sound of a gun firing) used to pinpoint targets, with accuracy as precise as 25 yards.[4] The British proved superior in these fields by pragmatically adopting the latest scientific methods. The technical lead in artillery tactics that emerged during 1917 was hugely facilitated by the proper use of advanced survey techniques. This was in marked contrast to the Germans, who had skilled individuals but often diluted their effec-tiveness by creating arcane or inefficient systems for solving simple problems – such as not standardising their grid projection so that their gunners often had to consult and cross-reference several maps. Another innovation was organisational: the Counter-Battery Staff Officer would not only have the full range of intelligence sources, he controlled the counter-battery artillery. Of course, the system was only as good as the men – one even resorted to using a ouija board – but it was better than in 1916.

The creeping barrage was also improved. It had proven invaluable in 1916, but the difficult months of experience on the Somme had indicated a number of ways it could be bettered: more depth (several lines of 18-pounder shells), different munitions (high explosive, shrapnel and – new for 1917 – smoke), and more guns (with 4.5-inch howitzers added ahead of the 18-pounders). This process of improvement would continue throughout 1917. Over the winter of 1916/17 the BEF reorganised its divisional artillery; instead of four pure (either all-gun or all-howitzer) field artillery brigades, divisions were now allocated two mixed brigades, each with three 18-pounder batteries and one 4.5-inch howitzer battery. This matched the tactics of the barrage: two 18-pounder batteries firing side-by-side, with the third also firing but available to switch to targets of opportunity, while the howitzers were firing on point targets ahead of the 18-pounders. This was also enough guns for a division just holding the line, while the remaining batteries were reorganised into independent Army Field Artillery (AFA) brigades that could be sent wherever they were needed. New technology also affected the field artillery: the new 'fuse no. 106' was more sensitive than previous models, detonating efficiently enough on impact to allow howitzers to slice through the tangled mass of barbed wire that earlier shells had merely rearranged. The howitzers' trajectory also meant that wire could be cut on reverse slopes and experience showed that the howitzers were more efficient, cutting circles in the wire instead of the cones that field guns made; the tactical possibilities were duly noticed and the BEF hoarded the available 'no. 106' fuses for the first attack.

Meanwhile, the Germans were not idle in improving their own tactical systems.[5] The new army doctrine, outlined in *The Principles of Command in the Defensive Battle in Position Warfare* in March 1917, sought to reduce losses by holding deeper zones with fewer forward troops (within range of enemy artillery), dispersing into more but smaller targets, and having better infantry–artillery coordination to both deal with enemy assaults and facilitate counter-attacks. The first zone consisted of outposts, strong enough to defeat small attacks and force a major effort, thus delaying large attacks so the Germans could move up reserves. The main battle zone had more defences and defenders, and its distance from enemy field artillery reduced the effectiveness of bombardments; it could be held against almost any attack. The rear battle zone was out of range of enemy heavy artillery (thus requiring sustained attacks to breach the German defences, and buying time for a German response) and would protect German counter-attack reserves. Artillery and *minenwerfers* were echeloned in camouflaged positions but the Germans were increasingly aware of the Allies' superior detection systems, and mobility was seen as the key to survival in the evolving battle: 'in battle or for special missions, the use of unprepared emplacements will often be advisable'.

For the artillery, the Germans tried to better coordinate with the infantry, including permanently attaching liaison officers to infantry regiments. Artillery command was altered a bit, with divisions getting an *Artillerie Kommandeur*, a general or senior colonel, who often stayed in a sector when the infantry were relieved to retain familiarity with the ground and conditions. In a quiet sector the *Kommandeur* would have around 18 batteries, one-third of them heavies (compared with 12 batteries in 1914, none of them heavy), while in an active sector he might have 30 batteries – probably too many for him and his small staff to readily control. A *minenwerfer* company (18 tubes of mixed calibres) was also intended for each infantry division. Conversely, counter-battery fire was handled by groups run from army level, mainly comprising 150mm and 210mm howitzers. Infantry tactics switched to defence-in-depth, and they sought to fight only for tactically important ground rather than trying to hold everything. The depth also created more defensive positions, and the Germans switched (mostly) from strong positions to many positions; they judged that since the Allied artillery would sooner or later demolish any position the gunners found, it made more sense to have lots of alternatives. Guns should either be protected against 9.2-inch shells or simply concealed; anything in-between was a waste. Long-range guns were emphasised, and new designs of guns (and shells) were arriving that provided more range. More and more shells were needed, but the Germans had to avoid firing too fast and over-heating the barrels, since this led to premature bursts. This, combined with limitations on production and battlefield transportation, led the Germans to end prolonged intense barrages, until they ended up with only 3 minutes' intense and 5 minutes' deliberate fire, unless signals indicated there was a serious attack in progress: observed fire 'executed calmly and well adjusted by observers, and methodical fires for annihilation, supports the infantry better than automatic barrages which use up an enormous amount of ammunition for a minimum result'. Observed fire was strongly encouraged since it was both more effective and needed fewer shells. By mid-1917 rigid unobserved barrages were deprecated and counter-preparation (essentially an attack-strength barrage fired in the defence) was recommended. This would not stop an attack, but would disorganise it and give the infantry a better chance.

An elastic defence would also allow attackers to penetrate but then bring counter-attacks to catch them when they were weakened, tired, disorganised and out of communication. Ludendorff described the new layered system as more effective 'because it forces the enemy in taking it to engage considerable forces and means, which he will lack when he comes to the principal attack. As his advance proceeds, he will encounter difficulties that constantly increase in number and which constantly become unexpected.'[6] Observation was the key to defence, both for controlling the artillery and for gathering information for effective counter-attacks; ensuring that the key positions were held also denied the Allies good observation posts. Observation was so important that 'the requirements of the artillery play a decisive part in the selection and preparation of positions' – in other words the infantry defended where the Allied artillery was minimised and fought to maximise the power of the German artillery. The Germans established a Division Commander School to test and explain all this but it was a new idea and was not easily implemented. The Germans around Arras kept too much strength forward and had their batteries too clumped together. (The British actually hit the isolated batteries first, then the clumps, which were easier to neutralise if destruction failed.)

At Arras the British used their new methods and had more guns. There were enough heavies to subordinate a bombardment group to each attacking division, ensuring better coordination. The Germans called the week-long intense bombardment (counter-battery fire and some trench bombardment had started two weeks earlier) the *Leidenswoche* (the week of suffering). On Vimy Ridge they knew the British were massing guns and also knew (from a map found on a downed pilot) that their own gun positions were well known to the British, but they could not reinforce fast enough to stem the tide. In one sector the British were throwing 12–15,000 shells per day at a single division, which was only able to fire 2,000 back.[7] The Vimy Ridge position was shallow and the defences needed work but the Germans judged that such work was only possible when the weather dried out. The hammering made it obvious that the British were going to attack but they still managed some tactical surprise, possibly because the new 106 impact fuse shortened the period needed for wire-cutting.

The foul weather on 9 April (Easter Monday) also helped the British plan as the SOS flares fired by the front-line German infantry could not be seen in the mist and blowing snow. Progress was therefore excellent on the first day, advancing several miles in some cases, and Vimy Ridge was quickly overrun as well. General Horne would later claim that Vimy had actually been over-bombarded, tearing up the ground and slowing the infantry. That was the flip side of a bombardment that reduced German regiments to battalion strength and filled the survivors with horror:

> The enemy had divided up the battlefield like a chessboard. Strip after strip was ploughed and torn up. The entire defensive works were to be demolished and the nerves of the defenders shredded. As it unfolded, it made for dreadful scenes. The explosion of the massive shells ripped great craters out of the earth, sending their contents skyward then, as they fell to ground once more, repeated the process in chaotic confusion.[8]

German batteries might fire up to 1,500 rounds that day, yet British numbers and planning told, and the Canadians captured over 120 guns, some of them heavies that had been deployed forwards to fire deeper into British lines.

With commendable skill the Germans reorganised during the battle, redeploying to take advantage of greater defence-in-depth, assisted by the BEF's tendency to launch too-small attacks, a brigade attacking quickly when it would have been safer (and cheaper) – but slower – to send a division. The Germans were actually perplexed by the British operation. Their opponents did not appear to understand how to attack where the ground favoured them, with observers controlling the artillery, but instead insisted on attacking over ridges and hills while relying on a timetabled barrage.

The crisis in the French army apparently caused Haig to prolong the attack. Too often the British would attack an objective their gunners could not see, the infantry would advance over a hill and never be seen again, cut off by German defensive barrages and torn up by German counter-attacks (the Germans also used what they termed mobile artillery – a battery or two attached to counter-attacking battalions – that could offer tactical fire support as long as the British aerial observers did not spot it).[9] Before fizzling out in May, the battle for Arras cost the BEF more than the Somme (on a per-day basis) but it had also inflicted significant losses on the Germans as well as wresting Vimy Ridge and a few other observation points out of enemy hands.

'We now have the formula!': Nivelle's Offensive and the Rise of Pétain

Nivelle's success at Fort Douaumont in 1916 had propelled him into the limelight and he proved remarkably adept at presenting the fire-plan that neutralised the German defensive system as the model for future success. His charm offensive was every bit as effective as the artillery he had deployed to retake the fort, and he was given command of the French army. He smugly informed a colleague that 'We now have the formula', confident that 1. the creeping barrage; 2. disrupting the defensive system with long-range batteries; 3. neutralising the defending artillery with gas shells; and 4. using the German technique of clearing specified zones through which the infantry could advance would enable a full-scale penetration and an 'audacious lateral exploitation' to roll up the whole system.[10] Entranced by his success at Verdun, Nivelle entirely ignored the harsh lessons of the first years of the war in the planning for his new offensive, even to the extent of ignoring the difficulties created by the German withdrawal in the sector in which he hoped to break through (Operation Alberich). The terrain between the Aisne and the Chemin-des-Dames was carefully chosen by the Germans; from here they overlooked the entire battlefield and had excellent cover for both observers and batteries. Most importantly, the Germans had studied the French successes at Verdun and now defended in depth with substantial reserves of artillery and counter-attack units. Even though GQG highlighted the importance of surprise, to the amazement of German intelligence officers details of the offensive were revealed in public discussions and plans for the offensive fell into their hands just before the assault was due to begin.[11]

French planners were concerned that the Germans would quickly seize the initiative, just as they had in 1916. Nivelle's plan focused on an Anglo-French operation on the flank of the Noyon Salient to fix the German reserves, followed by a main offensive based on 'rapidity and continuity of execution' on the Aisne.[12] The concept of methodical displacement developed by Pétain was almost but not entirely abandoned (Nivelle reminded his colleagues on 6 April that 'there is no such thing as a half battle'), with batteries sited as close to the front line as possible to minimise the time spent moving forwards:

The heavy artillery is to become a field warfare weapon. We must use it like the 75, and get it into position and open fire with it with equal speed . . . the constant, orderly, methodical and rapid thrust naturally leads to a return to the battle methods of open warfare, which should result in a breakthrough. As we approach the general offensive, we must definitely break away from the inertia and slowness which the excessive prolongation of trench warfare has introduced to our combat methods.[13]

On the Aisne Nivelle gathered 2,000 field guns, 1,650 heavy guns (of which 700 were modern and 160 were long-range pieces) and committed a further 1,650 trench mortars. In addition to the latest howitzers, the French deployed their first tanks but these were assigned to sectors where the terrain was poor and the tactical opportunities limited. Disappointingly for Nivelle, the Germans pre-empted his plan by withdrawing from the Noyon Salient to the Siegfried Stellung (Hindenburg Line), shortening their line by 40 kilometres. As a result the operation had to be radically altered. Due to the strength of the Siegfried Stellung, poor weather, enemy air activity, strong German reserves and the problem of reorganising logistics, the eventual preparatory bombardment made little impression on the German defensive system.

The core of the plan was based upon an unrealistic understanding of the limitations of the French artillery and infantry. Nivelle was fully aware that 'the complete destruction of enemy batteries is a utopia' but bewitched himself into believing that he could repeat his brutal but methodical success at Douaumont on a grander scale. Although there were successes (the Sixth Army took 5,300 prisoners and advanced over 6 kilometres), the offensive clearly failed to attain the objectives that Nivelle had claimed were possible. Compounding the failure to clear the wire and neutralise the German defending artillery, the creeping barrage (pre-planned at an absurd rate of advance for such poor conditions) soon out-ran the assaulting regiments and exposed them to withering fire from the concrete machine-gun nests the Germans had scattered throughout their defensive network.[14] German artillery fire soon eliminated the tanks (quaintly described as *l'artillerie spéciale*) and the entire French offensive ground to a bloody halt. Successive assaults received similar punishment, with Mangin's Sixth Army suffering particularly heavy casualties, and then German counter-attacks rapidly retook many of the positions lost in the initial operations. The plan had assumed that rapid advances would overrun some German artillery batteries but this time the French fire-plan was spread too thinly (Pétain later remarked that 'even the waters of Lake Geneva would have but little effect if dispersed over the length and breadth of the Sahara Desert'[15]) and those infantry who reached their objectives faced counter-assaults by enemy units that the supporting artillery could not interdict.[16] Understandably many French infantrymen felt betrayed by their commanders and units began to refuse to go into action. The mutinies of 1917 mostly emerged from the ranks of the hard-pressed infantry (129 infantry regiments mutinied but only 7 artillery regiments) and the failure of the 'pampered artillery' to support their comrades was one of the major grievances.[17]

Pétain's appointment as chief of staff calmed the simmering discontent and led to a new policy of conducting limited attacks, similar to the British 'bite and hold' concept, that would force the Germans to counter-attack into the teeth of artillery support. As Pétain dryly noted, 'artillery fire kills'. He intended to support the initial attacks (against suitable objectives) with overwhelming fire and then arrange his artillery reserves so that the main German counter-operations ran into a carefully orchestrated firestorm. On the Yser Canal in July, at Verdun in August and on the Chemin-des-Dames in October the French conducted a superb series of limited offensives based on this concept and their success did much to restore the morale of the French army.[18]

Pétain's concept centred on the idea that 'a breach can be envisaged only when successful pushes or attrition have created intervals in the enemy's line or have diminished German reserves considerably'.[19] These 'pushes' would be prepared in the utmost secrecy to ensure that the Germans could not counter the preparatory bombardment and would only seize the enemy's front line. Continuous methodical operations, such as those conducted in 1916 and by the British in Flanders, would be avoided as they led to high rates of attrition. The new artillery programme, outlined in May 1917, demanded increases in heavy artillery production (particularly 155s) and reduced the monthly output requirement for 75s. A mobile general reserve was established so that the new offensives could be supported and the key artillery units transferred to the next operational area as soon as the desired objectives were secured. Tank and aircraft production was also increased and a new 37mm infantry support gun was introduced to assist with enemy strong-points; Pétain had recognised that he had manpower problems and compensated for this weakness by focusing on materiel.[20]

After a series of successful German attacks during June and July, designed to secure key terrain features and delay French offensive preparations, French army group commanders bombarded GQG with reports on the high cost of ceding initiative to the Germans. Pétain reluctantly approved initial planning but was soon convinced that the time had come for his idea of conducting a series of limited offensives. The Verdun assault in August, designed to retake Le Morte Homme and Hill 304, used a six-day preparation with 3,000 guns plastering 3 million shells on the German system. Intriguingly, the French also began to copy British machine-gun barrage techniques and incorporated these into their fireplan. Thanks to the intelligence gathered by the *Service du Renseignements d'Artillerie* and the liberal amounts of gas shells fired in the final 6 hours, the relentless bombardment neutralised 187 of the 280 batteries in the sector. Even though the shell-scarred terrain was difficult to traverse, for the first time the French genuinely had both air and artillery superiority and all the German counter-attacks were rapidly scattered and their relatively limited objectives were efficiently seized and consolidated. Further attacks secured the final objectives required by the plan but the French avoided being drawn into an attritional contest that might shatter the French infantry's fragile recovery in morale.

The assault on the La Malmaison Sector occurred after lengthy discussions between Pétain and General Maistre on the Second Army's artillery at Verdun. The six-day preparatory bombardment, commencing on 17 October, shattered the front-line positions and interdicted reserve movements throughout the defensive system.[21] Unlike at Verdun, the counter-battery fire was delayed until the last day so that the Germans would have minimal warning of the final attack. This time the tanks were adequately supported and (although the terrain was poor and many broke down) enough of them reached their objectives to give welcome support to the infantry. The delighted GQG staff began planning increasingly effective ways of utilising the new weapons. As a result of Pétain's carefully planned operation, the Germans were forced to abandon the Chemin-des-Dames position for a tenth of the cost of Nivelle's failed enterprise.[22]

Pétain succeeded where Nivelle had failed because of an insistence on meticulous and thorough planning, increasing numbers of heavy guns, tanks and aircraft, extended preparatory bombardments and a fire-plan that made the most of the minimal displacement required by a 'bite and hold' attack. The recovery of French morale meant a return of some of the élan that Nivelle had hoped to encourage and French officers began to lobby for opportunities to show initiative during the assault. A report by the 16th

Corps after the Verdun attack illustrates this reawakening of Gallic panache:

> After a heavy preparation, the enemy is depressed, his liaison is destroyed and his command disorganised. The artillery is slow in delivering its barrages and executes them poorly; his counter-battery is weak on J-Day and remains almost inactive on following days. There is a feeling that he must undertake a complete reorganisation and before he again gets in shape, there will be some hours which will be very favourable to daring enterprises. Therefore in drawing up our plans we must not fail to discount the opportunities of a period of some length, following the attack, in which the enemy will not be in possession of his means. We will thus anticipate audacious exploitation in which the artillery, if the terrain makes its displacement possible, can play a capital part, and which will be fruitful in happy results.[23]

During the La Malmaison operation the French noted that the destructive barrage had little effect on enemy counter-batteries for the first three days but as soon as the neutralisation phase of the fire-plan commenced there was a notable decrease in enemy activity. The introduction of modern gas projectiles (and increased numbers of quick-firing heavy guns) had finally enabled the French to shorten their bombardments and thus created the possibility of reintroducing strategic surprise to the Western Front, a development that was further highlighted by the initial successes during the Battle of Cambrai.

An Explosive Beginning: Messines–Passchendaele

The British attacks of the summer of 1917 can be seen as the apogee of trench warfare. Given the problems of fighting through a brilliantly designed defensive system, the British did as well as possible, and at times the Germans felt not just defeated (which could happen by circumstance) but beaten – their best efforts were not enough and they could only withdraw slowly and hope for better results somewhere else.

The Battle of Messines was designed to mirror the operational success of the storming of Vimy Ridge, an attack that was limited to seizing a particular geographic objective rather than trying to break through.[24] There was detailed planning, a hallmark of Plumer's Second Army, assisted by several of the corps having been on the ground for months; they also borrowed ideas from the fighting at Vimy (Major Alan Brooke passed on information on how the Canadian Corps had handled its artillery at Vimy).[25]

The German guns were key, and Plumer had insisted that the objectives must include not just the crest of the ridge but the German artillery line: 'We must get those bally guns.' Counter-battery fire would make the attack possible. There was good intelligence on the German guns, and those that were identified in the main sector were targeted individually, with a British gun being tasked to hit each German one. The flanking German guns were outnumbered four to one, enough to harass and reduce their effectiveness. When Major-General Noel Birch of GHQ found a corps daring to put bombardment planning first, he was furious: 'this negation of all modern artillery thought appalled me'. There was tight organisation of the counter-battery work, with zones laid out, batteries assigned to grid squares, and the RFC employing as many aircraft as contemporary wireless technology could handle (it also forced down German balloons and drove off enemy aircraft). Effective counter-battery work was so important to the attack that Birch even raised the prospect of detonating the 19 immense mines days before the attack, suggesting it would cause the Germans to fire a defensive barrage, thus revealing their surviving batteries. Plumer thought this would be good for counter-battery work but bad for the overall battle, and promised that the last two days of the bombardment would have even more counter-battery fire than already planned. The scale of the British preparations was obvious for a month ahead of time, and the Germans reinforced with more artillery, but it only got them up to a ratio of 1:3, and the intense British counter-battery effort had succeeded in neutralising half the German guns by D-Day on 7 June. By then two weeks' bombardment (a week of it intense) from 2,266 guns had thrown 144,000 tons of shells. A German diarist recorded:

> The English have completely smashed in the whole trench and all the dugouts. I was almost buried in a dugout yesterday. It was a concrete one, and the English put a few 38cm shells on it, when it collapsed like a concertina. A whole crowd of men were buried and burnt. I cannot describe what it is like here; soon there will be no hope for us. . . . The English smash up everything with their artillery, we have frightful losses . . . and our artillery doesn't speak.[26]

The British troops were inspired by the same preparations, and it was indeed a remarkably easy battle for the Second Army, far easier than expected given that up to 50 per cent infantry casualties had been predicted in the original plan. The infantry swarmed forwards, overrunning the shelled and mine-stunned Germans, taking thousands of prisoners and capturing a large number of 'the bally guns'. Those counter-attacks the Germans succeeded in organising shattered on the protective barrage. Even that was pre-planned, with the field artillery from the British second-echelon divisions being deployed forwards (and staying silent to avoid German counter-battery fire) for this purpose, with other guns moving forwards to positions that had been surveyed, pre-prepared and with ammunition dumped for their use. Improved operational planning combined with limited objectives and overwhelming resources had yielded superb results.

Afterwards the Germans worried that the British would use the good observation positions gained on Messines Ridge to head northeast up the Gheluvelt Plateau. Instead, Haig shifted his focus a few miles further north into the heart of the Ypres Salient; he was after bigger fish than just clearing the Plateau: he wanted to punch through to Roulers, a key rail junction that would force the Germans to fall back and abandon U-boat bases on the Belgian coast. This would result in the Third Battle of Ypres, more widely known as Passchendaele.[27] Lloyd George was dubious about the proposed offensive, but acquiesced; his preference was to send heavy artillery to the Italian front, but this would take away the BEF's means of attack.[28] In turn Haig had also wavered about his objective. He told Hubert Gough, whose Fifth Army was to make the main attack, 'to wear down the enemy but at the same time, to have an objective', and that dual mission proved expensive in lives.[29] One of Haig's operations officers, Major-General J.H. Davidson, argued for one-mile steps, which would be tactically efficient. Everyone agreed there would not be a clean breakthrough on the first day, so the debate centred on how far to go in each step. Gough (and others with better reputations than Gough, including Lieutenant-General Ivor Maxse) wanted 2.5–3 mile steps, taking as much as possible with each attack, and Haig agreed with them – bigger bites were optimistically assumed to ensure a faster defeat of the Germans.

The cost of shifting into the Ypres Salient was a delay as infrastructure was expanded, and men and guns were moved. Then there would have to be a lengthy bombardment. The Germans used the time to build up their defences, building three zones (each 2–3 kilometres deep), with the second and third out of range of British field guns, thus forcing the British to pause after gaining each zone. The Germans also built large numbers of pillboxes.[30] The British infantry would ultimately develop new tactics to deal with these, and armour-piercing shells were borrowed from the Royal Navy to (literally) crack the pillboxes, but these new strong-points were a factor for several weeks. Meanwhile the Germans also deliberately used delaying tactics, such as night bombing and firing, using harassing fire instead of destructive fire, and introducing mustard gas. This killed few but it burned many, and a serious burn would take weeks to heal; it was also a persistent agent, so that (depending on weather) an area that had been gassed once could be hazardous for several days.

Haig's objective (Roulers) and the decision to attack from Ypres had the BEF attacking out of a salient. As far back as May Haig had set counter-battery dominance as a prerequisite for attacking here, and the day after Messines the Fifth Army had issued preliminary orders stressing counter-battery fire. With the Germans also building up, this meant a long bombardment. No fewer than 3,106 guns were assembled and they fired around 3 million shells over 18 days. Mediocre weather meant that the RFC observers and flash-spotting were less effective, and the Fifth Army won a delay for more bombardment (including wire-cutting) and then the French First Army (making a supporting attack) secured a delay for further counter-battery work. (Contrary winds and the noise from all the shellfire also made sound-ranging less effective.) Despite the problems, the volume of shells did plenty of damage: the Germans estimated 30,000 casualties, including 9,000 missing from the preliminary bombardment alone.[31] It lasted several weeks, but ultimately the counter-battery struggle ended with heavy German losses: *Gruppe Wytschaete* (on the eastern side of the salient, and not a major target of the British) lost 10 per cent of its field guns, 30 per cent of its heavy field howitzers, 17 per cent of its 8-inch and larger howitzers (what the Germans termed *Mörsers*) and half its heavy guns. So the Germans pulled their artillery back (and in a few places the German infantry also pulled back without orders to avoid the pummelling) and adopted a defensive posture. Their guns could still support the front lines, but could not hit deep into the Ypres Salient.

The attack on 31 July, the beginning of the Third Battle of Ypres, was supported by a stupendous creeping barrage, with about 24 tons of shells crashing down every minute. The poet Lieutenant Edmund Blunden wrote 'the British guns began; a flooded Amazon of steel flowed roaring, immensely fast, over our heads . . . one heard nothing from one's shouting neighbours'.[32] That was the perspective of a man watching; an officer responsible had a far more prosaic description:

It is now after midnight and I have just got zero hour and filled in the final details of the barrage tables. There are no fewer than 35 lifts, each involving a different range and angle for each gun. It would be simple enough if one had a room with a table and a good light to work with, but here in a mud-hole with a guttering candle, it is very difficult indeed . . .[33]

The Fifth Army had around 2,200 guns, while the Second Army's attack on the right flank had 320 and the French First Army on the left had 540. The depth of the objectives, however, meant that the field guns could not cover the infantry all the way, and the heavies had to be switched from counter-battery work to the creeper. Reducing counter-battery fire was one problem, but the greater danger zone from the large shells was another: the British infantry could not 'hug' the barrage as closely because the bigger shells would kill more of them. Moreover, the heavier guns had a lower rate of fire. After the infantry had moved through the German first position (which was fairly easy) they met the pillboxes and the struggle grew even more intense. Those inside the pillboxes had their own problems. Kapitän Kalepsky of *Infanterie Regiment 86* recorded:

The bunkers were reasonably strong and could withstand even direct hits from some of the heavy enemy shells, but owing to the ground conditions in the Flanders area they could not be erected over a strong foundation. When a couple of heavy shells opened a crater close to them, they would lean over, sometimes with the entrance down, with the soldiers trapped inside. There was no way of rescuing them, of course, and we suffered a rather heavy number of fatalities in this way – and the thought of the painfully slow death of those entombed haunted us all.[34]

These factors, combined with the increasing German shell fire, all added up and although the British infantry made impressive gains, the Germans were able to counter-attack under the cover of observed artillery fire (while the British guns sometimes held fire because they were unsure where their infantry was) and recaptured key areas. This was in contrast to the French method, where they used a handful of divisions, targeting modest objectives and using lots of artillery. General Anthoine had been picked for the French supporting operation because of his previous good use of artillery and Pétain had told him 'to lead an artillery battle supported by infantry'.[35]

The French had more trench mortars than 75s and more heavy artillery than mortars, and they had excellent results on the 31st.

Gough had gained ground, but had made the furthest advances where the Germans were least worried about it. The Second Army's supporting attack up part of the Gheluvelt Plateau had gained almost no ground (and faced fierce counter-attacks), while the Germans had not particularly contested an advance across a valley with both a stream and a canal. Throughout August Gough would continue attacking, but gains were relatively few and expensive. Marginal weather before the attack degraded into rain; it became hard to move the guns forwards, and the Germans frequently concentrated their fire on those guns that did move up. One British subaltern recorded:

> I received orders to move the guns further forwards under the lee of what had once been Sanctuary Wood. . . . And the weather worsened and it rained and rained, and the whole area became a great morass and ammunition could no longer be brought up in a wagon but had to be carried, eight rounds at a time, on a led pack-horse. All night and all day the German artillery pounded the gun lines and quite early on we had two guns damaged by shell-fire, one badly. We had had no time to dig gun-pits and, even if we had had time, we could not have done it in the flooded and boggy ground in which we stood. The best we could do for ourselves was to make a little scrape about one foot deep and try to get what shelter we could in that when it was our turn to sleep.[36]

The Germans also counter-attacked freely, using mobile artillery to support the attacks, sometimes getting close enough for direct fire.[37] Gough also rushed his attacks, many of which were too small to have a good chance. The French did little to assist, probably willing to attack if the British were clearly winning or if a big push was organised, but they did not take major risks for minor gains. The Germans, meanwhile, were rotating divisions into the area, both to hold the line and to counter-attack; they were not getting off free, and were concerned at how quickly divisions were getting 'fought out' (*abgekampft*). German divisions lasted about two weeks at the front, and from 31 July to 20 August a full 17 were used up.[38] The British planners were aware of this and fought a small battle at Lens to interrupt the German rotations. The Canadian Corps was ordered to attack the city, but on examining the tactical situation, Lieutenant-General Arthur Currie instead suggested taking Hill 70 which overlooked the sector. Massive artillery would cover the operation, and also protect against German counter-attacks, chewing up the Germans while minimising Canadian losses. On 15 August the Canadians duly took Hill 70, and for two days they smashed German counter-attacks with artillery fire until the Germans gave up. It was an effective tactic, and not only took the hill and forced a modest German withdrawal, ensuring that the British had good observation in the sector, but it battered several German divisions out of the Ypres rotation. However, it had serious limitations: the Canadians fired so many shells they wore out their guns (barrel wear increases at higher temperatures, and the guns were being fired until their barrels got hot), so that it was not a repeatable tactic.[39]

*   *   *

In Flanders Haig switched his main effort from Gough's Fifth Army to Plumer's Second Army. The drive now would be up and over the Gheluvelt Plateau. Plumer judged that 'success will depend primarily on the action of artillery',[40] and took three weeks to prepare and regain the edge in counter-battery work as well as pounding away with prolonged bombardment. Days alternated between counter-battery work and trench destruction; this allowed photo-interpretation of each day's results and time for new orders. Destructive counter-battery fire was carried out before attacks, with gas used against remaining German batteries at Zero Hour and follow-up barrages if the Germans stayed active. Over the years the Germans had built hundreds of gun-pits; since it was not possible to tell which were occupied, the British decided to hit as many as possible, but they also hit battery areas to destroy shell dumps and communications. At times Plumer had half his artillery firing counter-battery missions. The general bombardment was not neglected and Plumer's artillery methodically levelled trenches and pillboxes. He then sent fresh, prepared troops forwards to limited objectives. On top of this, heavy barrages (with multiple layers, totalling up to 1,000 yards of shell-fire and lasting up to 9 hours) helped the advance and protected against German counter-attacks. Harry Patch, Britain's last veteran of the Western Front, recalled the barrages as, 'like non-stop claps of thunder. It took your breath away. The noise was ferocious; you couldn't hear the man next to you speaking.'[41]

The Second Army attacked through September and October at roughly one-week intervals with fresh troops, benefiting at the start from a prolonged spell of good weather which is not how most people think of the 'Passchendaele' campaign. With heavy artillery preparation and support, the attacks readily gained ground. The Germans repeatedly changed tactics, putting more troops forwards, then holding the front weakly and counter-attacking even more. Narrowing the divisional fronts to concentrate manpower and firepower, assigning heavy artillery to the divisions (and typically then on to regiments), and even backing each front-line division with a complete reserve division were all tried. Nothing was working for them, and their commanders grew frustrated and nervous; one staff officer noted: 'We are going through a really awful experience. I do not know what to do in the face of the British.'[42] But Plumer's steps were so shallow that no guns were captured; in addition, his front narrowed as he advanced and thus generated another salient. Troops, vehicles and supplies were packed in so tight that almost any German shell could be expected to hit something, and wire-based communications were more often interrupted than functioning; carrier pigeons became unusually important. While the Second Army could concentrate its guns on the narrow sectors, so could the Germans – and theirs were more spread out, in better positions, with better road/rail links. A British junior officer wrote: 'It is pretty rotten taking stuff up to the guns though as the roads are shelled and are so full of ditched wagons [and] dead horses that we are having to rely on packs.'[43] But pack animals could only carry eight 18-pounder shells (two minutes for one gun) per trip, and fewer shells for heavier guns.

The Germans considered pulling back a few miles to buy time (as the British had to re-set their logistics), but they did not have to: the rain came instead. Crown Prince Rupprecht welcomed the October rain as 'our most effective ally'. The plight of the infantry is well known, but rain also affected every facet of the artillery's work. Aerial observation was hampered, as were flash-spotting and sound-ranging; ammunition supplies were slowed, and the guns themselves sank into the ooze, even when set atop heavy wooden platforms for support. Alternatively, guns would slip out of alignment and shells would fall all over the place. For example, on 4 October one division had only 25 guns firing the creeping barrage rather than the intended 96, and those 25 had less ammunition and were less accurate. While the infantry needed slower (and thus longer duration) creeping barrages, it was not possible to bring enough ammunition forwards to fire for hours, and the state of the roads meant the infantry got less support and took higher casualties. Lieutenant-Colonel C.E.L. Lyne recorded what it was like fighting his guns in mid-October:

It has rained in torrents all day, we were fighting at 3.30 this morning in a perfect deluge, until I was soaked and coated in mud. The mud which was horrible before became absolutely impassable. I had to get 2 guns into new places, one stuck muzzle deep in mud, and for hours defeated our most frenzied efforts. Finally the Hun strafed blue hell out of us unceasingly throughout the day . . .[44]

As the calendar advanced, progress on the ground slowed. Plumer tried attacking with less preparation but gained less ground each time, as there was no longer enough artillery support and the attacking infantry were neither fresh nor prepared. Finally he paused to regroup and also re-instituted strict limits on the attacks, this time only 500 yards deep. In late October and early November the Australians and Canadians clawed their way up the Passchendaele Ridge and finally gained observation down the far side. But they were miles from Roulers and all they had won was a reasonably dry position in which to spend the winter.

The battle ended up not much closer to Berlin, but the end of the war was measurably closer because of the rate of attrition. Yes, the Germans had to cut the size of their infantry battalions over the winter of 1917/18, but the British chose to disband some battalions instead of cutting all. Both sides had suffered savagely, but the campaign had proved that heavily prepared attacks could take ground and that shallow attacks could (usually) hold their gains. But the question was how to mount enough of these attacks to wear out the enemy?

Pétain and the French Recovery after the Mutiny

The French, in the *Instructions* of 31 October 1917, further developed the concept of Pétain's successive limited methodical operations, refining the concept that Lucas acidly described as the 'triumph of method over rapidity'. German defences were too formidable 'to think of making a breach in a single effort . . . As a result, offensive action will be characterised by successive attacks . . . against limited objectives where artillery can be most effectively employed.' Shorter preparatory bombardments and oper-ational security would contribute to strategic surprise and the use of both neutralisation and interdiction fire would enable tactical surprise. Air assets were now better integrated, with precise instructions outlined for their deployment and role in the new offensive system.

With the artillery now playing the decisive role, further instructions warily reintroduced the concept of individual initiative. 'All armies will be ready to exploit the confusion in the enemy's general dispositions which is produced by offensive actions; at each phase of any offensive action, they must prepare [for] the development of success', but officers should be 'prudent and methodical'.[45] Centralising artillery resources at division and corps level hugely assisted in planning an offensive but this approach unravelled as soon as the communication system broke down and the French struggled to find a solution to the vexed problem of maintaining contact with the units fighting their way forwards.

Lucas suggests that the dissemination of these instructions contributed to low morale in late 1917, plausibly suggesting that soldiers began to believe they could make little contribution to the success of operations that were increasingly dominated by impersonal, industrialised warfare. In reality, the French were still struggling to orchestrate the complementary technologies that might enable decisive success on the battlefield into a coherent symphony of destruction while allowing for opportunities for individual initiative. Without reliable artillery support, no officer could hope to forge beyond precisely planned objectives, but without flexibility both sides were doomed to fight a war of relentless attrition.

Pétain disseminated the latest French doctrine on defensive operations in December 1917, supplementing the instructions on the use of terrain issued in August 1917. Like the Germans the French highlighted the relationship between defensive and offensive operations and the importance of defence in depth. The French recognised that a layered defence was more effective than a strong forward position and, like their opponents, stipulated that each layer should be far enough from the next to require the attackers to move their guns forwards to commence the next artillery preparation; in many cases this meant widening the gaps between each line in the defensive system from 5 to as much as 8 kilometres. 'In order to escape the effects of artillery fire and aerial reconnaissance the essential elements of the defence must be dispersed. They must be detached from the visible lines of the defence and they must be dissimulated to the greatest possible extent. But such dispersion makes it more necessary than ever that there be a studied allotment of the means of the defence and good organisation of command.'[46] (The Germans learned the same lesson, reiterating it more and more forcefully in successive defensive guidelines, although they kept their traditional emphasis on decisions by forward leaders, and tried to keep the troops mobile and aggressive.[47]) The French were also coming to understand the value of a well timed counter-attack and instructed their army commanders to locate the optimum starting locations for their reserves and seize any opportunity to strike the flanks of any penetration. 'The army battlefield is the ensemble of organised terrain upon which it is the mission of the army to halt and defeat the enemy. The essential element of this battlefield is the position of resistance, selected so that the enemy will only be able to attack after a series of combats whose results shall have disordered both the assault dispositions of his infantry and the initial scheme of his artillery.' Crucially, GQG was beginning to understand that the Germans were just as keen to delay any French offensive through similar means. Operational planning was therefore increasingly based upon attaining strategic surprise, wearing down the defenders and absorbing their reserves by launching a sequence of closely timed and linked offensives. The problem was that the French had lost confidence in their ability to conduct major operations; it would take the failure of Germany's 1918 spring offensives to restore French confidence.

In addition to improving their doctrine, the French were also seeing increasing numbers of modern rapid-firing heavy guns in their arsenal. The artillery programme of 1917 enabled each division to have a *groupe* of 155mm howitzers and each corps to have a reserve regiment made up of two *groupes* of 105mm howitzers and a heavy *groupe* of 155s. The artillery available for an assault was finally strong enough and modern enough to quickly deliver a heavy bombardment. With the increasingly sophisticated use of aviation, camouflage and intelligence, specialist artillery units, adequate reserves, new tanks and the introduction of new gas shells designed to facilitate neutralisation, the French artillery arm was well placed to play a decisive role in the battles of 1918. To further enhance these elements, Pétain set up new training camps so that all-arms exercises could be conducted and artillery–infantry coordination improved. To ensure that the entire army was inculcated with the new approaches, senior officers were also sent on courses. In these courses, defence in depth was proposed for all sectors but not all had converted their defensive arrangements in time for the German spring offensive. As noted above, GQG was finally able to deploy a general artillery reserve that combined six formidable *groupes* of heavy artillery with the super-heavy *Artillerie Lourde à Grande Puissance*.[48]

The Orchestration of Destruction: The Battle of Riga

After the Czar's abdication in March, the Russian state and the army continued to disintegrate. A Provisional Government was formed but its authority was contested by the Council of Workers and Soldiers Deputies (the Soviet), which insisted that military planning should be approved by soldiers' committees. Oblivious to the political consequences, the French insisted on some kind of Russian offensive in 1917 and a chaotic process of operational planning began. German operations against the Stokhod bridgehead demonstrated Russian fragility but the Central Committee continued to assure its allies that they would honour their commitment to continue fighting. Kerensky, the charismatic War Minister, began planning a grand offensive. The two–day bombardment was one of the most impressive of the war but the assault collapsed as reserve units refused to support the initial successful advances or proved brittle under fire. Kerensky seized power from the Provisional Government and authorised further offensives but only the Romanians proved capable of fighting effectively, winning a bruising fight at Mărăşti in July, where they deployed their artillery under French tuition.

The German Eighth Army, commanded by Oskar von Hutier, was tasked in August 1917 with finally breaking through Kornilov's Russian Twelfth Army at Riga.[49] Plans had been under consideration since April, but the Russian positions were formidable and the garrison well prepared. Kornilov seems to have been aware that the offensive was imminent but appears to have played little role in the battle except authorising the retreat. Fresh divisions were assigned to Hutier's command but more importantly he planned to use a combination of the latest assault tactics to achieve a decisive breakthrough, with a fire-plan orchestrated by Colonel Bruch-müller. The infantry assault units were trained in infiltration methods – an approach initially suggested by Laffargue but perfected by Hauptmann Willy Rohr and others – on a grand scale for the first time. The Germans intended to use abbreviated registration in the first phase of the preparatory bombardment to mask the detailed fire-plan. This simple system was an effective solution to the problem of maintaining surprise. Instead of a long general bombardment or a slow methodical battering of key positions over several days, abbreviated registration required the batteries supporting the main assault to use pre-set registration points to first confirm their position on the battlefield and then shift their fire to targets identified within the carefully surveyed area around their initial registration point. Batteries could thus arrive during the night, pre-register at dawn, then fire on their main targets with a reasonable chance of hitting the target. Accuracy was worse than the old way but chemical rounds meant near-misses could still neutralise targets. Allied analysts would ultimately conclude the Germans had discovered a new way of delivering unobserved fire without registration.[50]

Mindful of the damage the Russian artillery could cause during the Duna river crossing, the first two hours of the fire-plan, planned for 1 September, also included a hurricane bombardment against identified battery positions. To ensure counter-battery success, the artillery was reinforced from both the Eastern and Western Fronts, with enough ammunition to provide a genuine test of Bruchmüller's methods. Given the scale of the bombardment, it is perhaps unsurprising that the Russians failed to notice the final phase of the abbreviated registration plan during the torrent of shellfire. The mix of shells (three-quarters gas and one-quarter high explosive) shattered the communication system and silenced most of the batteries. After 2 hours the majority of the heavies continued to focus on the Russian batteries while the rest, including the trench mortars, adjusted their sights according to the data gathered from the abbreviated registration phase and began to pound the front lines with a mix of shells dominated by high explosive (80:20). After another 3 hours of intense fire, the remaining heavy batteries joined the main barrage for a final terrifying few minutes before the creeping barrage commenced, leaving only one gun per battery to maintain the lethal miasma over the Russian gun positions.

The creeping barrage surged forwards after 5 hours and 10 minutes of pounding. As Zabecki notes in his biography of Bruchmüller, the main barrage had delivered 10,500 tons of high explosive on to the Russian defensive system – the equivalent of 500 B-52 bomber payloads. The devastation was made more horrific by the densest utilisation of gas shells since the technology was introduced and by the relative accuracy of the fire. Unlike the timed barrages at Verdun, the six lifts in the German creeping barrage were coordinated by the advancing infantry firing green flares. Bruchmüller's fire-plan fed additional silent batteries in to each phase while earmarked batteries pounded identified targets in the rear areas, sowing further chaos. Once the river crossing was complete (aided on the day by the morning mist), the heavy guns switched back to counter-battery fire. Light guns were rafted over for the attack on the second position, at which point the heavy guns switched targets to give supporting fire. The next phase of the fire-plan supported the consolidation units building the bridges, covered the movement of heavy guns over the river and assisted the assault units by disrupting counter-attacks on the bridgehead. Once these were in position the final phase of the fire-plan could begin and the exploitation phase could theoretically commence before the Russians could move any effective reserves into play.[51] The only aspect missing in the plan was the recognition that confusion was inevitable as soon as the assault units surged over the bridges and into the chaos created by the Russian retreat. This elaborate fire-plan confirmed Bruchmüller's reputation as a master gunner and his version of the creeping barrage was quickly nicknamed the '*feuerwalze*', a peculiarly light-hearted term which nevertheless captures his skilful orchestration of phased zone fire missions. While the intended effect is always entirely destructive, the creation of a complex fire-plan certainly shares some of the combination of art and precision that characterises musical composition.

Reluctant Students: Allied Assistance to the Russians

The British had relied on military attachés to assist the Russians with technical questions until 1917, when they belatedly decided to send one specialist gunner officer to oversee training on each type of gun. Charles Springfield was selected to train the Russians on the 26-inch 26cwt howitzer and the 12-inch super-heavy howitzer; when he asked for instructions, he found that the various departments of the War Office did not seem to understand what his mission actually involved and furthermore there was little enthusiasm for the task. On arrival at Tsarskoe Selo, Springfield discovered that his authority was undermined by his failure to wear a huge sword and a set of enormous epaulets so he borrowed a cavalry sabre from the embassy and bought some second-hand Russian rank markings. He also found that the Russians were depressingly inefficient: to his dismay, only one of the eight 12-inch pieces sent in early 1917 had actually fired at the enemy – a situation that had not been helped by the Royal Navy loading the dial sights (these enabled each artillery piece to be accurately positioned so that indirect fire missions could be calculated – see illustrations) with the final load of spares for the battery.

Springfield set about learning as much Russian as he could – in marked contrast to many other British officers – and soon discovered that his interpreter did not translate exactly what he said even when describing technical details vital to operating the guns. Technical knowledge can be seen as conferring authority in armies where a professional approach to training is weak, and the Russian officers that Springfield was forced to assist clearly saw controlling the arcane workings of the latest weaponry as a route to influence and promotion.[52]

As the revolution unfolded, Springfield was sent to Gatchina and was assigned an affable minor prince as an interpreter, after which the training process improved markedly. The Russian gunners were surprised to find the British instructor carefully maintaining a howitzer before anyone else arrived and asked if he was an ordinary gunner. Exasperated, Springfield indicated the nearest Russian NCO and informed them that English officers always pitched in to assist their men particularly 'when the damned Russian working party is too late and too lazy to do it for them'. The watching Russians were duly impressed. 'Our officers dance and drink and do other things, but work – no.' Inspired by Springfield's example, all the Russians who were previously inclined to stand around instead joined in and proved excellent gunners from then on.

Unsurprisingly, the Russians proved very stubborn when Springfield tried to inculcate the latest ideas in gunnery methods – the Russians 'had their methods and admired ours – but they preferred their own'. Calibration was one area where the Russians appeared completely disinterested and as the temperature variation in Russia could be as much as 80 degrees, it is not entirely surprising that the Russian artillery batteries often shelled their own men.[53] Sir John Headlam was sent to observe Russian methods in 1917 and was impressed with some aspects of what he saw but was surprised by the continuing contempt that artillery officers had for the infantry and the obvious lack of adequate liaison. He noticed that 'one battalion headquarters had an excellent sketch map, showing the zones of fire of all guns bearing on the front of the regiment' but also recorded that the artillery could be slow in reacting to requests for artillery support – 'especially if they were drinking tea'.[54]

A Vision of the Future: Russia's Artillery

While the overall quality of the artillery arm declined, the Russians continued to learn from their desperate efforts to stem the German tide. The most intriguing innovation, the experimental XLVIII Corps, continued to expand throughout 1917 and survived the Czar's abdication. The XLVIII Corps was made up of six artillery brigades and was theoretically designed to enable higher-level commanders to plan and coordinate advanced fire-planning. Alexeyev ordered that it be renamed the Heavy Artillery of Special Duty (*tiazhelaia artilleriia osobogo naznacheniia* or TAON) and, although there was little time to complete the necessary specialist training or logistic preparation, it was ordered into the line to support the summer offensive of 1917. The Front commanders found it difficult to position and coordinate their heavy batteries and, due to the preponderance of foreign guns, found TAON's logistic tail to be overly complex. With modern 9.2-inch howitzers emplaced but silent due a lack of ammunition, and other batteries firing with incorrect charges so that they could at least make a vague contribution to the battle, TAON's 1,000 heavy guns made little impact on the fighting. Some estimates even suggest that as many as 50 per cent of the heavy guns were put out of commission by the use of incorrect charges.

After-action reports from the TAON noted the importance of supplies, proper coordination with other units, target identification and the chaos caused by conducting a withdrawal without a clear plan. Few of the reforms required to reorganise TAON were completed before the Revolution. Some of the batteries decided that being designated 'separate' meant that they could ignore orders from their brigade or *divizional* commanders and the repair and maintenance workshops simply ceased to function at the levels required to keep TAON operating at full combat strength. As the chaos unfolded, Russia's first experiment in the coordination of massed artillery gradually rotted away or was sold for scrap but the concept remained in the institutional memory of Russia's artillerymen and saw a dramatic rebirth during the Second World War.[55]

Through Mud and Blood to the Green Fields Beyond: The Battle of Cambrai

The last battle on the Western Front in 1917 would be completely different; indeed, it arguably marked the end of conventional trench warfare. For the British, Cambrai was based on tanks (and new artillery techniques) while the German counter-attack relied on massively expanding the stormtroop tactics they had been developing at lower echelons since 1915. Both alternatives would restore surprise to the battlefield, with effects that are important enough to need exploring.

As noted at Riga, planners now recognised that surprise was the key to the enemy being at a disadvantage when an attack went in and considerable efforts went into ensuring that the redeployment of reserves was carefully concealed. As a result, when the British attacked on 20 November there was only one German division holding the 6,000-yard attack sector, and it was supported by only 34 field pieces and 20 heavy guns – some of which were captured guns with little ammunition. Later, when the Germans launched their counter-attack, the British were caught out because they did not expect an attack on such a scale (one corps' guns were, quite literally, facing the wrong direction). Surprise meant weak defenders, and that made success for the attackers far more likely.

Conventional trench warfare largely negated any element of surprise. Infantry could not attack through barbed wire without assistance but methodically cutting it before an attack by using an extended preparatory bombardment largely ruled out any chance of surprise. Infantry could not linger in no-man's-land using wire cutters or Bangalore Torpedoes, so the task of wire-cutting fell to the artillery. Using artillery took time – which allowed the defenders to move in reserves; those reserves then needed to be hit by the preliminary bombardment, so the tactical obstacle of barbed wire had an operational or even strategic effect. Not only did it take a week or more to prepare an attack, but it required huge amounts of guns and shells to prepare a sector for a conventional assault and there were finite quantities of both. Thus the sturdier the defences, the fewer attacks there would be. For the British, it took two developments to address the challenge of regaining surprise. First, tanks crushed the barbed wire; enough tanks would eventually allow a sizeable attack without any artillery wire-cutting. Secondly, a new technology allowed artillery to hit targets without first firing ranging shots. Calibration, an outgrowth of sound-ranging, involved checking each gun's muzzle velocity to see how it varied from the standard. Combining that with daily variations for temperature and weather allowed fall of shot to be accurately predicted. Once all the guns of a battery were calibrated, fire could be planned using a map instead of correcting the fall of shot for every battery before commencing 'fire for effect'. Thanks to the efforts of the excellent Field Survey Companies,[56] with 'predicted fire' there was no need for registering guns on targets (which itself ruined surprise) and the first shells would hit the target. Once the 'predicted' barrage was accurate enough for the infantry to follow safely, the British could dispense with all preliminary bombardment: the tanks would crush the wire, the barrage would be on target, and surprise meant the German artillery would be weak so that 'predicted' counter-battery fire would be enough to neutralise the outnumbered enemy batteries.

With surprise, other things also became possible. An attack needed less ammunition, since there would not be weeks of firing. Because the defending infantry would still be in their trenches and bunkers, it was possible to fire a lifting barrage (one that lifted from one trench to the next) rather than the slower creeping barrage that covered all the ground in between trench lines, and make final adjustments to the fall of shot for the heavier batteries. It was possible to put the attacking artillery close behind the front line because there would be no painful counter-battery struggle, and thus the attacking troops would have fire support deeper into enemy lines.

The British recognised how predicted fire would change tactics, but were astute enough not to cast aside proven tactical methods; they still planned to hit German observation posts, headquarters and telephone exchanges.

With tanks flourishing on the battlefield, anti-tank guns were a newly important target, and RFC patrols were assigned to watch for them; when news came back of an anti-tank gun, the British artillery covering that sector would be switched on to the guns for 5 minutes. (The Germans had no purpose-designed anti-tank guns. The Hindenburg Programme had focused on maximising production of existing models rather than developing new ones, and they had also not seen any need for a special anti-tank gun). A great deal of effort was put into camouflage, and poor weather for the ten days ahead of the attack at Cambrai helped maintain surprise.

The officer behind the development of 'silent registration' was the brilliant but irascible Hugh Tudor. Aided by the reports coming from the Eastern Front of a new subtle approach to registration, he was able to convince his sceptical colleagues that the Germans had already used 'silent registration' and that Britain could not afford to allow them to maintain this decisive lead in artillery tactics. Brigadier Hugo De Pree of IV Corps utilised Tudor's concept in the plan he submitted to the Third Army and, alongside Fuller's outline for the use of tanks, the British finally had the theoretical basis for a potentially decisive operation on the Western Front.[57]

On 20 November the supporting fire was all that could be asked. Private Kirkby of 2/6th West Yorkshires was among those who were surprised by the ferocity of the initial barrage: 'Suddenly the silence of the coming dawn was shattered by such an earthquake and fire that was never heard before by men. Though the ground shook with the thunder of our massed guns, it was the breathtaking circle of multi-coloured flames rising like gigantic fireworks which produced a sight so breathtaking, so all-together awe-inspiring, as to root us to the ground. . .'.[58] The barrage smashed into the German trenches. Smoke barrages blinded the German observation posts, counter-battery fire was effective, the advance was faster than the Germans expected and their weak defensive barrage missed the British attackers: everything appeared to have worked smoothly, everything except moving the reserves forwards to exploit the opening. Reserves had been designated (two cavalry divisions and one infantry division) and guns had been allocated to move with them. But getting the word back from the front line that there was a hole, then clearing and repairing the roads, clearing the wire (the tanks crushed the wire well enough for infantrymen to pick their way forwards, but not well enough for horses to haul guns or wagons over it), and keeping all the headquarters abreast of events was beyond the communications technology of the day. While the Tank Corps was the latest in military technology, it relied on carrier pigeons to communicate with headquarters. Thus the break-in was successful, but there was no break-through, and the Germans were able to paper over the gaps with reserves. The mobile guns had rendered good service, and showed that some of the tactics of 1914 were still valid. The direct fire of field guns (or even 6-inch howitzers) was an excellent way to smash a strong-point. There were not enough cases of it happening to be significant, but it reminded senior officers that they needed to refresh infantry–artillery training for mobile operations.

Even without a breakthrough, the results had been too good for the BEF to break off the battle, and since the Germans held some key observation posts the British would have to suffer the embarrassment of pulling back to their starting point or face having their new front line being dominated over the winter. But as they continued the battle, they were trying to implement standard bombardments and barrages with inadequate artillery – using only what could be hauled forwards and supplied with shells. At first the Germans were disorganised, but they could reinforce and resupply by railways and good roads while the British had to march several miles across the belts of wire and trenches of the Hindenburg Line. Once again logistics proved the leash that limited operations. The British were better organised but lacked enough support. The tired troops fought hard but made only minor gains and after a few days the British goal became simply smoothing out the front line for winter.

The Germans counter-attacked on 30 November; they also had surprise on their side. Part of it was due to careful planning, such as moving mainly at night and moving von Richthofen's *Jagdstaffel 11* into the sector for air superiority, but poor weather also hampered British reconnaissance. The British also had not established their full intelligence network, including sound-ranging stations that would have located additional German batteries. For reasons that are still unclear, GHQ was not particularly concerned about an attack and let itself be surprised even though the successful first phase had created an exposed salient that the Germans were extremely likely to exploit, and many of the divisional and corps commanders were increasingly concerned about their precarious position.[59] For Operation *Sturmflut* ('tidal wave'), the Germans used a Bruchmüller-model bombardment, an innovation in the West assisted by the redoubtable colonel being present as an observer at XXIII Reserve Korps HQ;[60] they had 350 heavy howitzers and 890 field guns and (as they were generally close to rail lines) the ammunition stocks were ample. While stormtrooper tactics had started at the battalion level, now whole divisions had been trained to penetrate and outflank enemy positions using smoke to increase the chaos created by the hurricane (admittedly with mixed results).[61]

The Germans aimed to roll up the British position from south to north, pinching out the British salient in the Hindenburg Line, and hitting both the north and south flanks to disguise the main objective of retaking the *Siegfried* positions. The southern attack hit a weak spot. The British troops were spread too thinly, the defences were weak, they had little artillery and much of what they had was facing north to support continued British attacks (what little wire had been deployed was dealt with by the German guns). After a brief hurricane bombardment, *trommelfeuer*, lasting just under an hour, the German infantry easily sliced through the gaps in the British line; where there were strong-points the *minenwerfer* and infantry guns, manhandled forwards by the infantry, provided mobile firepower that the British could not match. As much as anything, that gave the defenders an excuse to surrender ('Look, they've got a minnie and will eventually kill us all; it's fair for us to surrender') rather than providing overwhelming fire-power. The Germans swarmed on to the British gun positions, and despite some very gallant stands by the Royal Artillery (Lieutenant S.T.D. Wallace and Sergeant C.E. Gourley received the gunners' first Victoria Crosses since 1914) the Germans captured about 150 guns – roughly what the British had captured a few days earlier.

Some of the tanks, in the process of withdrawing, were thrown back into the battle but most were hurriedly pulled out to prevent the Germans from capturing them. The British desperately tried to establish a defensive line before the combination of infantry infiltration, strafing by aircraft and artillery fire overwhelmed any unit that tried to turn and fight. George McMurtrie of the 7/Somerset Light Infantry remarked after the battle: 'I never thought I should get back. We had no support from the artillery, not one of our aeroplanes appeared and there we were under a hail of machine-gun bullets from both aeroplanes and attacking troops, shells bursting everywhere.'[62] Even when the British were able to counter-attack, they risked being caught by their own artillery during the confused fighting.

The northern attack was almost a mirror image, although the British line was thicker there, with plenty of supporting guns. The Germans had relatively little information on British gun positions (one of the problems of poor weather and the British continuing to press forwards), and their counter-battery fire was ineffective. Reserve Infantry Regiment 226 noted in their war diary: 'Our own batteries were supposed to cover this move-ment by firing a smokescreen. In reality they only fired a few smoke shells and the protection they provided was illusory, because the wall of smoke was quickly dispersed by a strong wind.'[63] The 30–60 minute bombardment was inadequate – even though the British had done little digging, there were plenty of Hindenburg Line positions around for them to use. Without gaps for the stormtroops to flow through, they simply piled up in front of the British lines. One Royal Engineer observed that 'never have I seen so many Germans, the whole forward landscape seemed literally alive with them; thousands of them were attacking.'[64] While the plan hoped for a minor Cannae, it would have taken a complete collapse of the British defensive system for such a catastrophe to have occurred, As General Moser dryly noted in his diary during the planning phase, 'the transition from defensive to offensive operations is numbered amongst the most difficult tasks'.[65] There was hard fighting and plenty of casualties, but the British held easily. That did not mean there were no casualties:

> The gas in Bourlon Wood hung in the trees and bushes so thickly that all ranks were compelled to wear their respirators continuously . . . But men cannot dig for long without removing them and it was necessary to dig trenches to get any cover from the persistent shell-fire. Throughout November 30th there was, therefore, a steady stream of gassed and wounded men coming to the regimental aid-posts. Their clothes were full of gas, and as the medical officer could not dress wounds without removing his respirator, he, too, felt the effects. No fewer than seven medical officers went to hospital gassed as a result of this dilemma.[66]

Once the fighting subsided, the Germans drew very different lessons from the British from the battles of 1917. In order to make the Allied gunners waste their ammunition, officers were encouraged to further disperse and utilise every innovation in entrenchment and camouflage to conceal their men. 'The more works there are, the more objectives will exist for the adversary to fire upon and the more ammunition they will expend; a wide fortified zone in depth must therefore be prepared.' Zones were now standard: 'Battles should be conducted, not about lines, but within battle-zones.'[67] Shell-holes were increasingly used to support the defensive system and artillery was increasingly echeloned so batteries were more difficult for British and French gunners to locate and eliminate.

Unlike the French, the Germans were actively encouraged to use their initiative and to embrace mobility. The Germans were keen to reanimate the offensive spirit of the troops who had spent years defending on the Western Front but acknowledged that real operational flexibility only existed when troops recognised the value of the timely counter-attack and both tactical and strategic withdrawal:

> There are scarcely any points of terrain which must be held at all costs. There are a series of points which we believed that we could not give up in any case and which we had to resign ourselves to lose, after having made numerous and useless sacrifices. In such cases an opportune and voluntary withdrawal executed in accordance with orders does not affect the morale of the troops, while the arbitrary retention of points, which have evidently become unfavourable, shakes their confidence in [their officers].[68]

'It will crush us all': The Isonzo in 1917

On the Isonzo the morale of both armies was increasingly fragile. Cadorna ignored the growing criticism from his men and listened to the siren voices of Italian politicians (who wanted the Irredenta captured) and the demands of the Allies (who wanted constant pressure on all fronts). After considering the options, the Italian Third Army was ordered to attempt yet another attack into the Carso, but this time with more supporting artillery, including 166 new heavy batteries,[69] but there was little sign of sophistication in the fire-planning. Even though the Italians had doubled their number of guns, they still had little more than a quarter of the numbers seen on the Western Front and the uncertain ammunition supplies meant that the rate of fire for heavy guns was a fifth of that seen in the Heavy Artillery Groups of the Royal Artillery.[70] Field Marshal Robertson, visiting the front before the offensives of 1917, was stunned by the lack of pre-battle planning: 'no system of co-operation existed between the artillery and the infantry in the attack; in fact the relations between the two seemed strained.'[71]

Cadorna's tenth offensive on the Isonzo began a few weeks after Nivelle's offensive had collapsed and was delayed by the transfer of guns from the Trentino. On 10 May some 2,150 guns and 980 mortars blasted Austrian positions northwest of Gorizia for 44 hours. Initially the intention was to form a bridgehead at Hill 383 and then seize the Bainsizza Plateau. The Austrian artillery, firing at pre-planned sectors of the defensive system, shattered the first massed assaults. However, Italian numbers, a successful bombardment and dwindling Austrian ammunition stocks meant the Italians still managed to seize part of the Tri Santi position. Even then the

Austrians reacted quickly, retaking several key positions in night attacks.[72]

In other sectors the usual problems of coordination led to ruinously heavy casualties but the Italians grimly refocused their efforts. They shifted artillery from sector to sector and their methodical battering of Austrian positions enabled gradual progress. In some sectors intense shelling prevented either side from holding the objective. The attack on the Asiago Plateau was even less successful, with heavy rain disrupting the preparatory bombardment and Austrian machine guns slaughtering the *fanti* struggling through the mud and barbed wire. An Alpini captain described the aftermath: 'the mountain is infinitely taciturn, like a dead world, with its snowfields soiled, the shell-craters, the burnt pines. But the breath of battle wafts over all – a stench of excrement and dead bodies.' With typical petulance, Cadorna was furious with the slow progress of some units and blamed everyone but himself for the inadequacies of his own plan.[73]

To launch the second phase of the battle, on to the Bainsizza Plateau, the Italians fired a million shells in 10 hours – approximately 20 shells for every foot of the front line. Dust and smoke from the intense bombardment covered the advancing infantry and major gains were made wherever the artillery were able to dominate the battlefield. The Austrians retained the key observation posts and utilised units released from the Eastern Front, using more flexible tactics and working more closely with their artillery support, to counter-attack and many of the Italian gains were lost. During the savage fighting both sides expended prodigious amounts of ammunition – the Austrian Fifth Army fired almost 2 million shells during the battle – a rate of expenditure that Austria's industrial base could not support.

After a short pause, during which Cadorna displayed a ruthless disregard for the simmering discontent within the army,[74] the Italians began planning the Eleventh Battle, which Cadorna described as a 'general simultaneous attack'. The Second and Third Armies would take both Gorizia and the entire Bainsizza Plateau before capturing Tolmein, the Austrian Isonzo army's main railhead. However, even if Cadorna's plan succeeded, the Bainsizza was a rugged wilderness that would prove a poor basis for a fresh offensive, and Boroević recognised this flaw in the plan for the eleventh Italian offensive far better than did his Italian opposite number. The Italians massed 3,750 guns and 1,900 mortars, almost three times the Austrians' total (450 heavy guns and 1,250 field and mountain guns), and four times the ammunition; the artillery duel would be the largest on that front.[75] The barrage commenced on 18 August with the Italian guns, howitzers and mortars mercilessly hammering the entire front line. The quality of the artillery preparation was higher than in earlier battles and there were a small number of Allied batteries supporting the attack. In some sectors the defenders were rapidly cut off from headquarters and the defending corps commanders found it difficult to coordinate counter-attacks or to update the Isonzo army's headquarters on the progress of the battle. Elsewhere the difficult terrain and poor Italian planning gave the Austrians enough time to reorganise and prevent a breakthrough.

Weak planning left the Italians unable to capitalise on their gains. Despite their collapsing defences, the Austrians could choose to withdraw or to feed troops into the meat-grinder. Boroević was assured by the High Command that a counter-offensive was being planned and commenced a series of skilful Austrian withdrawals that delighted the Italians but ensured that he was able to consolidate on new positions on the eastern edge of the plateau. The end result was that the Italians secured most of the Bainsizza Plateau but stalled in front of Boroević's new position, unsure of how to proceed. Monte Santo was taken by coup de main but desperate assaults on San Gabriele by massed columns were torn apart by artillery and machine-gun fire. Desperate counter-attacks, supported by heavy artillery, prevented the last of the Tri Santi from falling; the mountain is said to have lost 10 metres in altitude due to the near-continuous bombardment by guns of calibres of up to 420mm. Angelo Gatti, a staff officer in the supreme command, described his mounting despair: 'I feel something collapsing inside me; I shall not be able to endure this much longer, none of us will; it is too gigantic, truly limitless, it will crush us all.'[76] The Austrians looked as if they had suffered a major defeat but, after Cadorna's grimly pyrrhic victory, the tide was about to turn.

There are excellent British sources on the quality of the Italian artillery at this stage of the war. Lieutenant Hugh Dalton served with the B2 Heavy Artillery Group assigned to the Isonzo sector while Lieutenant-Colonel Archibald Moberly commanded B1 Heavy Artillery Group. Dalton was particularly impressed with the individual technical skills of the Italian artillery and their incomparable mountain engineers but noted that local commanders were very keen to secure Royal Artillery support. While the total number of shells appears impressive on the Isonzo Front, Dalton noticed that the ammunition levels were lower than those in France and Flanders and noted that this was reflected in the rates of fire, RA 'ordinary' rate being 30 rounds per hour, five times Italy's *fuoco normale*.[77] Dalton also noted that the proportion of heavy guns was one quarter of what he had

experienced in France. The abundance of good observation post sites aston-
ished the Royal Artillery officers. Depending on the sector, there were
kavernen, mountain huts or treetop hides, all under cloudless skies. Such
luxury delighted one of Dalton's colleagues, who gleefully described Italy
as a 'gunner's heaven'.[78] The no. 101 fuse was almost as effective as the no.
106 in Italy due to the impact advantage of hitting solid rock. Wire-clearing
was relatively simple but a great deal of fire was required to destroy rock-
hewn trenches or *kavernen* – Moberly and his Italian colleagues naturally
preferred enfilade fire to lobbing shells straight into the enemy's defensive
line and both Dalton and Moberly were impressed by the 'man-killing'
effect of high explosive in the mountains (as at Gallipoli, the rocky terrain
increased the effectiveness of the artillery).

Moberly was equally impressed by the Italian engineers but rather less
impressed with the higher levels of command. The lack of telephone wire
for communications surprised him, particularly as the observations posts
that had so impressed Dalton tended to be distant from the battery and thus
required even more wire than usual. Italian HAG equivalents, the *raggruppamenti*, were allotted to sectors, not to particular assault or defensive units,
and Moberly was surprised by the fact that there was no expectation that
he would meet with the commander of the division he was supporting.
During the first operation supported by B1, Moberly noted the Italians
were still grappling with technical issues that had been identified and solved
on the Western Front years before, particularly regarding communication
between the assault units and the supporting artillery, a situation aggra-
vated by the smoke and dust created by the bombardment obscuring the
target. He was also troubled by the lack of specific missions assigned to his
men and the concentration on planned but uncoordinated support for
attacks.

Moberly noted that the ineffectiveness of Italian counter-battery fire was
due to the HAGs assigned to the task being allocated to army and not corps
command and thus lacking tactical coordination in the battles. As a result
the counter-battery staff soon lost touch with the progress of the battle and
found it difficult to coordinate fire. Moberly even received orders to shell
positions that his own observation posts had reported as silent for days.
Commando Supremo had made counter-battery work a priority for ammunition allocation, but had not realised that numbers did not equal results.
Counter-battery orders criss-crossed the chain of command, bypassing the
heavy artillery *raggruppamenti* and going to the field artillery *groupes*, a
system that naturally led to some confusion and to errors that made

counter-battery fire ineffective. Attempts to solve problems created others: the deliberate simplification of orders, for example, speeded up their transmission across scratchy telephone lines, but sometimes led to requests for a handful of shells so even a timely request lacked enough power. The only aspect that impressed Moberly was that counter-battery officers spent four days out of every eight at front-line observation posts and thus established a close relationship with the Forward Observation Officers.[79]

Breakthrough in the Mountains: Caporetto

The Austrian Emperor and his high command understood that the collapse of Russia presented an extraordinary opportunity, and the Germans understood that the resources of the Austro-Hungarian Empire were heavily overstretched on the Isonzo. Lieutenant-General Krafft von Dellmensigen was despatched to review the situation and returned to Berlin with an operational plan that centred on the small town of Caporetto. With detailed intelligence on Italian dispositions and half-amused by the weakness in the defences, Dellmensigen saw an opportunity to turn Cadorna's hard-won positions and drive the Italians deep into their own territory.

The Germans sent specialist units and seven experienced assault divisions to form the Fourteenth Army under General Otto von Bülow. Supported by twelve Austrian divisions and using both tactical and operational infiltration methods (the latter suggested by General Alfred Krauss, one of the Austrian corps commanders), they expected to pour down the valleys and utilise the complex terrain to encircle and bewilder the defenders before they had a chance to coordinate their reserves and stem the tide. No fewer than 1,076 guns and 174 mortars were assigned to the offensive, with reserves of 1.5 million shells.

On 24 October the massed batteries of the Central Powers commenced their bombardment on the Italian Second and Third Armies' positions. Hugh Dalton's unit witnessed the second phase opening up in the southern sector and described the area around Faiti becoming a 'sea of flame' as the shells rained down. After years of launching assaults on the Austrian defences, and with their positions arrayed to enable further attacks, the Italian command system appeared to completely collapse when expected to go over to the defensive. General Capello, commanding the Second Army, fluctuated between giving confusing statements about 'the thunderbolt of the counter-offensive' and being violently ill, while the usually competent Pietro Badoglio sacrificed the entire Tolmein sector by ordering his gunners to hold their fire due to a lack of ammunition. To compound the weakness of the defensive system, the Italians had poor-quality gas masks and the Germans used liberal amounts of gas shells to neutralise the higher positions so their infiltration units could proceed along the valleys.[80]

Isolated guns did their best but the Italian counter-battery effort was negligible. The shelling shattered their fragile communications system along the ridges, leaving the whole defensive system in disarray. Isolated units were left perched in their eyries, confused at the presence of enemy units all around them and unable (given the rigid command system) to do anything except await their fates. Among the assault units heading for Tolmein were the Württemberg Mountain Battalion with its own Mountain Howitzer Detachment. One of the company commanders was the youthful and exuberant Erwin Rommel, a keen student of the latest methods in assault tactics and an astute observer of the dynamics of the modern infantry battle. Rommel watched his own side's barrage with obvious delight but was also impressed by the Italians' use of harassing fire in the mountains. Instead of firing directly at the defences cut into the mountainsides, the Italians concentrated on the slopes above, showering the men below with boulders and shards of rock. Rommel copied this approach as soon as he had the chance, and as the offensive unfolded he casually hijacked a forward communications switchboard to contact a Forward Observation Officer near Tolmein to support his attack on the Kuk position. Given the possibilities of using landslides as a weapon, Rommel was bemused by the Italians' hastily entrenched positions on forward slopes – they made even meagre artillery support extremely useful.[81] On the other hand, he was impressed by the Italian searchlights illuminating the Austrian and German units passing below.

Once he had torn through the first layers of the Italian defences, Rommel quickly concluded that attacking a defence-in-depth required good artillery support;[82] even though his own unit captured a number of batteries, small numbers of guns could soon stall an assault. Even once the attackers clambered over the first ridge, signalling only served to give away their position and even the best assault timetable could not predict where the infantry might need close support.[83] As a result Rommel decided against using flares and instead used a heliograph to call in artillery against Italian positions on Mount Mrzli.[84] Just as Rommel had discovered in Romania, concealment and silence in the advance were essential for a successful breakthrough, but once the defences became too formidable to outflank or to assault, proper artillery support was required – such as during the Württemberg Battalion's attacks on Hill 1114 and the Kolovrat Ridge. Rommel noted that artillery batteries and Forward Observation Officers needed to be concentrated in positions from where they were able to observe the advancing troops in future attacks, but also realised that as soon as the direction of the assault was discerned by the defenders they could quickly assign carefully sighted artillery batteries to slow the momentum of the breakthrough.[85]

With the Germans and Austrians pouring through at Tolmein, Cadorna was forced to withdraw his forces from the Bainsizza Plateau; the pyrrhic victory of the summer had now turned into a bitter defeat. As ridge after ridge was retaken, Cadorna realised that he had to fall back on the River Piave before the enemy overwhelmed his confused forces. Crowds of men surged away from the bloody Isonzo battlefields and the engineers started the desperate process of blowing bridges to slow the triumphant enemy before they shattered the entire sector. Cadorna abandoned the Second Army to its fate and concentrated on saving the rest of his command. As so often happens in war, luck had not entirely abandoned him. Heavy rain made it difficult to get artillery across the swollen rivers, compounding the Austro-German logistic problems that followed the breakthrough. With his usual strategic myopia, Ludendorff, still focused on the continuing battle in Flanders, decided against further reinforcing von Hötzendorf's planned offensive in the Trentino until it was too late and, with the arrival of Allied units, the front eventually stabilised.

Conclusion

After Cambrai General Georg von der Marwitz was unimpressed by the deployment of tanks, and commented, after one-third of the lumbering mechanical beasts were knocked out during the battle, that 'I do not regard these things in their current form as battleworthy.'[86] This remark illustrates the fundamental weakness in the German approach to the overall direction of the war. The German army, with its preference for military direction of all projects, was superb at tactical innovation but 1917 saw it gradually fall behind the Allies in the broader pursuit of doctrinal and technological solutions to both tactical and strategic challenges. By the end of 1917 the British Field Survey Companies were providing excellent military maps while Allied scientists had produced advanced sound-ranging equipment capable of locating batteries far faster and more accurately than Germany's tracking systems.[87] At the same time French and British commercial companies improved their tanks and guns, made better fuses and built enhanced aircraft designs and more effective signals equipment, while improving both the production and distribution of traditional munitions.

The German focus on purely military solutions could win battles but the far broader Allied approach (based on applying a range of new technologies and adapting these to improved doctrine) had far greater potential to win the war. In the final analysis, while technology and doctrine were important, the outcome of the war also depended on which high command had the strategic vision to use these advances to end the war. It was the Germans who would be the first to seize the opportunity to test their own solution to the deadlock.

Chapter Five
1918

As the New Year dawned the Germans had the initiative: Russia had collapsed, freeing most of the German and Austrian troops on the Eastern Front. But the US was gradually deploying troops to Europe, so the Germans had to move fast or these fresh troops and the new Allied resources would grind them down. Ludendorff told his staff 'every thought must be turned away from trench warfare and towards the offensive . . . on the defensive, the army was bound to succumb little by little to the constantly increasing superiority of the enemy in men and materiel'.

The Germans pulled many divisions (and almost all men below 35 from the other units) out of the East. Many were retrained in Western Front tactics, and the thousands of guns were calibrated at firing ranges well in the rear,[1] although that would be the cause of some controversy. Fifty-six divisions were well enough trained as *stosstruppen*, storm troops, to be considered attack forces, but some others simply got a couple of weeks' training for mobile warfare, just shaking off the mud of the trenches, rather than full-scale training in infiltration, using *minenwerfer*, infantry guns, flamethrowers and the panoply of weapons. Stripping the East was not the limit of Germany's reorganisation: they also cut battalion sizes to more closely approximate their actual strength, and they pulled most of the younger men out of 'trench' divisions in the West. There was certainly a cutting edge of elite units, but the rest of the German army became a low-quality, line-holding force.

Munitions were less of a problem with only one front, but tactical distribution would remain difficult. There were too few horses (and the cavalry units were in the East where they could forage in the countryside), and there was a shortage of rubber for tyres. Steel tyres meant that lorries had no cross-country mobility, and chewed up the roads. Germany had only some 30,000 lorries (and it took 150 lorries to equal the cargo capacity of a single train) so the Germans were highly dependent on railways. Inevitably, they would have substantial problems supplying any breakthrough and sustaining momentum.

Austria was staggering. The economy was collapsing, and confidence in the government was fading; only the hope of Germany winning the war kept them lurching forwards. There were not even hopes of drawing resources from Rumania and Russia (the Germans made sure they got the lion's share) and the public was beginning to wonder whether victory might make anything better. Bulgaria was also fading. Her economy was mainly agricultural, and with so many men mobilised for so long, there was no labour. Turkey was a mixed bag. The Russian collapse meant one front went away, but the Turks decided to take advantage of that and grab land in the Caucasus rather than switching troops to hold off the British in Palestine and Mesopotamia – where they found themselves facing commanders adept at using the advanced artillery planning systems developed on the Western Front. Mesopotamia was a long way from anything vital but the Palestine front was wearing thin.

The British and French were holding on militarily as well as politically. After years of attacking, the armies were now making defensive preparations. Manpower was short. The French disbanded divisions (and took a few regiments of black troops from the US), while the British maintained the number of divisions by reducing the amount of infantry in each by a quarter. Knowing the Germans would attack, the British kept their other fronts quiet and also transferred more and more Indian troops to Palestine and Salonika to free up British troops for the Western Front. Factories were humming, and munitions would be no problem in the coming year. The British would be able to replace all guns lost in battle and from wearing out, and upgrade their quality as well.

Italy also recuperated on the defensive after Caporetto. Men were mobilised to refill the ranks, units were re-equipped and discipline restored. There were even some doctrinal improvements as the lessons of the past few years filtered into the army after Cadorna's dismissal. France and Britain each sent a corps of troops (the US sent a single regiment to show the flag), while the Italians sent a handful of divisions to the Western Front to reciprocate.

The US was mobilising as fast as possible, but going from an army of 100,000 to one several million strong was hard: there were few officers and NCOs, and schools and infrastructure were structured for a small force. Factories were switching to military production, but it was easier to make olive-drab socks than tanks or artillery. Moreover, many of the factories producing munitions were already fulfilling contracts for Britain, France or Italy, so their new capacity was limited. The US was forming divisions and training individuals, but there were few guns to train on. The plan was to issue artillery units with their guns once they reached France and give them several months of phased training 'over there'.

The Kaiserschlacht: Preparations

The Germans had been mulling where to attack – British or French; north, central or south — and started preparations in several sectors to deceive the Allies.[2] Digging gun positions, dumping ammunition and improving roads were visible to Allied aerial reconnaissance, so while they were real preparations they also assisted in the deception plan. Lack of guns (and the ability to rapidly move the guns they had from place to place) meant there would be no diversionary attacks to mislead the Allies and draw in reserves. There were some minor operations (on the French front) and troops all along the line were allowed to think they were taking part in something much bigger so any prisoners would mislead the Allies.

Ludendorff ultimately chose the British Fifth Army's sector because it had weak defences, not because of a key objective that could be reached; he famously wanted to break a hole and trusted that opportunities would develop as the battle evolved. The St Quentin/Somme area was selected not because it was particularly strategic, nor because it was where the French and British sectors met and it would be easier to split the two nations; instead, the ground would dry out here sooner than elsewhere and the attack could be launched weeks earlier than in the preferred sector, Flanders. While a strategic commander does have to work within tactical realities (something Haig should have borne in mind on the Somme), Ludendorff's mistake was in completely subordinating strategy to tactics: 'The whole matter depends on the advance of the artillery, and that depends on terrain.'[3] The focus on fighting and ignorance of logistics were typical of the German General Staff. (Ironically the Somme could have been an incredibly important sector because of the BEF's railway bottleneck at Amiens, but the Germans tended to analyse their plans at the tactical level and did not recognise the BEF's logistical weak points.) Even if the Germans broke through they would quickly be in the area they had devastated in the spring of 1917 as they pulled back to the Hindenburg Line, and then in the Somme battlefield of 1916. Those areas would test the German logistical capabilities while also giving the Allies ready-made defensive positions.

With Ludendorff looking at the front lines rather than at a deeper objective, the Germans assembled 6,473 guns and 3,532 mortars – 48 per cent of their guns and 40 per cent of their mortars.[4] Three armies would be attacking, but there was no single artillery commander: instead each army had a different chief. Among the Germans coming west was *Oberst* Georg Bruchmüller. While he was important in the upcoming offensive, he was not the key figure that he is sometimes made out to be. Bruchmüller certainly brought new techniques (including the 'Pulkowski method' of calibration and allowance for daily weather variations, which was essentially what the British had been doing for several months[5]) and his own gift for matching the right mix of munitions to targets. While he influenced Ludendorff (especially in getting the 'Pulkowski method' widely adopted so that the whole bombardment could be predicted instead of registered, thus preserving surprise), he was only in direct charge of the artillery for the Eighteenth Army. This meant that the impact of his talents was limited; the Second Army paid close attention to his suggestions but dedicated Westerners in the Seventeenth Army had to be forced to listen.

The Germans had not made a major attack on the Western Front since Verdun, over two years before. Bombardment methods had changed a great deal since Verdun, where areas had basically been drenched with shells; if the target area was trenches it was a 'trench bombardment' and if the area had French guns it was called 'counter-battery fire'. In 1918 far more precision was used, along with different types of artillery and a range of specialist shells. Bruchmüller was extremely confident in the Pulkowski method and planned to use a wholly predicted barrage. He also mixed gun types and shell types based on the effect he was trying to achieve, not on tradition. For instance, in the past counter-battery fire was often done with howitzers because they fired larger shells that were more likely to destroy enemy guns; meanwhile, field guns would fire at infantry. Bruchmüller turned this assumption around, trying to break up the infantry's positions (especially headquarters, observation posts and strong-points) with howitzer shells while field guns swamped the enemy artillery with gas shells. (He also mixed gas types, using a tearing/sneezing agent to make British gunners take off their masks and breathe in lethal phosgene.) At different phases of the bombardment Bruchmüller mixed field guns, field howitzers, gas and high explosive for counter-battery fire, and used various types of gun and shell to support the infantry. Trench mortars, *minenwerfer*, were used wherever possible, including during the barrage, but due to range limitations they could only reach the first British line. Bruchmüller kept the supportive role of artillery in mind all the time (he later wrote 'the thanks of the infantry, in my opinion, must be treasured more by every artilleryman than all decorations and citations"[6]), but took a wide range of routes to the objective. The artillery commanders for the Second and Seventeenth Armies were far more traditional; they lacked Bruchmüller's (uniformly successful) Eastern Front experience and confidence in his unorthodox methods. For instance Lieutenant-General Richard von Berendt of the Seventeenth Army would not fire a wholly predicted bombardment; there was a little registration fire before the attack, and he also had a pause in the fire on the morning of the attack to adjust fire. (Ludendorff had had to specifically order the Seventeenth Army to use the new principles and even suggested they use the same procedures, but the order came only two weeks before the attack, while Bruchmüller had used seven weeks.[7]) Another difference was in trusting the infantry. All the armies had a *feuerwalze* to cover the advancing infantry (including a creeping barrage advancing 200 metres every 4 minutes),[8] but Bruchmüller ended the fire at the guns' maximum range so the infantry could continue their advance, while von Berendt continued the barrage to protect against British counter-attacks.[9]

While there was a little registration fire, the Germans took strong measures to achieve secrecy,[10] including deploying most artillery as late as possible. The large number of guns, and accepting neutralising fire rather than destructive fire (both for counter-battery and against the infantry) allowed lower accuracy, which in turn allowed more surprise. Camouflage was also emphasised, and work was done all along the line to dupe the Allies. (This worked quite well against the French, who were concerned about being attacked.) Where precise fire was needed, the target was usually assigned to a battery that had been in the sector a long time and had already registered.

There were two more sources of artillery support during the attack. The forward battalions had infantry guns that used direct fire; sometimes they were even hauled forwards by men with ropes. In addition, *begleit* (escort) batteries would move with reserve regiments (typically the sections of the battery would leapfrog so some fire support was always available) and use observed indirect fire. Both would be more responsive than the main barrage, although the Germans tried to have as much flexibility as possible for that as well.[11] Some infantry units hauled small balloons forwards to mark their positions – obviously a double-edged sword since it would show the Allies where they were as well. Flares were also used, but as the Germans were counting on infiltration to break through somewhere and spread out, and the troops could not bring the barrage back – the timetable was sacrosanct – the flares could only tell the gunners to lengthen the range. Observers stayed in front-line observation posts, and others were sent forwards, but all would be at the mercy of circumstances, the proverbial fog of war. In those circumstances the infantry guns and *begleit* batteries were even more important.

It is easy for historians writing in warm, dry buildings to discuss numbers of guns and various planning factors but each of those guns was manned by very ordinary humans, who had to shove their weapon the last few feet, unload over 2 million rounds of ammunition from wagons and store them, dig gun-pits, and string up telephone and telegraph wire. Roads had to be mended: one of the British techniques to judge the sincerity of apparent attack preparations was to shell roads repeatedly; if the Germans doggedly mended the roads, an attack was likely. The staff, often maligned for working in comfort far behind the lines, had to devise and revise plans as circumstances developed. Every change of a battery or battalion, every alteration of a timetable, every move along a road had to be calculated. A unit's march-speed would differ depending whether it was day or night, and unit strength affected how much road space was needed. With those thousands of guns to move, plus the hundreds of trainloads of ammunition, and hundreds of thousands of infantry as well, the staff may have been safer but their work was not necessarily easier. On 19 March Herbert Sulzbach noted he 'could hardly get along the roads – it's a mass concentration of troops completely impossible to describe', and the next day 'there are still troops, troops and more troops moving up to the front'.[12] Ernst Junger's unit was moving around as well: 'All the roads were crowded with columns on the march, eagerly pressing forwards, with countless guns and endless transport. . . . Woe betide any unit whose movements were not up to scheduled time! They were ruthlessly relegated to the ditch and had to wait hours before they found a gap into which they could squeeze.'[13] This was no accident: German plans phased the arrival of new units.[14] First echelons (including artillery staff and munitions columns) arrived over 1–5 March; 8–10 March saw air units, engineers and supply units arrive; 9–20 March was timetabled for infantry and artillery; these overlapped with the medical and bridging units over 17–20 March. Sulzbach gratefully noted the overcast and rainy weather that hid the assembling forces from British fliers.

Bruchmüller used the time for his own detailed planning. Typically a corps would be attacking from the sector of a single defensive division, and he made use of local knowledge. Senior officers from the *stellungsdivision* would take on counter-battery or bombardment-planning roles for the attacking corps. The soldiers of the *stellungsdivision* also started work on the ammunition dumps, observation posts, communications network, camouflage and survey duties. With the work started, it was easier for the reinforcing units to continue it rather than starting from scratch. Most of the planning took place before the troops arrived. Leutnant Kurt Fisher of the 464th Regiment noted: 'Not a single gun was present – small yellow wooden stakes stuck in the ground instead, hundreds of them, under every bush and in the open. Two stood in line for the wheels of a gun, a bigger post behind for the trail. Every gun position was fixed geometrically [by survey].'[15]

The French had shortened their line by handing a sector over to the British Fifth Army; since the defences were in poor condition the British stayed generally quiet rather than indulging in 'active trench warfare' activities like bombardment and counter-battery fire. (Over the winter of 1916/17 the Fifth Army had fired over 2 million shells and never attacked in more than battalion strength; in the winter of 1917/18 they only fired in response to the Germans.) This quiet meant the Germans had little reason to conduct similar operations and allowed the BEF time to absorb replacements, reorganise divisions and build up defences. Lieutenant Arthur Behrend noted:

> Since the Cambrai 'show', the whole brigade had suffered barely a dozen casualties. Indeed, since Christmas, life on the Bapaume front had been delightful – a succession of invigorating canters across the overgrown downs to the batteries, joy-rides to Amiens through the snowy wastes of the Somme, early morning partridge shoots over the fields around our headquarters.[16]

The British were not simply enjoying themselves; worse, much of their work was not directed at strengthening the trenches that were about to be attacked.[17] Rear-area facilities (for instance stables, baths and billets) had to be built or improved. The longer British line meant a thinner line. Two things could have compensated for their precarious position: better defensive doctrine or better defences. The BEF had not faced a major German attack since 1915 at Ypres, and defensive doctrine for infantry and artillery alike was badly out of-date – the artillery pamphlet was titled 'Artillery in Holding the Line', suggesting how rigid the concept was. (The report on German techniques at Cambrai stayed at GHQ for far too long.) Haig's operations staff wrote new manuals over the winter of 1917/18 but they were not published in time to make much difference, although their principles were being implemented before actual publication. They also ran against everything the British troops had been told for years: it is difficult to change any organisation quickly and the BEF was no different. Troops were accustomed to standing and holding (and commanders had been sacked for losing ground), and while the idea of falling back and then counter-attacking could be taught, it was not a concept that the British army readily embraced. For instance, artillery were told that 'repulse of attacks' was the third priority, behind 'destruction of the enemy's fighting power' and 'hitting communications', but they still fired barrages whenever the infantry put up a SOS flare.

Moreover, there was not enough labour to dig the necessary defences for defence in depth. (W.H.F. Weber, an artillery brigade commander, noted that he had to dig positions not only for his own batteries in each line of defence, but also for a reinforcing brigade – so his four batteries had to prepare forty-eight battery positions, plus anti-tank gun-pits.) Britain was short of manpower, and the Cabinet made the army only its seventh priority: coalminers, farmers and munitions workers were more important not only to the British war effort but to the inter-connected Allied war effort. While that was theoretically prudent, it still left the BEF short-handed for digging defences and manning them. There were maps at divisional, corps and army headquarters with neatly coloured lines showing Forward, Battle and Rear zones of defences – while on the ground the Rear (and sometimes Battle) zones were only staked out, to be dug later. (The very open terrain made it hard to disguise positions from German air recon-naissance.) Haig was also substantially responsible for the St Quentin sector remaining weak: he looked at his line in much the same way that Ludendorff did and kept more troops in the centre and north. There was space to trade for time in the south, and if the British troops were thrown back, there was a good chance the French would come and help. So Hubert Gough's Fifth Army was left far weaker than it should have been, with only nine infantry divisions and three cavalry divisions (with a total of 1,566 guns) to cover 42 miles of front. (In contrast, the Third Army, which would take some of the German assault, had 14 infantry divisions for 28 miles of front.) With those sparse troops spread out over the three defensive zones (or even the front two), the artillery was also spread out (with around 10 per cent of the field guns scattered forwards as anti-tank guns), so concentrating firepower required even better communications than normal. And command was absurdly centralised: any counter-preparation fire required the approval of a division commander, and then brought down rather feeble fire: a field battery might be covering 200 yards – while in the attack it would cover at most 50 yards.

The regulations for the 'Attack in Position Warfare' of January 1918 noted that 'in every offensive action it is of decisive importance to produce surprise', and added that 'rapid progression [of the attack] offers the maximum protection and secures success'. The German army was determined to demonstrate these principles in the spring offensives. German morale was quite high; the troops believed they were winning the war, and were pleased to be finally attacking again after years of fending off the enemy, gradually losing ground and comrades. In contrast, the British troops were tired from digging all the time, and dispirited by the continual alerts. Weber commented derisively on 'daily, even hourly, warnings of an overwhelming attack to be supported by tanks of fabulous speed, size, armament, pattern and number'.

The Kaiser's Battle: Initial Operations

At 05.40 hrs on 21 March 1918 the German guns thundered. A German infantry officer described the sensation: 'If you put your hand over your ears and then drum your fingers vigorously on the back of your head, then you get some idea of what the drumfire [a hurricane barrage] sounded like to us.'[18] An artillery observer had a different perspective:

> Within seconds of the bombardment opening, we could see sparks and columns of fire in the enemy's trenches and their rear areas. A terrific roar, an immense noise greeted the young morning. . . . In the past the French and the Tommies had bombarded us for seven days without a pause; we would now do it for 5 hours. We laughed and looked happily at each other. Words were useless; the hell of the inferno outside saw to that. There was only lightning and noise.

The first salvoes of shells were largely gas (to catch men who were in the open or sleepy and slow to put their masks on) and high explosive, and focused on the front lines and headquarters. A British machine-gunner recalled: 'It seemed as if the bowels of the earth had erupted, while beyond the ridge there was one long and continuous yellow flash. It was the suddenness of the thing that struck me most, there being no preliminary shelling but just one vast momentary upheaval.'[19] After a few minutes everyone who was going to be caught by surprise was already caught, and the Germans shifted targets. Counter-battery fire was the next priority, once the first phase had drawn the gunners from their dugouts to their guns, and gas continued to play a major part because without gunners the guns were useless. Once the enemy guns were neutralised, counter-battery fire dwindled to a sustainable level and most guns switched back to pounding the enemy infantry. There were plenty of targets – wire to cut, strong-points to hammer, headquarters and communications links to disrupt, guns to silence – and the Germans shifted around among them. Locations would be shelled for a while then left alone, then the fire would return in case anyone had put their head up. *Minenwerfer* pounded the front lines and cut barbed wire, and infantry parties moved around to gather information about the progress of the attack and to snip wire where necessary. During the 5 hours of bombardment the Germans fired 2.3 million rounds.

There is no way to calculate British casualties from the bombardment but that was not the point of this deluge of shell-fire. It sought to break British command and control, shattering the defenders into groups who could not coordinate their fire or even call for help. By and large it worked. Weber remarked that his gunners could cover their front, but could make no differ-ence on the flanks. With the British trying to distribute in depth but weak and clumped up front (in strong-points that one old sergeant dismissed as 'bird cages'), the infantry were very vulnerable to infiltration as fog and the rolling barrage covered the advancing *stosstruppen*. German troops moved around British strong-points and their light *minenwerfer* and infantry guns gave them an edge: they had weapons the British infantry generally lacked. There is nothing more demoralising than being hit by weapons to which you cannot reply, and plenty of British troops honourably surrendered when they found themselves out-flanked and out-gunned.

In the Fifth Army sector the British artillery was willing to fight (despite the gas and counter-battery fire) and did what it could, but communications were impossible: the telephone lines to forward headquarters and observa-tion posts were wrecked, and the fog obscured the SOS flares. The forward anti-tank guns often fired off their ammunition (as did the 'sniping' guns that did much of the harassing work) because the Germans were almost on top of them and they could see targets. In contrast, 'silent' batteries were detached from their brigades and stationed in the rear to surprise the Germans. Many of them never received orders to fire and simply waited: such was the legacy of top-down control established by the years of trench warfare. One gun unit waited too long and surrendered: 'We came upon a position for four field guns. . . . The infantry had all gone, leaving the artillery on their own. They gave up quietly, forty or fifty men including some officers. None of them had been killed at all.'[20] At least the field artillery was mostly able to withdraw when the need arose; much of the heavy artillery was immobile (in winter the horses were frequently withdrawn to rear areas for better stabling) and had to be disabled before the Germans reached the positions. There was gallantry aplenty that day and in succeeding days, but it availed little at first. One gun, for example, fired 1,000 rounds and held up a German regiment (with a subaltern covering the gun's withdrawal with a machine gun),[21] but the Germans kept coming and overwhelmed the Fifth Army. For instance, XIX Corps had eight battalions holding the Forward Zone; at the end of 21 March these units mustered only 50 men ready for duty.

In the Third Army matters were substantially better for the defenders. With more infantry per mile, there were fewer gaps for infiltration. Better defences (especially a very deep forward zone, so the battle zone was out of range of the *minenwerfer*) meant the Germans needed a stronger bombardment, but not only did the Germans have fewer guns – especially heavy guns – per kilometre (despite recognising this as a key sector), but their stodgier commander used them less effectively. Soggy patches of ground slowed the Germans, especially hampering the gunners moving forwards where the stormtroopers had made some progress. Yet with the Fifth Army cracking under the repeated hammer blows, the Third Army soldiers also had to fall back to avoid being out-flanked.

That day the Germans shattered the deadlock but they did not break through the British line: they broke it open and destroyed the command system, but this tactical success did not mean a strategic triumph was now inevitable. The British had taken heavy casualties on 21 March (about 38,000, plus some 400 guns, while the Germans suffered roughly 35,000 casualties), and it would be two weeks before the defences stabilised, largely because the defenders would have trouble coordinating themselves even as reserves poured into the sector. Units could not coordinate with their neighbours and were extremely cautious about their flanks – a minor penetration (or a rumour of one) between two units could cause both to pull back, and that would ripple out along the Allied line. (French reserves soon joined the battle, but many of the first units arrived without their artillery and had little firepower.) It was easy to identify communications as a problem – one battery commander said 'the more [telephone] wire you give us the more Huns we shall kill' – but it was hard to connect units that were on the move and harder still to keep them connected. Of course, conditions were difficult for both sides: on the 21st the fog helped the German infantry infiltrate, but it lasted into mid-afternoon which made it hard to keep track of where the infantry was – flares, balloons and aircraft were of little use. After the first day the fog was less helpful to the Germans. The infantry still appreciated the cover it gave, but it actively hampered the artillery: on 21 March the British positions were generally known, but after the first day the Germans were also groping in the fog.

For those two weeks it was mainly a soldiers' battle, with battalions and batteries at times fighting semi-independent engagements. British batteries often engaged over open sights, and battery commanders spotted their own gunfire. They might well hold off a German advance, but with their flanks left 'in the air' units were falling back daily. Nobody can question the gunners' individual valour, but there was little opportunity for the artillery to have more than a local effect on the battle. Ammunition was often a problem since the shells dumped with the guns were left behind with the first move, and the light railway networks were laid out for the entrenched front. (Keeping the men fed was also a problem; Weber's group dined on the 26th on 'a tin of pork and beans from an abandoned dump, eaten off an envelope with a pen-knife'.) When a load of ammunition arrived it might have to be abandoned (or blown up) because nobody knew it was available. Divisional artillery commanders sometimes found themselves simply working as senior liaison officers, trying to pass information around from the quartermaster's staff to the guns.

The Germans were having problems too. Moving guns forwards through their old trench system was a simple exercise in planning, complex enough but predictable: routes could be prepared and bridges pre-positioned. Building roads across no-man's-land and then through the British lines was harder, and every kilometre of forward progress was a kilometre further from the supply points (up to 69km by the end of the first week) and many kilometres of communications wire would be needed to not only go forwards but laterally as well. It could take a full day for orders to get from an army headquarters to an infantry division, and then more time for it to reach the combat units. Moving across the old Somme battlefield did not help. Officer Candidate Paul Knoch wrote home:

The area where the Battle of the Somme was fought, around Peronne etc., is a scene of terrible destruction. Crater after crater, some villages such as Bouchavesne have disappeared completely, only metre-high stone walls remain. A few splintered stumps is all that remains of the trees. The roads are littered with dead horses, corpses of Germans, Englishmen and Frenchmen, strewn with equipment, weapons, ammunition, here and there damaged or abandoned English guns. One gets used to such sights, but one tries not to think about it.[22]

The infantry guns and *begleit* batteries could help, and they carried extra ammunition. But even the double stocks of the *begleit* batteries could be fired off in only 24 minutes, so it was hardly a solution. The Germans were so short of horses that the *begleit* batteries had to borrow (for how long nobody knew) horses from other units for their extra caisson of ammunition. And the heavy guns and minenwerfers could not be moved easily – some of them had to be broken into several loads and were not even scheduled to advance (they formed a 'battering train' that would be moved sideways to support each of the German offensives) – and all suffered from Germany's general lack of horses and lorries. By the 26th the German infantry was pulling ahead of the artillery and the artillery was having to cut back on shells because it was ahead of the supplies; *III Korps* had to cut its ammunition allotments in half that day.[23] The Germans had not had to deal with this situation before, and they encountered some of the logistic problems the Russians had faced at Tannenberg: they were marching men and moving supplies by horse-drawn wagons while the Allies were moving men and supplies by railway and lorries.

Sulzbach's unit was a *begleit* battery, sometimes engaging in direct fire and sometimes indirect, but the pace was draining.[24] For the first week casualties were light, although air attacks were more of a problem than in trench warfare as there were no dugouts to jump into. He was able to manoeuvre through a double-barrage, probably because it was fired blind, without an observer adjusting fire to catch the moving Germans. Nine days into the battle he had a close encounter as a German attack blundered into French troops, infantry and artillery:

> I bring the battery up behind, and now we've got so much shrapnel rattling down on us that you can hardly hear or see anything. The machine-gun fire, chattering away at us from only a few hundred metres distance, keeps on as heavy as ever. All hell has been let loose. The French seem transformed, they must have thrown completely fresh, properly rested, troops into the sector, and a large number of them too. . . . We pull up a steep track onto a plateau, and there is our No. 3 Battery next door to us. And up there it's a witches' cauldron,

compared with which the business we had before was child's play: the machine-gun and small-arms fire so strong that it might have been thousands and thousands of enemy gun-barrels being trained on our one Battery. The concentration of fire is so heavy that all we can do is lie on the ground beside the guns, with the infantry hardly 300 metres in front of us; and we haven't reached the peak yet, because suddenly we start being fired on from the right and left flanks as well, and it looks as if we are on a pointed wedge of ground offering a marvellous target to the French on all three sides. . . . Our own attack never gets off the ground . . . just in front of us, 2/Lt Mayer of No. 8 Battery gets killed in action; that's the tenth officer our Regiment has lost since 21 March. [At this stage of the war German batteries might have only two or three officers.] Now it gets even 'lovelier'. Our infantry start coming back, in groups or singly, because they can't stand it any more up there at the front, and finally there they are lying between the guns.

German casualties mounted, and units simply got tired as they moved further and further from their supply points. (Looting Allied supply dumps was hardly a long-term solution, not least because the German troops were demoralised to see how lavishly supplied the British were. The *landser* had been told that the U-boats were sinking hundreds of ships, yet now they saw that the ordinary British Tommy ate better, was dressed better and had more 'comforts' of life.) Ludendorff also proved an indecisive commander, spreading his resources and reinforcing in areas that offered no strategic results and refusing to withdraw units as they wore out.[25] By early April the Germans had inflicted just over 254,000 casualties on the Allies (including around 75,000 on the French) but had lost almost 240,000 men of their own – hardly the way to win the war, especially with Americans arriving every day; even capturing 1,300 guns was unimportant because Allied munitions factories were already producing more than they needed.

The next real German attack (a one-day attack on 28 March at Arras was slapped back) took place in Flanders between 9 and 29 April. On the first day a weak Portuguese division broke. Although the 55th (West Lancashire) Division held firm against the *stosstruppen*, the Portuguese hole created flanks and the Germans gained ground, although they never threatened to break through unless the British collapsed. Haig was sufficiently alarmed to issue an Order of the Day beginning 'With our backs against the wall and believing in the justice of our cause', but again the German attacks weakened and French reserves bailed out the BEF. One thing Ludendorff had learned was that putting Bruchmüller in charge made the artillery run better but even the individual genius of Bruchmüller (with 2,210 guns under his control) could not wipe out stout defences and determined defenders. The British had held firm against two fierce offensives but Ludendorff identified French reserves as the reason, so he aimed his next offensive against the French. Hindenburg wrote in his memoirs: 'Twice had England been saved by France at a moment of extreme crisis' through 'massed attacks and skilful artillery.'[26]

The British were also looking for ways to improve their defensive performance. Infantry lost the 'right' to supporting firepower; SOS signals now were for information and not a demand for fire-support. Counter-preparation had to be fired as intensely as for an attack, not just desultory fire to hamper attacking infantry. Guns might be sacrificed if the gains – in dead Germans, or a sector held – outweighed the losses. And the training on mobile artillery operations that had seemed so useless over the winter of 1917/18 now had a relevance that even the lowliest soldier could see, and units out of the line trained as much as they could. With the Germans attacking the French, this training would pay off when the British finally attacked, and it would pay off handsomely.

A Period of Balance

After the May offensive ran out of steam, there was a pause on the Western Front. The Germans were largely spent; Ludendorff knew he lacked fresh troops to attack soon, but he could not pull back both for diplomatic reasons and because of domestic politics in Germany. Unable to decide what to do, he dithered while hoping that Germany could regroup faster than the Allies could. The German troops were not optimistic and aggressive (a result of concentrating the younger and more aggressive men in the *stoss* divisions earlier in the year), but they also were not mutinying nor surrendering. Many would not waste time entrenching newly gained ground but they would fight reasonably well if attacked. In some places the logistic system had problems bringing supplies forward (even basics like barbed wire) but Germany was also running out of food and bandages.

The Allies were feeling far more confident – they had weathered the storm so far – but were not certain who had the advantage. They had a Supreme Commander, Ferdinand Foch, who was aggressive by nature and ordered the Allies to commence a series of small attacks. If these went well, they would restore confidence among the troops and on the home fronts, keep the Germans off balance, clear bulges in the line and exploit tactical advantages. If they did not go well, they could be broken off until there were (in Petain's phrase) more tanks and more Americans. Foch was Supreme Commander but he was more a coordinator of the various countries; he encouraged them and set the tone but could not fire his subordinates. The decision to launch a number of small attacks rather than try a major offensive was the right one. Typically the Germans were poorly fortified, and there could be surprise attacks even without tanks; there simply was not much barbed wire to cut. A small attack could be broken off once it ran out of steam, when losses mounted and gains slowed. The succession of small battles drained the German reserves and were demoralising, since almost no unit could be sure it would not be attacked the next dawn. (By late September the Germans were breaking up divisions and cutting battalion strengths further, but nothing could hide the haemorrhage of manpower.) Once the Allies had pushed the Germans back to the original (spring 1918) defences, the German troops were demoralised and the Allies could bash their way through the Hindenburg Line, as the British and Americans proved.

The Second Battle of the Marne

Pétain and his staff recognised that they were likely to face a major German offensive in the spring of 1918 but unlike Foch, Pétain failed to see the Western Front as a whole and focused on the direct threat to his own men. His defensive strategy was based upon an initial defence phase where casualties would be minimised while the 'first shock' of the German offensive was absorbed and then a second phase with powerful artillery reserves rapidly transferred to bolster the defence and support limited counterattacks. The German assault on the Chemin-des-Dames Ridge in the Aisne sector, made on 27 May, was supported by 4,000 guns firing a night barrage that lasted 2 hours and 40 minutes. The density was roughly one gun for every 7-metre section of the front line. Ernst Jünger would later write:

A flaming curtain went up, followed by unprecedentedly brutal roaring. A wild thunder, capable of submerging even the loudest detonations in its rolling, made the earth shake. The gigantic roaring of the innumerable guns behind us was so atrocious that even the greatest of the battles we had experienced seemed like a tea party in comparison. What we hadn't dared hope for happened: the enemy artillery was silenced; a prodigious blow had been laid out. . . . we gasped at the colossal wall of flame over the English lines, gradually obscuring itself behind crimson, surging clouds.[27]

The advances were impressive, largely due to General Duchêne's failure to reorganise (and deepen) the Sixth Army's defensive system, but the failure to exploit the initial successes and the survival of major flanking positions at Soissons and Rheims prevented a full-scale breakthrough. The next offensive was delayed until 9 June but by this stage the French were adept at recognising German offensive preparations. Even though the Germans only moved their guns forwards under cover of darkness (many to as close as 1,000 metres from the front line) on 7 June, the French intelligence service discerned their objectives and the Third Army belatedly began to redeploy their reserves for prompt counter-attacks. This time the French counter-preparation shattered the cohesion of the assault and although the Third Army's defensive preparations were incomplete, the French reserves stemmed the German tide. The intuitive approach used by the German stormtroopers left them disorientated when faced by an organised opponent, particularly when their enemy was able to deploy large numbers of tanks in a properly supported counter-attack (163 were used on 11 June).

On 9 June the Germans did penetrate the primitive defensive system between Noyon and Montdidier. But the Allies had learned how to defend: echeloned in depth and supported by reserves of artillery and infantry. Delighted by the tactical success, Ludendorff was pleased with the progress of his stormtrooper assault teams, but recognised that the artillery was the real key to making a full-scale breakthrough. That day he noted that 'a greater density [of infantry] serves only to increase losses. The most vigorous resistance is broken more readily by reinforcing the artillery than by adding to the infantry . . .'. If the Allies built up their reserves then the artillery would have to be deployed even more flexibly to support the attacks that were making progress. The problem was identifying these before the Allied reserves moved into position. The German General Staff and commanders were slowly coming to the view that the process of breaking through was an objective in itself but that the cost of such offensives could quickly wear down the attacking units in pointless assaults on objectives other than those which maintained the momentum of the attack. In mid-June OHL noted that gaining artillery dominance in the first phase was essential to success. Pushing artillery forwards to support minor break-throughs could disperse it before the real opportunities became apparent. As a result, planners were advised to allow organic divisional artillery to advance but to leave the allocation of heavier reserves to the judgement of the corps commander. The final assault was expected to combine all the lessons of the spring offensive in one final push to break through the French positions along the river Marne. However, the Germans had used the same 'battering train' for each of their offensives and their artillerymen were weary and the guns increasingly worn, while Allied intelligence could hardly miss the arrival of the battering train.[28] Without tanks, the Germans depended wholly on artillery and *stosstruppen* to create any kind of momentum and found that the process of force-marching reserve units into the breach tended to exhaust the infantry before they even entered the battle. The Germans had 78 fresh divisions in reserve in March, 62 in May, 43 in July and only 21 in August. Thus the Allied commanders were able to gather and redeploy reserves in good time, and because Ludendorff's objectives were created by tactical successes, Foch was able to secure and support the strategic keys to the campaign and focus on building an ever-expanding reserve capable of shattering the momentum of any German offensives. The initial successes of March and April impressed the attacking infantry and the artillerymen that supported them, but the failure to win the 'Peace Offensive' before July wore down their morale and made a direct contribution to their second defeat on the Marne.

Foch hoped that the Germans would persist in using the same assault tactics they had used since March and was convinced that Ludendorff's clumsy strategy had created an opportunity for a series of coordinated counter-offensives once the Germans exhausted themselves creating pockets they would find difficult to hold.[29] If the pressure continued, GQG hoped that the defensive lessons of 1917 would be sufficient to frustrate the offensive. The German attack was launched towards Chalons and Epernay on a front of 90 kilometres. Although they still outnumbered the French, many reserve units were still being reconstituted after being burned up in the spring offensives. The French Fourth Army had time to reorganise its entire defensive system, using the lessons of 1917, but the Fifth and Sixth Armies had less time to prepare and fought in the early 1917 dispositions, thus leaving historians an opportunity to compare the two systems. It is important to note that the British and French adjusted their front lines several times during the spring and neither was entirely satisfied with their ally's defensive doctrine.[30] As early as 9 April Pétain outlined his views on the initial attacks. Counter-attacks were to be organised as quickly as possible; the local commander's discretion was preferable to detailed fixed plans; infiltration and flanking movements were to be encouraged;

strong-points and enemy batteries should be rapidly identified and subjected, respectively, to destructive or neutralising fire; and potential routes of reinforcement should be cut off with curtain barrages. In summary, Pétain expected 'rapid and violent preparation' and the 'full use of the [potential] flexibility of the infantry and artillery'. As Mangin noted after the war, 'the enemy was a good teacher, but his lessons cost us dearly'.[31] Collating the views of various officers on the initial battles, the *Instruction* of 10 May 1918 added details on the most efficient allocation of assets when making methodical attacks in position warfare.

Foch's insistence on counter-offensive preparations enabled the French to gather 27 divisions, and the key was in recognising the culminating point of Ludendorff's offensive plan. Mangin was selected to conduct an initial operation towards Soissons on 28 June and identified an opportunity that might bear fruit if the Germans blundered forwards again without realising they were over-extended. On 15 July, after a 3 hour and 20 minute bombardment, the French Fourth Army was attacked by 50 German divisions, 27 of them in the first wave. The French had 8 divisions holding the 42 kilometre front line and 5 in reserve. The stormtroopers penetrated the main battle zone but after seven bitterly contested attempts the Germans finally realised that the French defensive preparations and artillery reserves had completely neutralised the German system. On the Marne itself the Germans attacked with 13 divisions, after a bombardment that lasted 3 hours and 40 minutes.[32] Securing the bridges across the river delayed the main attack but the Germans still penetrated 5 kilometres into the Sixth Army's defences. French artillery and aircraft focused on interdicting the bridges, so the Germans were unable to bring up their artillery to support further advances.

Against the Sixth Army the Germans made major gains and drove some 10 kilometres towards Epernay. Foch was confident of holding the sectors being defended by the Fourth and Sixth Armies and unleashed his counter-attack between Sisne and Belley, sending Mangin's Tenth Army crashing into the German right flank on 18 July. No fewer than 18 infantry divisions, 470 batteries (comprising 1,545 pieces), and 469 light and medium tanks joined the Sixth Army's 9 divisions, 230 batteries and 273 light and medium tanks. Mangin's Franco-American force used no artillery preparation, instead attacking with a powerful creeping barrage (one battery fired a round per gun per minute for almost 8 hours), while Degoutte's Sixth Army attacked after a 1½ hour preparatory bombardment. The Germans were completely surprised by the strength of the

counter-offensive and were flung back 8 kilometres on a front of 20 kilometres. The Sixth Army and Berthelot's Fifth Army joined the offensive
and the German army was forced to recross the Marne and to withdraw
from part of the salient that had been created in the spring.[33] While the
Germans would refine their offensive doctrine, they had lost the initiative
and would never attack again.

Foch noted, 'if we attack it must be to beat him, to disorganise him to
the greatest extent possible . . . a battle engaged by us for this purpose
must be pushed with the greatest possible speed and to the greatest
possible distance, with the utmost energy'. Directive No. 5 of 12 July 1918
summed up the new French approach to warfare. Obtaining strategic
surprise was essential to success, with maintaining secrecy being seen as
'a question of honour'. Tactical surprise would be exploited by sudden
attacks with short but violent preparation, using gas barrages and aircraft
to neutralise the defending batteries. Deep penetration was to be enabled
by aiming for distant objectives but employing 'simple and concise orders,
which leave the greatest part to the initiative and temperament of each for
the accomplishment of his mission'. Tanks were recognised as a vital
innovation to assist but the French recognised that German gunners could
rapidly neutralise unsupported tanks.[34] The artillery batteries were no
longer the conductors of the orchestra of battle but were still the primary
factor in failure or success: 'the capture, as rapidly as possible, of the mass
of the hostile artillery, in every case, will be the surest guarantee of rapid
and deep progress'. Like the Germans, the French now used the preparatory bombardment to neutralise enemy batteries, promptly moved their
own guns forwards to support the advancing units, including placing
'batteries or sections of the artillery at the immediate disposal of division
infantry commanders, regimental, or battalion commanders'. Over time
the French learned when it was best to decentralise command and when a
piece-meal approach was risky and it was time to reconcentrate. As
Colonel Lucas noted after the war, the French now believed that an
'audacious infantry, knowing how to dispense with the aid of the artillery;
artillery, whose constant and primary preoccupation is constantly to
support the infantry . . . seemed to be the true formula for the exploitation of success'.[35] The British and French learned valuable lessons about
the value of initiative during an improvised defensive situation, lessons
that helped prepare them for the counter-offensives that would follow.
Mobile warfare, *à la* 1914, had to be relearned.[36] Many division commanders intuitively realised that artillery had to be decentralised, and

directly allocated to front-line units; the problem was that liaison was still difficult and effective communications took time to set up.

After the Second Battle of the Marne, Foch coordinated a series of successive Allied offensives designed to scatter and destroy the German strategic reserves and shatter the German defensive system. Foch made sure that these offensives penetrated deeply enough to force the Germans to commit reserves to the battle but halted them before they created salients that might give the Germans a chance to regain the initiative. When the Germans withdrew to preprepared positions (shortening their line by 200 kilometres), the Allied armies rapidly advanced and immediately commenced preparations for the next series of offensives, preventing Ludendorff from resting his men and reconstituting his reserves. The Germans had worn out their best units in the spring offensives and Foch's hammer blows continued to rain down on their defensive system, switching between pugnacious British and Dominion troops, rapidly improving Americans and the weary French. In contrast, the Germans were declining in numbers and quality. In May, forced by Lloyd George's increasingly petty intrigues to undermine GHQ, Haig had considered creating B class British units to do no more than hold the line but was urged to abandon this decision by Foch, who argued that units of uneven quality would create opportunities for the enemy. As soon as the Germans were forced to adopt such desperate measures, Foch was delighted, recognising the problems for units without experience of liaison and incapable of tactical flexibility. 'This is a weakness of which we must take advantage by undertaking important offensives.'[37]

Each successive offensive drove the Germans back, then forced them into delaying actions as they tried to consolidate their next position faster than the Allies could exploit, while the Allies moved their guns forwards to begin the grinding process anew. Both sides had to develop methods of alternating positional and mobile warfare to suit this new paradigm but at least the deadlock appeared broken. As Mangin confidently observed, 'it is time to shake off the mud of the trenches'. General Debeney, of the First Army, agreed wholeheartedly, noting in his orders for 8 August 1918, 'I approve in advance every act of initiative, no matter what its result may be.' The German defensive system (especially as thin as it often was) could be shattered with brutal efficiency by the Allies and there is little evidence for the Germans managing to formulate a strategic solution to complement their otherwise impressively elastic tactical approach to defence. The key to success in the assault was the availability of reserves, with even the most formidable positions falling when they were poorly garrisoned. Even vigorous counter-attacks had lost much of their value in the defensive, Ludendorff informing commanders on 4 September that 'counter-attacks should be delivered only when there is a chance of success', arguing that such an attack, 'under unfavourable conditions, leads solely to useless losses'.

'The Black Day': Amiens to the Hindenburg Line

The first deliberate Allied step was the British Fourth Army's attack at Amiens.[38] Sir Henry Rawlinson wanted to attack to clear the Germans away from the key railway junction at that city, and detailed why it was tactically feasible as well as strategically desirable. His top two reasons were weak German defences and weak German defenders – a far cry from 1916 when the Allies attacked without much regard to the German situation. (The German defences were weak because they wanted to attack Amiens themselves, and thus had little incentive to dig elaborate defences; as long as they held the initiative there was little risk in weak defences, but when circumstances changed they did not react. Troop strengths were also reduced by the influenza epidemic.)

While Rawlinson wanted to attack, he was also cautious. He wanted all the tanks in the BEF, the best infantry (the Canadians and Australians), and strong artillery support, eventually totalling 60 train-loads of artillery. By 1918 the artillery units formed in 1916 and 1917 were in action, and there were finally enough guns to do all the tasks at one time, so destructive and neutralising fire could be one simultaneous deluge of shells. He also wanted surprise, which would keep the Germans weak, and would also have other tactical repercussions. For instance, surprise meant counter-battery fire would be far more effective: the Germans would not be moving their guns around to dodge increasing British fire, but would be stunned on Z-Day. Since the Germans would not be reinforcing their artillery, the British barrage guns could be further forwards and thus the creeping barrage could reach deeper into the German positions. (Without a preliminary counter-battery battle, more British guns were functional on Z-Day – 98.5 per cent.) A bit of registration could be concealed through having newly arrived guns fire the routine 'daily hate' and harassment missions, but not all guns could be registered. Surprise was so important to Rawlinson that he gained approval for a BEF-wide deception plan, with a series of rumours, and also made sure every man in the Fourth Army received a leaflet headed KEEP YOUR MOUTH SHUT. Revealing the build-up would put so much at risk that he decided the reinforcing guns would only fire if there were a major German attack – a simple probe or raid would not trigger massive defensive firepower – and the decision about what to fire was decentralised to the CBSOs, presumably because they would have plenty of information and they controlled much of the heavy artillery. It was a remarkable display of how the BEF could be at once centralised and decentralised.

The battle began at 04.20 hrs on 8 August. Surprise was total, and most of the artillery elements worked like clockwork; even when mist meant the infantry could not see the barrage, they could hear it and follow it. Two-thirds of the heavy guns were firing counter-battery missions, and 95 per cent of the German artillery had been correctly located. Many batteries were abandoned without firing (some still had their muzzle-caps fitted) since German artillerists' morale was no higher than their infantry's. (The Germans had been reorganising their artillery, and were now mixing a bit of heavy artillery with the field artillery as 'close-range groups' to support the infantry regiments, while a 'long-range group' of heavy artillery was responsible for other missions. It hardly mattered on the first day at Amiens, but they were trying out new methods.[39]) Other batteries were found demolished with their horses dead and the gunners fled once there was no point in trying to continue the fight. The Canadians had somewhat poorer artillery support since they had been the last to arrive and were not permitted to fire any preliminary rounds; it did not help them much that the French First Army (on their right) was also attacking but at H+40. The French had no tanks and needed a short bombardment, but for the first few minutes the Canadian flank was only supported by fire instead of by advancing troops. The Canadians did something unusual for counter-battery fire: instead of one battery firing on a German battery, they assigned one gun from three or four different batteries to each German battery. They knew their accuracy would not be perfect, but by blending in several guns with different errors, on average the targets would be hit. It worked, and they continued the technique through to the end of the war – despite the extra paperwork involved.

The creeping barrage was fired as far as the field artillery could reach, and then the barrage was held on that line until H+240 as a protective barrage for the infantry to mop up and reserves to start moving. The barrage then stopped, and the infantry/cavalry/tank forces could fight their own way forwards. Some field artillery did advance (about a brigade per infantry division, and it advanced when ordered to by the supported infantry) and there were thorough plans to open lanes in the wire and have signallers to connect the guns to the infantry, but these guns fired concentrations where Germans were resisting rather than a barrage. While the problems of cavalry–tank coordination are better known, it was equally hard to co-ordinate guns (even the Royal Horse Artillery) and cavalry because mobility was so different. The RAF provided valuable support to both infantry and artillery. Many zone calls provided information and targeting, and there was some strafing of German artillery where it was beyond the range of counter-battery guns. Smoke barrages had formed part of the original plan (not just providing some cover to the advancing infantry but blinding specific German observation posts) and in later phases, when smoke was needed beyond artillery range, the RAF tried dropping large quantities of smoke bombs.

The results on 8 August were excellent: up to 8 kilometres gained across the 24-kilometre front, about 18,000 prisoners (plus probably 10,000 killed and wounded who retreated) and around 400 guns. In yet another way surprise paid off: the Royal Artillery suffered no casualties from German shelling. When the attack continued on 9 August, progress slowed markedly. The Germans flung in more reserves than the BEF had antici-pated, and the Allied forces were fatigued and had suffered casualties. They were also far less organised (16 British brigades would attack on 9 August, but they had 13 different start times as coordination broke down; individual attacks also had far less artillery support), and it was harder to move supplies forwards and get information back. All these were familiar problems in the Great War, indeed in warfare in general. Still, the Allies had the advantage and fought their way forwards, gaining ground and taking prisoners. (The artillery had its sound-ranging specialists and observers moving forwards on the 9th to support the fight when the RAF could not.) But on the 10th Rawlinson was already suggesting to Haig that his attack be wound down and the attack widened to the flanks, with the British Third Army on the left and the French First Army on the right.

Rawlinson's attack was continued for a few more days, partly to wring maximum effect from the initial success but partly to cover the preparations of Sir Julian Byng's Third Army. (The attack would ultimately take over 25,000 prisoners, inflict roughly 50,000 more casualties on the Germans, take 600 guns, and take up to 19 kilometres of ground.) Intangibly, Amiens was proof of the momentum swing on the Western Front and in the whole war. The Germans were not to attack again, but the Allies would continue to rain down blows throughout the 'Hundred Days' until the German army was defeated. When Ludendorff referred to 8 August as a 'Black Day' for the Germans, he was not just referring to the casualties (although they were heavy, and the large number of prisoners showed how fragile German morale was); he had been shown that he was no longer calling the shots. The Allies were, and Foch's plans for successive attacks would continue along the front.

Byng had been making phony attack preparations as part of the deception plan, and now the BEF could make Third Army's phony preparations real while the Fourth Army's real attack (which was becoming more cautious) became the deception. Byng had few tanks, which made protecting them from German artillery even more important, so the Third Army stressed its counter-battery efforts. This included integrating the RAF and artillery; aircraft were earmarked to hunt for German anti-tank guns and not only strafe them but call in the 60-pounder batteries which were on call – their sole mission was to hit anti-tank guns. At first Byng just cleared the German outpost zone, although in places the German artillery resisted stoutly and delayed the British; he then paused and brought up his guns and prepared (while beating off German counter-attacks) for the main attack. After only a day of preparations (and the Germans weakening themselves through ineffective counter-attacks), he was ready and cracked the German main line with only modest resources. Even in the V Corps' sector, where the German artillery had caused problems on 21 August, the attack on 23 August gained ground readily. The results (up to 4 miles of ground, over 10,000 prisoners plus other casualties) were far less dramatic than in the surprise attack at Amiens, but they showed both sides that the Germans could be driven out of their positions by an 'ordinary' attack – tanks were not necessarily the key to an attack, nor were Dominion 'shock troops'.

German reserve divisions were getting little time to rest before having to go back into battle. On the 23rd Herbert Sulzbach heard the battle over the horizon. His reserve positions in a pretty village were 'invaded by the rumbling and rolling of the new large-scale battle between Noyon and Laon; it seems to be the fourth phase of the Foch offensive, directed against our Fourth Army'.[40]

Ludendorff recognised the weakness of his position and tried to pull back to a 'winter' line in front of the Hindenburg Line where he could reorganise. But he needed time to actually build the winter line and time to rest his troops and restore morale. He tried to buy time with rearguards, and both sides had to coordinate semi-mobile operations. There were few or no trenches, so it was not trench warfare, but there was a reasonable front line so it was not quite the mobile operations that had been taught before the war. The Germans found it hard to meld artillery into the rearguards for a range of reasons, not least because the gunners might simply not know where the infantry was, as units were moving every day or two. Meanwhile, the Germans had identified tanks as a key Allied weapon, not just for their firepower and mobility but because they demoralised the German infantry. New guidelines and methods came down from on high that looked rather like the British methods of the late spring of 1918: guns to be mobile, distributed in depth, withdraw if losing the battle, counter-battery fire in lulls in the overall fighting, counter-preparation fire instead of defensive barrages, and the like.[41] The anti-tank instructions were unrealistic: it was all very well to say that the field artillery needed to be even more mobile and move to support the infantry, but where were the horses to come from?[42] Supplies might be a problem too, as resupply points changed erratically. But morale seems to have been the worst issue, as infantry frequently simply pulled back past batteries, or batteries fired off the ammunition they had (at whatever target they selected) and then pulled back themselves. At the end of August the British broke Ludendorff's planned winter line in two places, the Canadians breaking through the heavy fortifications of the Drocourt–Queant Line (an extension of the Hindenburg Line) while the Australians fought their way up Mont St Quentin.

These actions set off another round of German withdrawals, this time back to the Hindenburg Line itself. For the BEF much of September would consist of day after day of semi-mobile operations, and they became fairly adept at it. Infantry divisions were typically rotated every two or three days to rest and reorganise, but because the artillery did not rotate as frequently, so there were 4 to 6 brigades of field artillery available to support each infantry division, and also a brigade of heavy artillery.[43] No more than one-third would be moving at once, so plenty of fire support was available. These brigades may have been available, but they were not necessarily engaged; ammunition supplies were problematic, and if the Germans were not entrenched there was no need to fire much of a barrage. There was seldom a bombardment, just a creeping barrage in the morning to help the infantry get started and suppress whatever defences the Germans had organised overnight. When ammunition was short, the creeping barrage might do little more than guide the infantry forwards, and the few smoke (and incendiary) shells mixed in were very useful because they stood out. Some days the infantry did not even know where they were, and the barrage would start firing along a terrain feature (such as a road) and the infantry would advance to the start line before the barrage even began moving. German strong-points would receive concentrated fire, and there might also be enough of a bombardment plan to shell suspected strong-points ahead of the barrage. Much fire was observed rather than planned from the map; that this was a novelty shows how much things had changed since 1914. Against lighter defences the concentrated heavy artillery was enormously potent: 'Sections of trench were flattened out in minutes, dug-outs blown in, walls collapsed, machine guns and mortars were covered by earth and rubbish, and ammunition dumps exploded.'[44] Artillery support did not stop with the barrage; typically a field battery moved forwards with each infantry brigade headquarters to provide on-call indirect fire, while the leading battalions could have a section (two guns) pushed forwards to blast machine-gun nests. A number of 6-inch mortars were also pushed forwards on wagons, with improvised mounts on the wagon bed so the mortar did not have to be dismounted.

This sort of fighting led to average gains of 1–3 miles per day, not much more than the range of a creeping barrage (showing how much the infantry wanted and needed support – which was understandable, with them fighting every day). Often the attack would peter out by midday, with the afternoon spent organising for the next day's attack, scouting, laying tele-phone cable and bringing up supplies. With few tanks available and the ever-variable weather limiting the RAF's activities, artillery was the most reliable support for the infantry and the BEF recognised that artillery support reduced casualties. The senior gunner at GHQ reported: 'All army commanders are at me not to reduce the artillery and say with the present state of the infantry they cannot do with a gun less . . .'.[45]

Where the German defences were thicker, as at the Hindenburg Line, the BEF slowed down and brought up the panoply of trench-warfare tools. More guns and ammunition were sent forwards, and for the artillery the sound-ranging and flash-spotting sections also moved up. Survey units needed only 40 hours to identify friendly positions to a reasonable standard, allowing good (if not perfect) shooting in only two days. It helped that the BEF did not face the same challenges as in previous years: German morale was so much lower that there was no need to demolish the defences, only to crack a way in and let the infantry fight their way through, albeit with artillery support.

Rawlinson's Fourth Army would be tackling the Hindenburg Line, and as his men reached it and drove in the outposts, they had an inestimable advantage: on 8 August they had captured a detailed map of the sector they would be attacking. It marked the locations of all the key German installations, so the British could select exactly what they needed to hit and not waste shells from their 1,600 guns. The pinpoint targeting probably increased the demoralising effect on the German troops, who would have seen an uncannily accurate bombardment. As the British noted at the time, 'Prisoners state that our 48 hours' bombardment prior to the attack was extremely effective, and that it was owing to this that the pioneers of the 2nd Division were unable to blow up the bridges over the canal at Bellenglise, as they did not receive food for two days and dared not leave their dugouts owing to the artillery fire.' Increasing the demoralisation was the first British use of mustard gas. The Germans had used it during the Third Battle of Ypres, but it took British industry roughly a year to identify the chemical, develop a production process and make a substantial quantity of shells. Now they were being used and were fired early so that the Germans would experience the worst effects. In theory (after the four-day bombardment), there would be little residual effect for the attacking British troops.

Mustard gas certainly helped the bombardment, but there were plenty of problems to counter-balance. The weather was mediocre, with rain and cloud producing a murk that seriously reduced observation (from air or ground) and affected the counter-battery effort. The Germans also moved guns around as best they could, given their serious shortage of horses, and the net result was that the German artillery was not particularly well suppressed. Ammunition supply was also a weak point for Rawlinson. Only one main railway line was in working order and the roads were clogged with units and vehicles. Shells could be brought up, but often arrived late. With other operations under way or in preparation (Foch had Belgian, British, French and American attacks scheduled for the end of September), there were simply not enough guns to go around, and the Fourth Army had fewer than they would have liked. But the bombardment still involved 750,000 shells (including 32,000 mustard gas ones) over four days, starting on 26 September. Counter-battery fire was vigorous, while wire-cutting was absolutely vital since there were few tanks available and much wire; harassing and interdicting fire were also important across the depth of the German position, and there were of course the machine-gun nests and dugouts to hammer.

Rawlinson was attacking the toughest point of the Hindenburg Line in two sectors: the Americans and Australians faced the Bellicourt Tunnel, which was heavily fortified because the tunnel was an obvious weak point, while IX Corps was planning to cross the St Quentin Canal, a formidable feature in itself (35 feet across and up to 50 feet below the natural level of the ground) with lots of barbed wire and a good number of machine-gun positions. However, IX Corps was attacking the Bellenglise Salient, and it was simple to concentrate shells on the salient and get advantageous angles of fire.

On the 29th there was fog (in addition to the smoke shells mixed into the barrage) which substantially bothered the Germans. Their artillery observers could not see what was happening and infantry could not see very far. This fog was bad for the RAF but it was still a net benefit for the attacking Allies because air support was only a modest benefit. One brigade commander wrote later: 'The night 28/29 had been an unpleasant one – very dark and wet, everyone on the move, heavy shelling and much gas, and quite a number of casualties; but the morning found us merrily firing our barrage, which lasted several hours (3,000 rounds by Zero + 512) and left us in the immediate necessity to bring up more ammunition.'[46]

The attacks developed very differently. The US 27th Division attacked without a creeping barrage (because of fears that isolated groups of friendly infantry were still scattered around after a preliminary attack) and barely captured the German forward line. The 30th American Division did better, largely due to having better observation posts (so their preliminary bombardment had been more effective) and a creeping barrage for cover, but they pushed too hard without mopping up effectively. They punched through the German line but reserve troops got held up by the by-passed Germans and spent their strength mopping up and fending off the inevitable German counter-attacks. The American/Australian attack had pushed the Germans back and partly broken through, but hitting the Germans in this heavily fortified and defended sector had proven problematic.

Meanwhile IX Corps led its attack with the 46th (North Midland) Division crossing the canal. The terrain problems were formidable, but the bombardment had done much to help, for instance by knocking down sections of the brick walls to make it easier to get out of the canal. But the unit needed ladders to get down to the canal, boats to get across and ladders to climb back out. Good staff work provided all that and more, including life-jackets from cross-Channel steamers, to get more men across the canal quickly. On the 29th their careful planning was only part of the explanation for their success. The Germans were extremely surprised by the bold frontal attack, and that threw them off guard. Their reactions were also slowed by the fog. A heavy bombardment had played a role, with the men of the 46th covered by an exceptionally dense creeping barrage: no fewer than 54 18-pounders each firing two rounds per minute and 18 4.5-inch howitzers each firing one round per minute covered the 500-yard bridge-head. The leading brigade cleared the German advanced positions, crossed the canal and reorganised; reserves crossed under a protective barrage and then turned laterally to widen the hole. When the fog cleared, the Germans were able to direct in more artillery fire, but thanks to the preliminary bombardment their communications were patchy and they simply lacked the strength. The corps' reserve division moved through the hole and by the end of the day the corps had taken 5,100 prisoners and 90 guns. It was a stunning accomplishment: the Main Hindenburg System and the Hindenburg Support System had both been broken on a corps' width, and the BEF had overwhelmed the Germans' last prepared defensive line. It was made possible by a combination of good infantry training, effective artillery preparation and support, and intelligent leadership. As Charles Budworth, the Fourth Army's senior artilleryman, boasted in his report, 'The results of our artillery fire as a death-dealer and as a life-saver are written on the ground and in the trenches by German corpses and unused rifles and ammunition.'[47]

Bad news was pouring in to Hindenburg, Ludendorff and the Kaiser. The Turks had been routed in Palestine; the Bulgarians were breaking under attack around Salonika; repeated Allied attacks were hitting the Western Front. Their last hope had been to fall back to a winter defensive line and hope the Allies exhausted themselves in fruitless attacks, but now all they could do was retreat as slowly as possible and hope to gain better terms as armistice negotiations began. Ludendorff continued trying to tweak tactics to win, possibly trying to avoid thinking about the collapsing strategic position. The same day that Rawlinson broke through the Hindenburg Line and the Salonika front collapsed, Ludendorff was sending out new instructions: 'The selection of a position is dependent on artillery observation, by which the ground in front of and behind the main line of resistance must be watched. This generally entails a reverse slope position. The possession of high ground is not of so great importance for the infantry defence.' Moreover, artillery machine guns were to be integrated into the overall checkerboard of resistance and 'the guns will fight to the last . . . their fire over open sights forms an extraordinarily effective support to the infantry'.[48] He was at least realising that Allied attacks were routinely reaching the artillery positions, but paper instructions from the First Quartermaster General could not make the German artillerymen fight to the last: Germany was defeated.

The Americans Enter the Fray

From mid-September the US was an important factor on the Western Front. The American Expeditionary Forces (AEF) were over a million strong and growing as fast as the transports could bring over more men.[49] Artillery, however, was not one of the AEF's great strengths. The AEF was organised in enormous divisions of around 28,000 men – about the strength of a European corps. (This was largely due to the Americans' lack of trained staff officers: the few available could make more impact with fewer divisions. The huge divisions may have been one reason why the American creeping barrages were planned by divisions rather than by corps.) With four infantry regiments of around 16,000 men, each division also had four artillery regiments, three light and one heavy. But the US lacked enough artillery of its own (at home, units trained on log cannons), and production was hampered by a series of bad decisions about what to produce – the US pre-war 3-inch gun, a 1916 variant, a blend of the 1916 gun and a French 75, or a blend of the British 18-pounder and the 1916 gun.[50] It seems the desire to have 'Made in USA' stamped on the guns drove the decision for domestic manufacture, but in nineteen months of war the US built only 109 guns suitable for the front. Instead, the French offered them guns, the 75 for the light regiments and 155mm howitzers for the heavy regiments. (This made the Americans the only force to have 155mm weapons at divisional level.) But most American units only received their equipment in France, so training was greatly curtailed; trench-mortar units were even worse off, because there was not even obsolete or dummy equipment in the US for minimal training.[51]

The Americans had similar problems with doctrine. General John Pershing, their commander, was obsessed with mobile warfare and avoiding the ills of trench warfare; he held that after so many years in the trenches the Europeans lacked aggressiveness and dynamism and insisted that Americans should not learn too much about trench warfare or their native superiority would be diluted. American *Field Service Regulations* even held that 'pre-concerted plans' were 'objectionable', looking back to a simpler day when a general on horseback could run his battle.[52] For artillery, this approach even included disdaining indirect fire as it was 'tainted' with the trenches and lacked the aggressiveness of moving forwards to conduct direct fire. However, given the shortage of horses in

France, there was not much opportunity for mobile warfare training and so trench warfare training was the default, largely because the US lacked experienced officers (there were only 275 artillery officers with more than one year of experience) and European officers were the main instructors. There was also much publishing of European experience and methods, for example a full reprint of the British IX Corps' artillery plans for attacking Messines Ridge, which was essentially a siege operation – about as far from mobile warfare as possible.[53] Thus, whatever Pershing might think, his artillery crews had to learn about modern methods. Implementing them would be more difficult, as the Americans would have as much problem moving on from pre-war methods as the Europeans had done, and they were trying to do it faster.

The first major American battle was a mid-September attack on the St Mihiel Salient, as part of Foch's series of limited attacks. For the American soldiers, it was their first battle as an army; always before they had been scattered in separate divisions. (While a number of divisions had seen action, their infantry had suffered heavily, and even Pershing was now seeing the merits of artillery preparation; he had issued new instructions encouraging more fire support, albeit still emphasising deep penetrations.) It was also the Americans' first battle with their own corps, and they had to borrow much of their non-divisional artillery from the French, including artillery-support units such as balloons and aircraft, and even borrow some corps–artillery commanders. Probably as a result, the Americans followed French doctrine in a number of ways, including concentrating counter-battery work at corps level. Pershing was determined that the US First Army would not falter in its first battle (and under his personal command), and he assembled overwhelming force and his most experienced units. After Verdun, the Germans had treated the St Mihiel sector as a quiet area, and rested divisions there. It was undermanned if well fortified, but units there had very limited transportation service to move supplies and equipment; they were even starting a withdrawal from the salient as the American preparations were finalised.) One change for the Americans was a strong emphasis on forward guns, a battalion of 75s being attached to each infantry brigade; one battery was to stay around the headquarters of each infantry regiment for quick-response fire while the third battery was broken up into single guns (dubbed 'Pirate Guns') that were to provide direct fire support to the infantry.[54] These were a decent compromise: Pershing could be pleased with the aggressiveness of these guns, while the French advisers might not mind losing a small part of the field artillery.

There is little to say about the artillery at St Mihiel except to say it worked. Massive artillery support for a massive attack against defenders who were weak in numbers (and in spirit) was ample. An American infantryman remembered his battle: 'Shrapnel bursting and sending down its deadly iron. High explosives bursting on the ground and sending bricks, mud and iron . . . A mad dash of 50 feet, then look for cover. A stop for a minute . . . then another mad dash!'[55] The Germans were broken in two days (12–13 September) and the Americans took more prisoners than they suffered total casualties. Looking back, communications were identified as a problem (as they always were in the Great War), especially where the infantry advanced quickly and outran the telephone cables.

However, the next attack (actually a sustained offensive) was not so easy. Pershing had agreed to the St Mihiel attack but he had also promised to take the Meuse–Argonne sector for the Americans, and he was keen to launch an attack there as soon as possible. Unfortunately, he rushed the offensive. Road links were poor, delaying troops, guns and ammunition. With the experienced divisions busy disentangling themselves from St Mihiel, the Meuse–Argonne attack would open with inexperienced divisions to meet the timetable. And nobody had asked for gas shells to neutralise the German guns. Trying to advance 16 kilometres in two days with all these problems – plus no artillery support after the initial creeping barrage because the infantry would be too far ahead – was asking for trouble. Unsurprisingly, the opening attack on 26 September had mixed results, rather like an attack in 1916, and in subsequent days the Americans laboured mightily to even out the line. The Germans held on to key observation positions in the centre and on both flanks; continued battering would eventually take Montfaucon in the centre, but the AEF only gradually realised that a new phase was needed to clear the flanks. Each day casualties rose, cohesion fell and there was less and less progress despite Pershing's hectoring: 'we must push on, night and day, regardless of men or guns' and his firing of commanders who were insufficiently aggressive.[56] (In contrast, one of his corps commanders commented: 'If we are to be economical with our men, we must be prodigal with guns and ammunition.'[57]) After a week they had indeed taken the German first line, at least in the centre, but there were a number of German lines – this area protected key rail junctions in Germany and was heavily fortified, even if there were too few troops to hold all the lines. (German troops fought almost fatalistically, knowing they were protecting the supply lines to their comrades further north. Machine-gun teams might fight to the death, but there were relatively few counter-attacks and artillery fire was often on a zone and not adjusted to where the American troops actually were.)

The Americans paused, reorganised and brought up fresh troops, and finally succeeded in clearing their flanks. By 14 October they had taken all the objectives set for 27 September. As elsewhere on the Western Front, the Germans were exhausted and the Allies gained ground in spurts: the Germans could easily be knocked back when an attack was well prepared and well supported, but it took time to organise such an attack and the Germans could resist poorly supported attacks. But Pershing's insistence on always pressing home the attack, rather than accepting that attacks inevitably ran out of steam, ran up casualties and only burned divisions out sooner. Repeated American attacks in early October and then on 1 November (with 'cannon enough to conquer Hell'[58]) each drove the Germans back but lost momentum. The attack on 1 November was especially well planned, with gas being used, German battery and reserve positions identified, and interdiction fire to isolate hills while trained infantry teams wormed through gaps. That attack kept its momentum as the Germans finally lost heart with the war, and the leading American troops reached the German border by the Armistice. An infantry regimental commander gushed:

> The initial attack was marked by a brilliant coordination of arms, the artillery laying down an absolutely smothering barrage which the infantry followed closely . . . Attention must again be called to the wonderful work of our artillery in the first fighting. Our troops have never advanced behind a more perfect barrage.[59]

The Americans had plenty of guns for dense creeping barrages, and also experimented with deep ones, using 6-inch and even 8-inch guns firing ahead of the infantry. Counter-battery fire also improved, and at times the Americans had enough shells to hit areas where German batteries were suspected but not proven.[60] (Ammunition supply was more a question of the roads and light railways; sometimes guns were held to the rear because supply links were too poor, and sometimes there were enough shells to fire on possible but unproven positions.)

The Americans did not live up to their own expectations, but they learned fast and they were certainly able to bash the Germans. However, their tactical clumsiness cost them more casualties than experienced troops would have suffered.

Salonika, 1918

After 1915, when the Franco–British landing force at Salonika had failed to link up with the retreating Serbs, the Salonika front remained a backwater for years; the Germans sarcastically referred to it as an internment camp since the Allied troops were hardly fighting.[61] It caused a certain amount of inter-Allied diplomatic and military friction: the French generally wanted to sustain the troops there (partly as a counter-balance to the British forces in Palestine that stood to expand British influence in the eastern Mediterranean after the war), while the British were less enthusiastic. The Greeks sat on the fence, with factions arguing the pros and cons of entering the war on either side, and the question marks about that also kept the Allies on tenterhooks. There was some fighting in 1916 (the Allies attacked just ahead of Rumania's declaration of war, trying to draw Central Power forces away from Rumania) and 1917 (tied to Nivelle's attack), but the battles gained little ground and none of what they gained was strategic. That is not to say units got off scot-free: a battalion or brigade could be savaged by a day's fighting.

The Allies under-resourced the forces they had there, and their ideas on artillery employment were also outdated. Salonika was, unsurprisingly, a low priority for equipment – the first battery of 8-inch howitzers arrived in January 1918, and was actually discussed at Cabinet level.[62] (Imagine if Western Front operations had been that tightly controlled!) Until the late summer of 1916 the British had no heavy artillery, and only gained ten batteries then – again very low quantities for multiple divisions. Trench mortars only began arriving in December 1916. There was also not much specialist equipment: the British army had only three batteries of mountain guns, and while they were sent to Salonika, they were, after all, only three batteries. (The Indian army had more mountain guns, but Indian troops were not sent to Salonika.) The British had problems with both high explosive and gas shells. The high explosive 'sweated' (or chemically separated) in the summer heat and had a high dud rate, while of the few gas shells that were shipped, some must have leaked during shipment because they had no effect either. Then the British (at least) showed their low regard for Salonika by not shipping doctrinal manuals: for the April–May 1917 attacks they were using pre-Somme handbooks. The 1916 and 1917 attacks often had problems with counter-battery fire (Bulgarian guns were hard to locate and often well protected against the sparse Allied fire, and the first sound-ranging equipment only arrived in January 1918), barrages were hard to coordinate without much experience and in rough ground, and lengthy preparatory bombardments gave the Bulgarians warning of where to move their operational reserves.

The front was a backwater for the Central Powers as well. The Austrians never had enough troops, while the Germans sent only enough to stiffen to the Bulgarians. Instead, they built up the Bulgarian forces.[63] The Bulgarians had decent artillery in the Balkan Wars, and had captured a fair number of modern guns from the Turks in the First Balkan War. Then they had captured a good number from the Serbs in 1915, and although many of those were obsolete fortress guns, they were useful on a semi-static front like Salonika. With all these guns, they not only increased the number of guns, but divisions were upgraded with quick-firing batteries. Trench mortars were also delivered, while the Germans supplied gas shells and sound-ranging equipment. The Bulgarians organised new artillery formations, including a separate artillery brigade for counter-battery fire, drawing in the sound-rangers but also observers from the dominating heights such as the Grand Couronne – called the 'Devil's Eye' by the British who could see the observation post on top – that looked out over Allied positions on the Salonika plains. Captain A.D. Thorburn, who commanded a British howitzer battery, commented, 'Accurate counter-battery work they understood, and executed with unpleasant results to us on more than one occasion. They had most efficiently handled 8-inch and 5.9-inch and 4.2-inch howitzer batteries whose shooting was at least as good as that of German gunners we came across . . .'.[64] It was lucky for the Allies that Bulgarian ammunition was often limited, and so was not wasted on counter-battery or harassing fire but saved for when there was an attack. Bulgarian troops were fierce in defence, and counter-attacked as much as the Germans did, and those counter-attacks presented some of the best artillery targets: 28th Division laconically recorded one action: '07.50 hours. A counter-attack by the Bulgars was launched on Yenikoi from Topalova. 3rd Brigade RFA engaged and stopped it.' A second counter-attack in the same spot at 08.20 hrs 'was pushed forwards with very heavy losses until about 09.40 when it dwindled away and was crushed'.

Yet seizing a few farms or villages was not the result the Allies sought: nevertheless, there was no easy end-run around the Western Front. It was not somehow easier to coordinate infantry and artillery just because they were fighting the Bulgarians. The Salonika Front saw its own halting advances in tactical ideas, and steady progress in thickening defences and the build-up of troops.[65]

By 1918 the melange of Allied troops (not just French and British, but

Serb, Greek and Italians, with some Russian troops disarmed after the Bolshevik revolution and used for labour) had an increasing advantage. The Germans had never put many troops on the Bulgarian front – at most about three divisions and 72 batteries – but to maximise their forces for the Kaiserschlacht they had withdrawn almost all the infantry and much of the artillery. The Bulgarians could not effectively use the guns that were left behind; they were already over-mobilised, with more men in uniform than the country could support – about one-third of the agricultural land was not under cultivation in 1918 because of a lack of farmers and draught animals. Bulgarian morale was dropping because they knew the conditions on their home front, they knew the Germans were expropriating some of what food was being produced, they knew their uniforms and boots were wearing out, and by September they knew the Germans were losing battles on the Western Front.[66] As a result, while the Germans left some of their guns with the Bulgarians, it hardly strengthened the front. The lack of reserves (and the lack of draught animals to move guns and supplies) proved more disastrous as Foch spread his range of limited attacks beyond the Western Front. He had been urging the Italians to attack, but they were resisting. Since the troops at Salonika were under Anglo-French control, they could more easily be sent forwards, and an attack was approved for mid-September.

The tactical details are almost beside the point. Allied operational planning had misled the German commander (the Germans retained command, despite having only three infantry battalions in the theatre) and the reserves were in the wrong place.[67] (This was helped by British preliminary attacks that took heavy casualties for limited gains, but pinned down more Bulgarians.) When the bombardment started on 14 September (in what a German officer called an 'iron storm' in 'hurricane force'),[68] it caught the Bulgarians off balance. The front-line troops resisted as best they could and counter-attacked as much as they could, but the Allies seized the front line at Dobropolje, which gave them observation over the second and third lines and meant that their interdiction fire was even more effective against the limited Bulgarian reserves. Their morale was already brittle, and once the front was broken the Bulgarians cracked and streamed for home. The Allied advance northwards was limited by their inability to repair the railway, but by November the Allies were well into Serbia and threatening central Austria-Hungary.

Swansong of Empire: Austria on the Isonzo

The Germans transferred their artillery and divisions to the Western Front in late 1917 and the Austro-Hungarian army was left to deal with the Allied armies on the Piave. General Armando Diaz set about rebuilding the Italian army and organising it for the battles of 1918. The artillery was a particular priority and Diaz was far keener to learn from his allies than Cadorna had been. The Austrians benefited from the transfer of troops from the Eastern Front but the Empire was already on the verge of collapse. Boroević was ordered to plan a new summer offensive but received little of the vital equipment or reinforcements that might ensure success.[69] Of particular concern was the absence of substantial numbers of heavy batteries on the Trentino and the empire's critical weakness in the air (there were just 53 aircraft to take on the Allies' 486). The Austrians would have to attack with limited ammunition and without detailed intelligence on the dispositions of Allied units, while blissfully unaware that 'the most minute details of the coming bombardment and the assault were in the hand of the Italian command previous to the attack'.[70] Operation *Lawine* ('avalanche') went in on 15 June. The bombardment phase, broadly based upon Bruchmüller's approach to fire-planning,[71] used large quantities of gas but the majority of Italian batteries remained unsilenced and their counter-barrage hit the Austrian assault divisions as they struggled across the river Piave and attempted to break through near the Asigo Plateau. The Austrian Official History bitterly noted that 'our artillery fire had – as prisoners related – shot badly and inflicted hardly any loss on the enemy'.[72] The Austrians made surprising progress in some sectors but overall the offensive faltered against Badoglio's more 'elastic' defensive system. The Battle of the Solstice gave the Italians new hope and, although there were Allied units in their order of battle, they savoured the feeling that they had finally beaten their old enemy without being the handmaiden of more powerful Allied forces.

As Germany's offensives also ground to a halt and Foch's counter-offensives began, Diaz came under pressure from both his government and the Allies to go on the offensive. The reluctant Italian commander-in-chief decided on a breakthrough in the central sector, between Vittorio Veneto and Sacile, as his main objective and began the agonising process of planning what he privately suspected would be another disastrous offensive. The Fourth, Eighth, Tenth and Twelfth Armies were to initiate the offensive, with an attack by the Fourth Army on Mount Grappa unhinging the entire Austrian position. Some 400 additional guns were transferred in to support the attack and Diaz sensibly assigned key objectives to some of his most experienced Allied units. The Fourth Army ran into trouble at Mount Grappa on 23 October, attacking clumsily after days of shelling, but the Tenth Army had more success, benefiting from the presence of two notably pugnacious British divisions under Lord Cavan's command and a bombardment that one British veteran described as 'thousands of gun flashes coalescing to form a continuous blaze of light along the bank'.[73] The Piave line shattered after six days of fighting. The assaulting units quickly left their artillery support behind and only the headlong retreat of the demoralised Austrians prevented the Allies from suffering heavy casualties as the offensive gathered momentum in what Diaz gleefully described as 'Caporetto in reverse'.

Symphony of Fire: Valenciennes

On 1 November 1918 the Canadian Corps would take Valenciennes. The small city was only 30 kilometres from Le Cateau but the artillery tactics and techniques were four years apart, and it made a world of difference.[74]

In late October Haig reckoned the Germans were on their last legs, with Turkey and Bulgaria knocked out of the war and Italy preparing to attack the tottering Austrians. With the Americans and French attacking, it was time for the BEF to launch one final blow. To get the British First Army in position for the anticipated Battle of the Scheldt, they first needed to take Valenciennes, which lay east of the Scheldt Canal. Because of the rain and German-controlled flooding, the low ground west of the canal was flooded for a distance of perhaps a thousand yards; in addition, there was barbed wire on the eastern bank and the German troops (and machine guns) were safely positioned in houses. A frontal assault across the canal was out of the question. However, the canal swung round the city and to the south XXII Corps had got across. If the Germans could be thrown off Mt Houy (which was only 150ft high, but about 50ft higher than the surrounding countryside, and blocking observation of German artillery to the east), they could be levered out of Valenciennes.

However, the Germans recognised the key ground and they had plenty of guns; in addition, troop morale was reasonably firm. From 24 to 28 October several British attacks were made, all rushed and poorly supported, more in hopes that the Germans were weak than in confidence that the attacks would succeed. But the British troops were at the limit of their supply lines (railheads were 30 miles back, and lorries were in short supply), casualties had thinned the ranks and everyone was tired. The Scots of the 51st (Highland) Division pushed up Mt Houy, but their last attack on 28

October was driven back from the crest by a German counter-attack, despite support from nine brigades of field artillery and fourteen batteries of heavies.

The Canadian Corps was now moved in to make the attack. The Canadians had been facing the canal, but since the main thrust could not be made there, they were available. The 4th Canadian Division relieved the 51st Highlanders, and moved up guns and shells; they took several days to plan their attack. Few infantry and plenty of support was a key element of their plan: 'to pay the price of victory, so far as possible, in shells and not in the lives of men'.[75] The delay also allowed time to coordinate infantry, machine guns and artillery. The Canadians knew there had been several failed efforts to take Mt Houy, and steadily increasing German artillery fire showed the enemy's determination to hold the position; however, the Canadian gunners were just as determined to crush German resistance by weight of shell.

The attack would be some 2,500 yards wide (about 1½ miles). One Canadian infantry brigade would attack (by this stage of the war, that meant about 1,200 men). Generally speaking, about 10 per cent of any unit was left out of battle in case there were heavy casualties. For that one infantry brigade, there were eight brigades of field artillery and six of heavy artillery. The first objective was basically Mt Houy, and the second was 2,000 yards beyond it, clearing a few villages and the suburbs of Valenciennes.

There was no preliminary bombardment, but most of the heavy artillery fired well ahead of the infantry, hitting the German defence in depth and the reserves. No fewer than 39 6-inch howitzers were assigned to fire one round per minute over the front of the attack, a ratio that equated to 1.6 shells per 100 yards and the bursting radius was over 500 yards. McNaughton was putting 'a practically continuous rain of chunks of steel across the whole front of the attack'. That was the first phase; when the Germans were pushed off Mt Houy and lost their observation posts there, more Canadian guns could fire, and the second phase of the attack narrowed to 1,000 yards. Some 55 howitzers would fire 2 rounds every 3 minutes, so it became 3.6 rounds per minute per 100 yards.

In all, 144 18-pounders and 48 4.5-inch howitzers would fire a creeping barrage (effectively 7 tons of shells per minute), deliberately moving at only 100 yards in four minutes (later slowing to five minutes) so that the infantry would have no problem keeping up. The field howitzers would fire some smoke shells but would also hit selected strong-points ahead of the 18-pounders. The infantry, in turn, pulled back from the foremost positions on the lower slopes of Mt Houy so the artillery would have a straight (and convenient) line for its starting barrage. Machine guns fired both forward and flanking barrages, taking advantage of the topography: Mt Houy was an exposed salient. The infantry would be attacking from the southwest with machine guns firing from the south and heavy artillery firing from the north. Additional machine-gun and heavy artillery barrages were planned for the right flank of the attack, covering the ground with fire instead of sending more infantry into battle. Planning also took into account where German reserves were likely to be and thus where counter-attacks were likely to start. Since the towns and villages were full of refugees, the French had forbidden unnecessary shelling. (The Germans were continuing to use gas shells, and the Canadian troops were upset about its use around unprotected civilians; they were prone to confiscate gas-masks from German prisoners and give them to civilians. They were also taking relatively few prisoners at this stage in the war.) The Canadians decided only to hit counter-attacks on the edge of towns; this meant that the Germans had a good night's sleep in a building but they were easier to kill in the open. The half-circle of British positions allowed enfilade fire not only on the front line but on roads (for harassing fire) and on reserves. Counter-battery work was not neglected, with 49 guns assigned to obliterate the 26 known German battery positions. The gunners slept by their guns in case the Germans got wind of the attack.

One battery was assigned a particularly devious mission. It was deliberately sited where it could fire into the rear of the German positions, and shortened its range as the attack progressed. Not only did this prevent it from hitting the Canadian infantry, but the Germans would think their own artillery was shelling them and their morale would suffer accordingly.[76]

At dawn, 05.15 hrs, on All Saints' Day the bombardment crashed out and the infantry moved forwards. German artillery fired promptly and accurately but mainly at the British artillery, with little or no effect. (Gibbs called it a 'fierce line of fire' but noted that it quickly ended as counter-battery fire took effect.) The hapless German infantry soldiers, meanwhile, were deluged with shell-fire. Gibbs wrote, 'our barrage rolled like a tide wiping them off the map of France', and the *New York Times* headlined the story 'British Gunfire Paralyses Foe'. Prisoners, 'stupefied and demoralised', surrendered freely, including a complete company that was trapped in the fog and smoke; perhaps the first thing they saw of the Canadians was their bayonet points. With these advantages, the first objective was reached on time. A few machine-gun nests and a single field gun held out during the advance to the second objective, inflicting casualties before being overrun by the experienced infantry. The heavy artillery fire stayed ahead of the barrage and deliberately smashed some rows of houses where the Germans were known to have positions (any refugees killed here were regarded as collateral damage). Once the objectives were secured, it was time to see what the Germans would do. Each of the infantry battalions moved a 6-inch trench mortar forwards, and three brigades of field artillery moved on to the slopes of Mt Houy. Their observers moved to the top, so they could quickly engage any target they saw. Shortly after noon German infantry was seen forming up and the planned protective barrage was employed: 11 batteries of 6-inch howitzers rolled a barrage over the Germans. The survivors lost all interest in attacking. Between 15.00 and 16.00 hrs more movement was seen on the right flank, and on-the-fly plans were made to hit the Germans once they had fully formed up. At 16.35 hrs the situation was judged ripe, and 9 batteries of 6-inch howitzers obliterated another counter-attack.

The results were gratifying. Mt Houy was taken and the Germans were levered out of Valenciennes. (Another Canadian brigade had squelched forwards to the canal to test the German positions, and found almost no resistance. By mid-morning two Canadian battalions were solidly across. The German infantry had withdrawn very quickly, probably realising from the noise of the bombardment on their left rear flank that their comrades could not hold under such a maelstrom.) Over 800 dead Germans were found around Mt Houy alone, and 1,800 prisoners taken. The 2,149 tons of shells had done their work.[77] But the Canadians also suffered 501 casualties,[78] out of the 1,200 infantry in the attack. Massive (and well handled) firepower could reduce casualties – not least by allowing fewer infantry to attack – but there was no avoiding a substantial percentage of casualties. The three British divisions attacking further to the south took over 1,600 prisoners and counted 300 dead; their casualties were higher than the Canadians', but by this stage of the war a well supported Allied attack could easily break any German line. The Canadians had used every trick in the Allied arsenal and noted a number of ideas for the future but their brutally effective use of artillery had not solved all the problems of the Great War.

Conclusion

All the combatants adapted their tactics as the unrelenting warfare threw up new challenges and created fresh opportunities for tactical or technological innovation. Every nation adapted and improved its technology and tactics as its experience of warfare intensified, though only the great powers could mobilise their economies to industrialise almost every aspect of armed conflict. Not every nation's learning curve was the same: Italy's doctrinal inertia appears to have partly stemmed from Luigi Cadorna's flawed personality, while Romania's recovery and success at the battles of Mărăşti and Mărăşeşti (July and August 1917) showed that French advice combined with native resolve could eventually turn bitter experience into battlefield effectiveness. While other armies did as well as they could with the tools and techniques they had available, the major powers also struggled with challenges created by their industrial limitations and cultural peculiarities and a great deal can be learned from comparing the experience of the three largest forces on the Western Front.

The Germans started with a technical advantage and an approach to artillery technology and doctrine that appears to have encouraged innovation from below. There is strong evidence to suggest that the policy of temporarily assigning relatively junior officers to operational roles typically filled by a more senior rank (such as Bruchmüller) enabled tactical innovation, but such a system did not appear to encourage continuity of development or dissemination of ideas. The problem was that the same flexibility often gave credit to senior commanders who oversaw the campaign (such as Hutier), instead of the officer responsible for planning the operations or introducing the technology, and arguably prevented the key innovator from being assigned a role that made the best use of his talents – some innovations were even ignored because they were seen as having originated on other fronts. The German army's tradition of military patronage made them highly adaptable and able to continue innovating in peacetime but their habit of celebrating individuals and not processes meant that their major successes were limited to relatively few units and their strategic ideas often focused on purely tactical challenges.

The French started behind the Germans in almost every aspect of artillery development (except their superlative field gun) and were forced to make do with what was available; inevitably they paid a high price in casualties. As soon as they were able to introduce a reasonable quantity of suitable weapons, they rapidly disseminated new ideas and French commanders were generally happy to share their insights with other officers and to absorb the advances that originated from other armies. Nivelle's over-confidence caused progress to falter in 1917 but by 1918 the French were fully capable of halting German offensives and then battering through almost any defensive system. As Foch noted after the war,

> the Germans had more powerful guns than ours [in the first years of the war], but they, in their turn, failed because they did not use them advantageously. As a matter of fact, the offensive never recovered its full power until we had increased more than ten-fold the number of our heavy pieces and the allowance of ammunition of all kinds. We next learned to regulate our artillery methodically, and finally we perfected armoured appliances which could seek out and destroy the hostile machine guns.[79]

The problem was that the lessons of the Great War were almost entirely forgotten. French planners mistook success in 1918 as a vindication of their overall military system instead of as evidence of a need to review and understand how warfare was changing as a result of technologies and techniques discovered in the war. Instead of reviewing the impact of new developments, the enthusiastic adoption of flawed doctrinal panaceas ensured that France began the Second World War even less prepared than she had been in 1914.

The British had started with useful equipment but nothing in quantity. The Royal Artillery learnt fast, however, and by 1918 its crews were rather more effective than the Germans and the French at weaving new technologies into their general planning. The lack of a large pre-war military establishment was a weakness, and the British struggled to adapt to large-scale warfare, but once the army demonstrated that it was capable of major operations, it also proved adept at drawing upon skills and technologies that the Germans failed to utilise effectively. Like the French, these innovations were rapidly disseminated to other units but, once the guns fell silent, the British army assumed that the operational challenges of the Great War were unique and discarded key elements in the adaptive ethos that made them the most effective artillery force on the Western Front.[80]

The story of the artillery in the Great War tells us a great deal about how organisations adapt in fast-moving conditions and, most importantly, how the efforts of the opposing armies served to rapidly neutralise their opponent's attempts at innovation. All the generals of the Great War had to contend with expanding armies, new technologies and the unprecedented logistic requirements of modern war – and the way that each army dealt with these challenges was largely based upon the way in which their military culture approached innovation.[81] The Great War saw increasingly sophisticated integrated artillery fire-planning in both attack and defence. Nevertheless, even with all the technical and tactical innovations combined, even when they were orchestrated as part of a coherent strategy, success in battle still depended on the infantry advancing into a grim and confusing wasteland strewn with strong-points, machine-gun nests and pockets of desperate men driven into a primeval need for revenge by the artillery fire they had just survived. Even the most efficient operational fire-plan could not completely overcome the fog and friction of warfare and thus only served to create a framework for success in the otherwise relentless chaos of battle.

Notes

Prologue
1. Beck, MD1115/16 Le Cateau, Woolwich Archive.

Chapter One
1. See Stephan van Evera, 'The Cult of the Offensive and the Origins of the First World War', *International Security*, vol. 9, no. 1 (Summer 1984), pp. 58–107.
2. There is still debate on the influence of the original Schlieffen concept – for the purpose of this study it is important to note that the General Staff operated using a mobilisation/operations plan and some of the factors that prevented a breakthrough in 1914 saw their genesis in pre-war planning assumptions.
3. *Encyclopaedia Britannica*, 11th edn (New York: Encyclopaedia Britannica Co., 1911), vol. 16, p. 593.
4. See Holger Herwig, *The Marne 1914: The Opening of World War I and the Battle that Changed the World* (Random House, 2009), pp. 72–3, for a description of the garrison.
5. See Captain Becker, 'The 42cm Mortar: Fact and Fancy', *Field Artillery Journal* (May–June 1922), pp. 224–31, for technical details of these weapons.
6. General von Berendt, 'Use of Heavy Artillery in Attacking Fortifications', *Field Artillery Journal* (November–December 1939), p. 549.
7. Becker, 'The 42cm Mortar', p. 227. This was at Antwerp, which was protected by forts very similar to those around Liege.
8. Lieutenant-General H. Rohne, 'Concerning the Fall of the Belgian Forts', *Field Artillery Journal* (October–December 1914), pp. 589–90. They inevitably celebrated Krupps' role (instead of the Austrians who had built the 305mm howitzers).
9. Berendt, 'Use of Heavy Artillery in Attacking Fortifications'.
10. Generalleutnant Wilhelm Balck, *Development of Tactics – World War*, trans. Harry Bell (General Service School's Press, Fort Leavenworth, 1922), p. 240.
11. Bruce Gudmundsson, *On Artillery* (Praeger, 1993), p. 3.
12. During pre-war exercises a few German corps commanders, keen to maintain the offensive momentum in a mobile battle, expressed resentment at

dragging such heavy guns into battle, one officer memorably describing the draught horses as 'thirsty elephants'.

13. Balck, *Development of Tactics*, pp. 242–6.

14. Gudmundsson, *On Artillery*, p. 22.

15. Supporting his assumption, Langlois estimated that a quick-firing gun could, on average, deliver up to 40kg a minute while a heavier gun could only deliver 15 or 16kg in the same period. Even if the heavy gun fired a far heavier shell, such as a 40kg 155mm shell, it lost in flexibility what it gained in weight of shell due to the extra time required to deploy the battery.

16. Robert M. Ripperger, 'The Development of the French Artillery for the Offensive, 1890–1914', *Journal of Military History*, 59 (October 1995), pp. 599–618.

17. James K. Hogue, 'Puissance de Feu: The Struggle for New Artillery Doctrine in the French Army, 1914–1916', MA Thesis (Ohio State University, 1988), p. 5, quoting Herr, *L'Artillerie: ce qu'elle est, ce quelle doit etre* (Paris, 1923), p. 6

18. Pascal M.H. Lucas, *The Evolution of Tactical Ideas in France and Germany During the War of 1914–1918* (GCG, Paris, 1923; trans. F.A. Kieffer, US Army, 1925), pp. 4–6. Lieutenant-Colonel Lucas, writing after the war, noted: 'We did not pay enough attention to the effect of fire, we went on using formations that were too dense [and] we neglected liaison . . . [The French army] threw itself into battle with an ardour that was superb, but with a disdain for fire for which it had to pay dearly.'

19. Lucas, *The Evolution of Tactical Ideas*, p. 7.

20. Ripperger, 'The Development of the French Artillery', p. 613, quoting Captain Bellenger.

21. *Ibid.*, p. 608. To De Lamothe, ensuring 'maximum mobility combined with firepower' was a 'fundamental principle', and while he conducted multiple trials of proposed weapons as war approached, he found it difficult to escape his own narrow definition of the role of heavy artillery.

22. Anthony Clayton, *Paths of Glory: The French Army 1914–1918* (New York, Cassell, 2003), p. 22; and Ripperger, 'The Development of the French Artillery', p. 606

23. Lucas, *The Evolution of Tactical Ideas*, pp. 9–16. Lucas, while reviewing these reforms, noted that the French were not alone in harbouring this delusion and found only one pre-war writer, a Swiss officer writing in 1902 about the 'Battle of the Future', who correctly identified the advent of operational siege warfare. Aviation was notably absent from the proposed system.

24. Alistair Horne, *The Price of Glory: Verdun 1916* (London, Penguin, 1993), p. 13.

25. *Ibid.*, p. 13. Weygand ruefully noted that the 75 was seen as the entire Holy Trinity but 'one would have liked to have seen it surrounded by a few saints'.

26. Robert B. Bruce, *Petain: Verdun to Vichy* (Washington DC, Potomac, 2008); see also Ferdinand Foch, *The Principles of War*, trans. Hilaire Belloc (Paris, 1903; repr. London, Chapman & Hall, 1918). Foch's writings, although often bewilderingly frenetic, included moments of insight that gave him a precious intellectual advantage over many of his contemporaries. In *Principles*, like Pétain, he stated that 'fire has become the decisive argument' and noted the importance of combining the efforts of the infantry and artillery in the decisive battle, remarking that 'the union of both arms has become more necessary than ever'. Foch instinctively recognised that launching an attack without artillery preparation was folly, a process he methodically divided into 'the artillery struggle', 'clearing the way', 'breaching the objective' and 'following up the attack', but his lectures were frenetic affairs and few officers remembered the dry technical details about firepower and the increasing 'necessity of cover' after hearing him describe his cherished theories on the primacy of morale. While Foch underestimated the number of guns required to support an attack – he assumed that quick-firing guns meant that fewer artillery pieces would be necessary – he did understand that counter-battery fire would be essential to a breakthrough, that concentration of fire was vital to success and that the increased range of artillery could use sudden concentrations of firepower to facilitate strategic surprise.

27. Hogue, 'Puissance de Feu', pp. 2, 8–9.

28. Anon, *The French Artillery after August 1914, Armies of the First World War, Tactical Notebook* (Quantico, Institute for Tactical Education, August 1992).

29. Lucas, *The Evolution of Tactical Ideas*, p. 24. Lucas notes that the 75s did prove effective in several crucial encounters and that the German batteries sometimes fired too high; this is supported by Balck, *Development of Tactics*, p. 240.

30. *Ibid.*, p. 28.

31. Hogue, 'Puissance de Feu', pp. 19–20. Some 75 per cent of casualties were inflicted by artillery, compared with less than 20 per cent in the Russo-Japanese War. See also Lucas, *The Evolution of Tactical Ideas*, p. 8; and Ferdinand Foch, *The Memoirs of Marshal Foch* (London, Windmill, 1931), pp. 16, 39–41, 217.

32. Lucas, *The Evolution of Tactical Ideas*, pp. 25–33.

33. Hogue, 'Puissance de Feu', pp. 22–3. The most modern howitzers available had originally been destined for export as the domestic armaments industry had been rather less convinced by the overwhelming superiority of *offensive à outrance* than either the French government or the General Staff.

34. *Ibid.*, pp. 29–32.

35. Gudmundsson, *On Artillery*, pp. 77–8. The reliable 58T spigot mortar, firing a 6kg winged projectile, was finally made the standard piece in February 1915.

36. Clayton, *Paths of Glory*, p. 20.
37. As with many things, scholars debate the quality of German training. Terence Zuber, *Ardennes 1914: The Battle of the Frontiers* (Tempus, 2007) is very positive, while Eric Brose, *The Kaiser's Army: the politics of military technology in Germany during the Machine Age, 1870–1918* (Oxford University Press, 2001) is more mixed.
38. There are few detailed accounts in English of the Battle of the Frontiers. Robert Doughty's *Pyrrhic Victory: French Strategy and Operations in the Great War* (Harvard, 2005) is very good, while John Keegan's older *August 1914: Opening Moves* (Ballantine, 1973) has a chapter about the battles in Lorraine. Paddy Griffith, *Forward into Battle: Fighting Tactics from Waterloo to the Near Future* (Presidio Press, 1991 edn), pp. 90–3 mentions these battles. Herwig, *The Marne, 1914*, covers the whole campaign and ch. 3 examines the Lorraine campaign.
39. Douglas Johnson, *Battlefields of the World War: A Study in Military Geography* (Oxford University Press, 1921), pp. 476–9, has comments about the topography.
40. Max Arthur, *Forgotten Voices of the Great War* (Globe Pequot, 2004), pp. 25–6.
41. Joseph Joffre, *His Memoirs* (Harpers, 1932) show him expecting further French attacks.
42. Shelford Bidwell and Dominick Graham, *Firepower: British Army Weapons and Theories of War 1904–1945* (Pen & Sword, 2004).
43. C.E.D. Budworth, 'Artillery in Co-operation with Infantry', *Journal of the Royal Artillery*, vol. 37, no. 1 (1910), pp. 1–14. *Field Artillery Training 1914* (London, HMSO, 1914), pp. 252, 259. Budworth later served as artillery commander for Rawlinson's Fourth Army from May 1916 until the Armistice.
44. Henry Hugh Tudor, Papers (Woolwich Archive, MD1060). Tudor correctly identified Murray as the man most likely to become Chief of Staff to the British Expeditionary Force.
45. A.G. Bates, *To Ypres for a Haircut, The War Diaries and Letters of Lieutenant A.G. Bates RA* (Winkfield, 2006). With thanks to Jonathan Bailey for noting this reference in the BCMH journal in 2009.
46. Nik Cornish, *The Russian Army and the First World War* (London, Spellmount, 2006). For the Russian view see http://www.artillery-museum.ru/en/schema-2.html. Headlam (Woolwich, MD183) notes that the Russian artillery called the infantry 'black bones' and the artillery 'white bones'.
47. Karl von Wiegand, 'On The Firing Line, Near Wirballen, Russian Poland', United Press, 8 October 1914.

48. Norman Stone, *The Eastern Front 1914 to 1917* (London, Penguin, 1998), p. 93.

49. *Ibid.*, chs 1 and 2 cover the pre-war Russian artillery and army in general. Dennis Showalter, *Tannenberg: Clash of Empires, 1914* (Brassey's, 2004), chs 1 to 3 give an overview of Russian–German antagonism building up to the war. Chs 4 and 5 give backgrounds on both the German and Russian armies.

50. Allan R. Millett and Murray Williamson (eds), *Military Effectiveness, Vol. 1: The First World War*, Mershon Center Series on International Security and Foreign Policy (Allen & Unwin, Australia, 1989), p. 309.

51. Showalter, *Tannenberg*, p. 161.

52. Edward T. Donnelly, 'Russian Field Artillery Drill Regulations, 1912', *Field Artillery Journal* (April–June 1915), pp. 403–6 is largely about coordination.

53. Showalter, *Tannenberg*, p. 214.

54. Hew Strachan, *To Arms* (Oxford University Press, 2001), p. 321.

55. N.N. Golovin, *The Russian Army in the World War* (Yale University Press, 1931), p. 143.

56. Stone, *The Eastern Front*, p. 62.

57. A. Kearsey, *A Study of the Strategy and Tactics of the East Prussian Campaign 1914* (Sifton Praed, 1932), p. 11.

58. Showalter, *Tannenberg*, p. 220. It might have been true but the Russian reaction was to shell Neidenburg, the nearest town.

59. Stone, *The Eastern Front*, pp. 55–8.

60. Kearsey, *East Prussian Campaign*, p. 47.

61. *Ibid.*, p. 13, claims Russian infantry fled during the bombardment and German infantry simply had to occupy the positions.

62. Showalter, *Tannenberg*, pp. 230, 238, 254.

63. *Ibid.*, p. 259.

64. Kearsey, *East Prussian Campaign*, p. 39; Stone, *The Eastern Front*, p. 51.

65. *Ibid.*, p. 278.

66. Stone, *The Eastern Front*, p. 66.

67. Christian Ortner, *The Austro-Hungarian Artillery from 1867 to 1918* (Verlag Militaria, 2007), pp. 10–21.

68. Norman Stone, 'Army and Society in the Habsburg Monarchy, 1900–1914', *Past and Present*, 33 (April 1966), pp. 95–111, offers an excellent overview of the disfunctionality of Imperial–Royal politics as they relate to the military.

69. Lawrence Sondhaus, *Franz Conrad von Hötzendorf: architect of the apocalypse* (Humanities Press, 2000), p. 121. There was also somewhat more money for fortifications, but most of those were on the Italian frontier. Gunther Rothenberg, *The Army of Francis Joseph* (Perdue University Press, 1976), p. 160.

70. This section draws on Sondhaus, *Franz Conrad von Hötzendorf*, pp. 92, 103

and 158, and Ludwig Elmannsberger, 'The Austro-Hungarian Artillery in the World War', *Coast Artillery Journal,* 62 (1925), pp. 192–206.

71.   Janos Decsy, 'The Habsburg Army on the Threshold of Total War', in Bela A. Kiraly, Nandor F. Dreisziger and Albert A. Nofi (eds), *East Central European Society in World War I* (Columbia University Press, 1985), p. 285.

72.   Istvan Deak, 'The Habsburg Army in the First and Last Days of World War I: A Comparative Analysis', in Kiraly, Dreisziger and Nofi (eds), *East Central European Society in World War I,* p. 303.

73.   This section draws on Rothenberg, *The Army of Francis Joseph,* pp. 126-7, 149, 164 and 174; and Strachan, *To Arms,* p. 28.

74.   Every year the Austrians spent three times as much on tobacco, beer and wine as they did on their military – but this is not all that different from modern societies so it might be prudent not to criticise the Austro-Hungarians for being more interested in pleasure than preparing for war!

75.   The standard history of Austrian war planning is Graydon A. Tunstall, *Planning for War Against Russia and Serbia: Austro-Hungarian and German Military Strategies, 1871–1914* (Columbia University Press, 1993), especially ch. 9. Stone, *The Eastern Front,* is older but more widely available, and chs 2 and 4 cover the Austrians. Holger Herwig, *The First World War: Germany and Austria-Hungary 1914–1918* (Arnold, 1997) is an excellent overview. Italy was nominally an ally, although the Austrians had prepared to fight Italy as well.

76.   http://cgsc.cdmhost.com/cgi-bin/showfile.exe?CISOROOT=/p4013coll14&CISOPTR=583&filename=584.pdf#search=%22Forces%22 has maps and an operational/strategic overview but does not mention artillery.

77.   Tunstall, *Planning for War Against Russia and Serbia,* pp. 239, 241.

78.   Herwig, *The First World War,* p. 91.

79.   Ortner, *The Austro-Hungarian Artillery from 1867 to 1918,* p. 605.

80.   Tunstall, *Planning for War Against Russia and Serbia,* p. 242.

81.   Ludwig Elmannsberger, 'The Austro-Hungarian Artillery in the World War', *Coast Artillery Journal,* vol. 62 (1925).

82.   Alexei Brusilov, *A Soldier's Note-Book* (Macmillan, 1930), pp. 49, 56, 67.

83.   http://net.lib.byu.edu/estu/wwi/memoir/Kreisler/Kreisler.htm.   Most shells in the First World War were low-velocity projectiles and thus sub-sonic. Troops learned to recognise the incoming rounds by the distinctive whine they made as they approached. Most were given colourful nicknames: Pip-Squeaks (small or gas shell), Whizz-Bangs (77mm), Coal-Boxes (5.9-inch), Woolly Bears (shrapnel shell), Moaning Minnies (*minenwerfer*), Black Marias (high explosive) and Jack Johnsons (heavy shells). Howitzer shells that were incorrectly rammed into the breech made a distinctive undulating whistle as they hurtled overhead. High-velocity guns were dreaded by both

sides as there was little warning before their projectiles exploded, and thus they were used for harassment and sniping fire missions, where the unexpected arrival of their shells could do the most damage. C.A. Rose, *Three Years in France with the Guns* (London, Leonaur, 2007), pp. 39 and 76, notes two such guns which were nicknamed 'Quick Dick' and 'Silent Sue' by the British.

84. English language sources on Serbia are relatively few. Most recent, and with the best research in Serbian archives, is James Lyon, '"A Peasant Mob": The Serbian Army on the Eve of the Great War', *Journal of Military History*, vol. 61, no. 3, (1997), pp. 481–502, which covers the army but not the campaign. Dimitrije Djordgevic, 'Vojvoda Putnik, The Serbian High Command and Strategy in 1914', in Kiraly, Dreisziger and Nofi (eds), *East Central European Society in World War I*, pp. 569–89, has a useful overview of the campaign but is older; Andrej Mitrovic, *Serbia's Great War, 1914–1918* (Perdue University Press, 2007), has little on the fighting and more on the occupation policies of the Austrians. Gunther Rothenberg, 'The Austro-Hungarian Campaign Against Serbia in 1914', *Journal of Military History*, 53 (April 1989), pp. 127–46, gives a good overview of the campaign. John Schindler, 'Disaster on the Drina: The Austro-Hungarian Army in Serbia, 1914', *War in History*, 9/2 (2002), pp. 159–95, is an excellent review of the campaign, with an overwhelming emphasis on the 21st Landwehr Division. While this division was at the centre of the battle at Cer, its role later on was less dramatic and Schindler becomes a weaker source for the later stages.

85. Schindler, 'Disaster on the Drina', p. 165.

86. http://cgsc.cdmhost.com/cdm4/item_viewer.php?CISOROOT=/p4013 coll14&CISOPTR=927&CISOBOX=1&REC=1 has maps of the operational area.

87. Djordgevic, 'Vojvoda Putnik, The Serbian High Command and Strategy in 1914', p. 577.

88. www.heroesofserbia.com/2009/08/battle-of-cer-first-allied-victory-of.html.

89. Both quotations from Schindler, 'Disaster on the Drina', p. 181.

90. Both quotations from Djordgevic, 'Vojvoda Putnik, The Serbian High Command and Strategy in 1914', p. 581.

91. Elmannsberger, 'The Austro-Hungarian Artillery in the World War', p. 199. Even Elmannsberger, who was highly sympathetic to the Austrians, admits this was exceptional. Schindler, 'Disaster on the Drina', pp. 185–6, covers the same events in more detail.

92. Schindler, 'Disaster on the Drina', p. 187.

93. Quoted in Herwig, *The First World War*, p. 112.

94. Quoted in Schindler, 'Disaster on the Drina', p. 161.

95. Ortner, *The Austro-Hungarian Artillery from 1867 to 1918*, pp. 346–7.
96. Ypres is covered in Strachan, *To Arms*, pp. 275–80, and two English-language monographs, Ian F.W. Beckett, *Ypres: The First Battle, 1914* (Pearson Longman, 2004) and Anthony Farrar-Hockley, *Death of an Army* (William Morrow, 1968).
97. Beckett, *Ypres: The First Battle*, pp. 113–17, has the best detail on this.
98. Farrar-Hockley, *Death of an Army*, pp. 147–8.
99. Alan Palmer, *The Salient: Ypres, 1914–1918* (Constable, 2007), p. 80, quoting Gunner Barrows.
100. Edward J. Erickson, *Ordered to Die: A History of the Ottoman Army in the First World War* (Greenwood, 2001). Erickson suggests that the low figure of artillery casualties indicates that the Ottoman army had problems getting their guns forward (pp. 60–1).
101. There is a substantial literature on the shell shortage and on industrial mobilisation in the Great War. An excellent one-chapter summary is in Strachan, *To Arms*, pp. 993–1113.
102. Doughty, *Pyrrhic Victory*, pp. 105–65, covers French operations and the shell shortage.
103. Wilhelm Diest, 'Strategy and Unlimited Warfare in Germany: Moltke, Falkenhayn and Ludendorff', in Roger Chickering and Stig Forster (eds), *Great War, Total War: Combat and Mobilisation on the Western Front, 1914–1918* (Cambridge University Press, 2000), p. 271.
104. Roger Chickering, *Imperial Germany and the Great War, 1914–1918* (Cambridge University Press, 1998), p. 37.
105. The shell shortages in Russia became an excuse for the ex-Czarist officers to avoid blame for losing the war. Golovin, *The Russian Army in the World War*, has long sections (e.g. pp. 133–48) on how the army was let down. Stone, *The Eastern Front*, ch. 7, delves into this.
106. Chickering, *Imperial Germany and the Great War*, p. 36.
107. Ian Hogg and L.F. Thurston, *British Artillery Weapons and Ammunition, 1914–1918* (Allan, 1972), and David Nash, *German Artillery, 1914–1918* (Altmark, 1970), cover many of the various weapons.
108. Stone, *The Eastern Front*, p. 123.

Chapter Two

1. Doughty, *Pyrrhic Victory*, p. 121.
2. Sources for Neuve Chapelle are plentiful. Robin Prior and Trevor Wilson, *Command on the Western Front: The Military Career of Sir Henry Rawlinson 1914–1918* (Pen & Sword, 2004), pp. 19–73; Bidwell and Graham, *Firepower*, pp. 72–6, 102–3; Sir Martin Farndale, *History of the Royal Regiment of Artillery: Western Front 1914–18* (Royal Artillery Institution, 1986), pp. 86–92; Doughty, *Pyrrhic Victory*, pp. 136–40 covers the alliance background;

Sanders Marble, *'The Infantry Cannot Do with a Gun Less': The Place of the Artillery in the British Expeditionary Force, 1914–1918* (Columbia University Press, 2003), pp. 55–63, 120–1, 156–7 covers various aspects.

3.   Quoted in Prior and Wilson, *Command on the Western Front*, p. 45.

4.   W.L. Andrews, *Haunting Years: The Commentaries of a War Territorial* (London, 1930), cited in J.H. Johnson, *Stalemate: The Real Story of Trench Warfare* (London, 1995), p. 23.

5.   Quoted in Prior and Wilson, *Command on the Western Front*, p. 61.

6.   Cornish, *The Russian Army and the First World War*, p. 227.

7.   Stone, *The Eastern Front*, pp. 132, 163.

8.   *Ibid.*, p. 134. Astonishingly, X Corps lost one regiment from each division for this outrageous presumption!

9.   According to German records, Von Mackensen was amused by this quaint custom.

10.   http://www.greatwardifferent.com/Great_War/Galicia/Onslaught_01.htm.

11.   Stone, *The Eastern Front*, pp. 136–8.

12.   Hermann von François, *Gorlice 1915. The Piercing of the Carpathian Mountains and the Liberation of Galicia*, trans. Alfred R.W. Jonge (US Army Military History Institute, 1931), pp. 41–2.

13.   Stone, *The Eastern Front*, pp. 138–40. The Germans faced far fewer problems and Mackensen was soon happily contemplating a reserve of 1,000 rounds per gun – almost ten times the Russian reserves in the same sector.

14.   Richard DiNardo, 'The Gorlice-Tarnow Offensive, May 1915', US Marine Corps Command and Staff College, http://bobrowen.com/nymas/podcasts/diNardo%20WWI%203.mp3; Gudmundsson, *On Artillery*, pp. 53–7.

15.   Timothy C. Dowling, *The Brusilov Offensive* (Indiana University Press, 2008), p. 31.

16.   Stone, *The Eastern Front*, pp. 145–52.

17.   *Ibid.*, p. 168. Stone describes Russian infantry burning telegraph poles to cook their meals, so one can understand why the artillerymen could get irritated.

18.   There are numerous sources on the Gallipoli campaign but the continuing controversy means that most have to be approached with considerable caution. Among the most useful works are Tim Travers, *Gallipoli 1915* (London, History Press, 2001); Erickson, *Ordered to Die*; and John Lee, *A Soldier's Life: General Sir Ian Hamilton 1853–1947* (London, Pan Books, 2000). L.A. Carlyon, *Gallipoli* (Doubleday, 2002) is a very worthy and readable example of narrative history that fails to recognise the technical challenges of the campaign faced by commanders on both sides.

19.   Erickson, *Ordered to Die*, pp. 78–9.

20. Travers, *Gallipoli 1915*, p. 27.
21. Ross Anderson, 'The Battle of Tanga, 2–5 November 1914', *War In History*, vol. 8 (2001), pp. 294–322 is the best recent coverage.
22. Lee, *A Soldier's Life*, pp. 152, 187. See A.J. Barker, *The First Iraq War 1914–1918* (Enigma, 2009), pp. 387–8.
23. Travers, *Gallipoli 1915*, pp. 226–7.
24. *Ibid.*, p. 93.
25. William Birdwood, *Khaki and Gown: an Autobiography* (Ward Lock, 1941), p. 258.
26. Lee, *A Soldier's Life*, pp. 167–201. Only 18,500 rounds were fired during the Second Battle of Krithia. Hamilton requested 300,000 rounds a month of 18-pounder and 30,000 rounds of 4.5-inch, with half being high explosive, over the summer but was informed that this was impossible; he was not even told how much ammunition he would actually receive, thus preventing the MEF from planning effectively. Even when shells did arrive, the fuse keys turned out to be on a different ship! Travers, *Gallipoli 1915*, pp. 226–8. Travers suggests there were 102 Allied guns.
27. Travers, *Gallipoli 1915*, p. 128.
28. Lee, *A Soldier's Life*, pp. 137–225. Travers, *Gallipoli 1915*, pp. 226–8, suggests that the complaints about the quantities of artillery only arose after the war but this is contradicted by contemporary letters and notes by a number of officers, including Hamilton and Stopford – although they were entirely correct to criticise the inability of planners, on both sides, who failed to recognise the difficulties created by the complex terrain. See also Birdwood, *Khaki and Gown*, pp. 267, 280, who notes that some of the guns received were elderly and inaccurate.
29. Erickson, *Ordered to Die*, pp. 88–9. Lee, *A Soldier's Life*, p. 182. The arrival of German specialist engineers helped.
30. Lee, *A Soldier's Life*, pp. 183, 192. One French barrage, made by 75s, inflicted 7,000 casualties on 22 June.
31. Travers, *Gallipoli 1915*, pp. 132–7.
32. *Ibid.*, pp. 154–60.
33. *Ibid.*, p. 216, quoting Captain Drury.
34. *Ibid.*, p. 234. Travers notes how Allied soldiers saw rapid improvements in Turkish gunnery.
35. Birdwood, *Khaki and Gown*, p. 296. A disgusted Kemal remarked to a colleague after the war, 'Had I been there, and the British had got away without loss, as they did, I would have blown out my brains.'
36. Lucas, *The Evolution of Tactical Ideas*, p. 40.
37. *Ibid.*, pp. 37–8; Bruce Gudmundsson, *Stormtroop Tactics: Innovation in the German Army, 1914-1918* (Praeger, 1995), pp. 193–6. Gudmundsson assumes no link between French ideas and German innovations but it is

extremely difficult to imagine the Germans ignoring confirmation of their own ideas! See also Hogue, 'Puissance de Feu', pp. 44–6.

38. Anon, *French Trench Artillery, Tactical Notebook* (Quantico, Institute for Tactical Education), vol. I (10/91–9/92). Innovations such as the *Lance-mines Gatard* and the *Cellerier Mortar* eventually led to the workmanlike and effective '58 T', also called the *appareil Duchêsne*. There were 75 batteries of the latter by June 1915.

39. Lucas, *The Evolution of Tactical Ideas*, p. 42.

40. *Ibid.*, p. 44, quoting an amended GQG report of 26 May 1915.

41. *Ibid.*, pp. 46–9.

42. Ian F.W. Beckett, *The Great War: 1914–1918* (London, Longman, 2001), p. 167.

43. Efisio Luigi Marras, *Evolution of the Employment of Artillery in the World War*, trans. US Military Attaché in Rome for the Office of the Chief of Artillery (Army Military History Institute, 1924). They were based on German ideas and focused on the artillery 'overpowering' the enemy batteries.

44. James F. Gentsch in his chapter, 'General Luigi Cadorna: Italy and the First World War', in Matthew Seligmann (ed.), *Leadership in Conflict 1914–1918* (Leo Cooper, 2000), attempts a spirited defence but Cadorna appears to be one of the genuine donkeys of the Great War.

45. Marras, *Evolution of the Employment of Artillery*, pp. 5, 14. There were also fourteen super-heavy guns of obsolete design.

46. Laura Bobbio and Stefano Illing (eds), *The Great War on the Little Lagazuoi*, trans. Paolo Giacomel and Robert Striffler (Cortina d'Ampezzo, Belluno, Italy, 1998).

47. Archduke Eugen later noted that 'Rock splinters and fragments caused by heavy shells striking frequently causes far more serious wounds than the shells themselves, since the rock splinters are razor-sharp and frequently carry dirt into the wounds they inflict.' See also John R. Schindler, *Isonzo: The Forgotten Sacrifice of the Great War* (Greenwood, 2001), p. 181; Hugh Dalton, *With the British Guns in Italy* (London, Leonaur, 2007), p. 140.

48. Marras, *Evolution of the Employment of Artillery*, p. 15.

49. Schindler, *Isonzo*, p. 67.

50. *Ibid.*, p. 75, 2 August 1915. See also p. 100.

51. *Ibid.*, p. 69. The 20th *Honvéd* on 20 July 1915 on Mont San Michele.

52. Gentsch notes Cadorna's support for expanding this system, including *teleferiche* railways.

53. Schindler, *Isonzo*, p. 98. In one case the supporting artillery blew away the only cover.

54. Lucas, *The Evolution of Tactical Ideas*, p. 52.

55. *Ibid.*, pp. 51–3.

56. *Ibid.*, p. 52.

57. James Marshall-Cornwell, *Foch as Military Commander* (London, Batsford, 1972), pp. 178–9.

58. Hogue, 'Puissance de Feu', p. 48.

59. *Ibid.*, p. 52. The creeping barrage is best outlined in J.B.A. Bailey, *Field Artillery and Firepower* (Naval Institute Press, 2004). The concept evolved over time with improvements to the profile of the lifts – improving from a straight line to one that conformed to the defensive being attacked. Creeping barrages could advance over the target area or 'pile up' on top of the target. Creeping barrages could also move along the defence system or sweep areas diagonally.

60. Lucas, *The Evolution of Tactical Ideas*, pp. 55–7.

61. Loos is covered in C.R.M.F. Cruttwell, A history of the great war, 1914-1918 (Oxford, 1936), pp. 161–3, Doughty, *Pyrrhic Victory*, pp. 176–82, Bidwell and Graham, *Firepower*, pp. 77–9, Farndale, History of the Royal Regiment of Artillery, Western Front 1914–1918, pp. 116–27, Prior and Wilson, Command on the western front : the military career of Sir Henry Rawlinson, 1914–18, pp. 100–34, Marble, *'The Infantry Cannot Do with a Gun Less'*, pp. 63–6, 122–3, 162 and 251–4. There are also two recent books about this battle: Nick Lloyd, *Loos 1915* (Tempus, 2006), has events and analysis, while Niall Cherry, *Most Unfavourable Ground: the Battle of Loos, 1915* (Helion, 2005), has more fine detail but little analysis.

62. The only book that deals specifically with this campaign is C.E.J. Fryer, *The Destruction of Serbia in 1915* (New York, 1997).

Chapter Three

1. Lucas, *The Evolution of Tactical Ideas*, p. 71. In a sense Verdun was to the Germans in the Great War what Stalingrad would be a generation later. Joffre certainly expected that the city's symbolism warranted a German attack but was surprised by the scale of the offensive. Doughty, *Pyrrhic Victory*, pp. 260–4.

2. Particularly one created by Vauban and improved by Seré de Rivières!

3. Lucas, *The Evolution of Tactical Ideas*, p. 72. Orders for the 10th Bavarian Division noted 'the construction of special assault positions [is] not necessary; such positions serve only to attract the attention of the adversary, and it is impossible, in a very short time, to fortify them sufficiently to give troops protection from a systematic bombardment'.

4. Horne, *The Price of Glory*, p. 54.

5. Malcolm Brown, *Verdun: 1916* (Tempus, 2000), p. 46. The 20th Bavarian Brigade's orders noted 'To determine whether a position is ripe for the assault, intervals of time must be left in the last "fire for effects", reconnaissances are conducted in these openings . . . The infantry should blame nobody

but itself if the position has not been effectively and completely bombarded.'
Lucas, *The Evolution of Tactical Ideas*, p. 74.

6. William Philpott, *Bloody Victory: The Sacrifice on the Somme and the Making of the Twentieth Century* (London, Little Brown, 2009), p. 88.
7. Lucas, *The Evolution of Tactical Ideas*, p. 73.
8. Philpott, *Bloody Victory*, p. 114.
9. Brown, *Verdun: 1916*, pp. 45–6.
10. Lucas, *The Evolution of Tactical Ideas*, p. 79.
11. Doughty, *Pyrrhic Victory*, p. 276.
12. *Ibid.*, p. 274.
13. Clayton, *Paths of Glory*, p. 122.
14. Brown, *Verdun: 1916*, pp. 14–15.
15. Hogue, 'Puissance de Feu', p. 65: 'Instruction sur l'emploi de l'artillerie loude dans la défensive'.
16. *Ibid.*, p. 65. The number of infantry regiments fell from 489 to 368 by 1918.
17. Horne, *The Price of Glory*, p. 145.
18. *Ibid.*, p. 153.
19. Brown, *Verdun: 1916*, p. 76, quoting a sergeant of the 24th Infantry Regiment.
20. Bruce, *Pétain: Verdun to Vichy*, p. 40.
21. Doughty, *Pyrrhic Victory*, pp. 277–8. Pétain estimated that it took 8 to 10 days before a division was worn out.
22. *Ibid.*, p. 286.
23. Horne, *The Price of Glory*, p. 308; Doughty, *Pyrrhic Victory*, pp. 286–90. Previous attempts had failed due to counter-preparatory fire and defensive barrages.
24. Horne, *The Price of Glory*, p. 311.
25. Hogue, 'Puissance de Feu', p. 68.
26. Horne, *The Price of Glory*, p. 310.
27. *Ibid.*, p. 311.
28. *Ibid.*, p. 313.
29. *Ibid.*, pp. 314–18. The 10th Division famously advanced into the line bleating like sheep going to the slaughterhouse and the *Voie Sacrée* was briefly renamed *Le Chemin de l'Abattoir* by an enterprising graffiti artist. See also Lucas, *The Evolution of Tactical Ideas*, p. 77. Lucas estimates that 30 per cent of the German batteries were destroyed and 40 per cent silenced by the counter-battery fire-plan. Doughty, *Pyrrhic Victory*, pp. 306–8.
30. Hogue, 'Puissance de Feu', pp. 77–8. Hogue plausibly suggests that Tim Travers' concept of 'group think' applies to the French army before the Great War.
31. The literature on the Somme is vast, and only sources used here will be mentioned. Prior and Wilson, *Command on the Western Front*, has a lengthy

section, pp. 137–259. The same authors' *The Somme* (New Haven, 2005) is also excellent. Jack Sheldon, *The German Army on the Somme, 1914–1916* (Pen & Sword, 2005) comprises mainly individual German accounts. Christopher Duffy, *Through German Eyes: The British and the Somme* (Weidenfeld & Nicholson, 2006) mines the archives to a greater extent than Sheldon. Comments on the French come from Doughty, *Pyrrhic Victory*. Marble, *'The Infantry Cannot Do with a Gun Less'*, covers the battle in various sections, and Farndale, *Western Front 1914–18*, pp. 141–57, is the regimental history. Much of the analysis of the Germans presented here is drawn from primary sources that are available on-line, including *Notes On Recent Operations* (captured documents printed by the US General Staff, Washington, DC, 1917), www.archive.org/details/notesonrecentope00unitrich and *German and Austrian Tactical Studies* (captured documents printed by the US General Staff, Washington, DC, 1918), www.archive.org/detailsgermanaus trianta00germiala. The most interesting recent volume is Philpott, *Bloody Victory*, which is the first to combine the perspectives of all sides and promises to be the standard work for some time to come.

32. Numerous German accounts show a terror of being buried alive; a typical one is in Sheldon, *German Army on the Somme*, pp. 133–4.

33. See Sheldon, *German Army on the Somme*, pp. 80–82, for a German document about the lessons of 1915.

34. Neil Fraser-Tytler, *Field Guns in France* (Hutchinson, 1922), pp. 75–80, has a lengthy account.

35. Philpott, *Bloody Victory*, p. 235. Philpott notes that the 7th Division copied the concept from the French.

36. Quoted in Ian Passingham, *All The Kaiser's Men, The Life and Death of the German Army on the Western Front 1914–1918* (History Press, 2005), p. 107.

37. Duffy, *Through German Eyes*, pp. 313–19, has several accounts.

38. *German and Austrian Tactical Studies*.

39. Prior and Wilson, *The Somme*, esp. pp. 112–15.

40. Philpott, *Bloody Victory*, p. 147. Philpott reveals that Colonel Herring was Brooke's French source for the approach. There were 35 lifts, travelling at 50 yards every 90 seconds, instead of one lift for each defensive line.

41. Quoted in Sheldon, *German Army on the Somme*, p. 185.

42. Herwig, *The First World War*, p. 204.

43. Quoted in Duffy, *Through German Eyes*, p. 208.

44. Fraser-Tytler, *Field Guns in France*, p. 93.

45. Robert Asprey, *The German High Command At War: Hindenburg and Ludendorff and the First World War* (New York, 1991), p. 269.

46. Quoted in Duffy, *Through German Eyes*, p. 215. The barrage was twice as concentrated as that on 1 July but only half as heavy as that on 14 July.

47. Fraser-Tytler, *Field Guns in France,* pp. 106–7.

48. Quoted in Passingham, *All The Kaiser's Men,* p. 123.

49. *Notes on Recent Operations,* pp. 8–9.

50. Quoted in Sheldon, *German Army on the Somme,* p. 292.

51. Quoted in Duffy, *Through German Eyes,* p. 255.

52. Fraser-Tytler, *Field Guns in France,* p. 115.

53. Philpott, Bloody Victory, pp. 265, 418. Sir John French was sent to review French artillery practices.

54. *Notes on Recent Operations,* pp. 24–32, contains a German order (over Hindenburg's signature) about the lessons of Verdun.

55. See G.C. Wynne, *If Germany Attacks* (Faber, 1940) and Timothy Lupfer, *Dynamics of Doctrine: the changes in German tactical doctrine during the First World War* (Kansas, Fort Leavenworth, 1981), also several parts of *Notes on Recent Operations* and *German and Austrian Tactical Studies.* Philpott, *Bloody Victory,* p. 253, quotes an artillery officer during the Battle of the Somme: 'The shape of the ground is so much in favour of the Germans, there is not a single point hereabouts in our possession whence we can see their country.'

56. Philpott, *Bloody Victory,* pp. 245–7. The Australians experienced this tactic at first hand at Pozières after they drove off a series of counter-attacks on 23 July 1916.

57. Lucas, *The Evolution of Tactical Ideas,* p. 84.

58. Philpott, *Bloody Victory,* p. 226.

59. *Ibid.,* p. 438.

60. *Ibid.,* p. 112. Even in 1914 Fayolle remarked, 'I attack with the greatest care, with all the artillery and fewest infantry possible.' Philpott (p. 224) suggests that Fayolle was perhaps too methodical at times.

61. Doughty, *Pyrrhic Victory,* p. 291. The actual casualties suffered by the French on the Somme were 202,000.

62. Lucas, *The Evolution of Tactical Ideas,* p. 82; Fayolle, commenting on 8 June 1916, and Foch on 20 April 1916. Foch, commanding the Army Group North, added that surprise, momentum and concentration of fire were vital in any plan to reach the second position – an aspiration that was to prove unrealistic when the overall doctrine still stressed the methodical approach.

63. Philpott, *Bloody Victory,* pp. 117, 145. Army Group North's briefing ran to 82 pages.

64. Gudmundsson, *On Artillery,* pp. 81–2; see Philpott, *Bloody Victory,* p. 133, for Foch's shopping list for the Somme battle.

65. Philpott, *Bloody Victory,* pp. 142, 270. Each French corps had a squadron assigned to it and each artillery regiment had a half squadron.

66. Lucas, *The Evolution of Tactical Ideas,* p. 85. Lucas claims that only 116 were quick-firing.

67. Philpott, *Bloody Victory*, pp. 205, 225, 241.
68. Elizabeth Greenhalgh, 'The Experience of Fighting with Allies: The Case of the Capture of Falfemont Farm during the Battle of the Somme, 1916', *War In History*, vol. 10 (2003), pp. 157–83; Doughty, *Pyrrhic Victory*, pp. 294–5.
69. Philpott, *Bloody Victory*, pp. 352–6, 377.
70. *Ibid.*, p. 220. Henry Wilson noted in his diary that 'Foch and Weygand can well be proud of themselves'.
71. Quoted in Lucas, *The Evolution of Tactical Ideas*, p. 86.
72. Doughty, *Pyrrhic Victory*, p. 306.
73. Lucas, *The Evolution of Tactical Ideas*, pp. 86–7.
74. Philpott, *Bloody Victory*, p. 348. These heavy guns were increasingly moved into position by caterpillar-tracked vehicles.
75. Lucas, *The Evolution of Tactical Ideas*, pp. 88–91.
76. Philpott, *Bloody Victory*, pp. 129, 258, 267. Fayolle concurred with Foch on the key elements but found his overenthusiastic Gascon colleague exasperating! Doughty, *Pyrrhic Victory*, p. 218.
77. Doughty, *Pyrrhic Victory*, p. 296.
78. Cornish, *The Russian Army and the First World War*, p. 99. Evert and Kuropatkin both opposed the idea of any major offensive on this basis.
79. Stone, *The Eastern Front*, p. 237.
80. Dowling, *The Brusilov Offensive*, pp. 42–3.
81. Stone, *The Eastern Front*, p. 234.
82. *Ibid.*, p. 249. Some units tunnelled under their own wire instead of removing the wire during the night to conceal their final preparations.
83. Cornish, *The Russian Army and the First World War*, p. 104.
84. Chris Bellamy, *Red God of War: Soviet Artillery and Rocket Forces* (Brassey's, 1986), pp. 36–43.
85. Cornish, *The Russian Army and the First World War*, p. 104.
86. Graydon A. Tunstall, 'Austria-Hungary and the Brusilov Offensive of 1916', *The Historian*, vol. 70 (2008), pp. 30–53.
87. Tunstall, 'Austria-Hungary and the Brusilov Offensive of 1916', p. 41. Fifteen batteries had been transferred.
88. Dowling, *The Brusilov Offensive*, p. 59.
89. *Ibid.*, pp. 72–3; Cornish, *The Russian Army and the First World War*, pp. 105–6; Tunstall, 'Austria-Hungary and the Brusilov Offensive of 1916', p. 40.
90. Stone, *The Eastern Front*, p. 252.
91. *Ibid.*, p. 240. This unusual burst of initiative followed the realisation that he was attacking the enemy with 'an extremely insignificant quantity of heavy artillery'.
92. *Ibid.*, p. 251.
93. *Ibid.*, p. 242.

94. Dowling, *The Brusilov Offensive*, pp. 42–54, 175.

95. *Ibid.*, p. 171.

96. *Ibid.*, p. 169.

97. Cornish, *The Russian Army and the First World War*, pp. 110–11. Some of the artillery was motorised. The infantry were excellent, with high morale, and the equipment was first rate but the officers, from the army commander downwards, were directly appointed by the Tsar for reasons that rarely included professionalism.

98. Dowling, *The Brusilov Offensive*, p. 100.

99. *Ibid.*, p. 130.

100. Cornish, *The Russian Army and the First World War*, p. 112.

101. Dowling, *The Brusilov Offensive*, p. 146.

102. *Ibid.*, pp. 148–9.

103. Charles Springfield, *Firepower* (Woolwich Arsenal Archive, MD2096), p. 29. Norman Stone notes a scathing remark by a British officer that 'the operations of the Romanian Army would make a public school field day look like the execution of the Schlieffen Plan'.

104. Glenn E. Torrey, 'The Battle of Turtucaia (Tutrakan) (2–6 September 1916): Romania's Grief, Bulgaria's Glory', *East European Quarterly*, XXVII, no. 4 (Winter 2003/4), pp. 379–402.

105. Marras, *Evolution of the Employment of Artillery*.

106. There is an excellent museum and the preserved galleries are open to the public.

107. *New York Times*, 2 July 1916, quoting a cable from the Berliner Tageblatt based on an interview on 30 June conducted by Leonard Adelt.

108. Schindler, *Isonzo*, p. 176.

109. *Ibid.*, p. 179.

110. Archibald H. Moberly, 'Report on B1 Group Heavy Artillery, 1917' (RHAT Archive, Woolwich, 7/1), p. 3.

111. Philpott, *Bloody Victory*, p. 95.

112. *Ibid.*, p. 379.

113. *Ibid.*, p. 271.

Chapter Four

1. Quoted in Passingham, *Pillars of Fire*, xxiii.

2. Millett and Williamson (eds), *Military Effectiveness, Vol. 1: The First World War*, p. 39. Shell production was 0.5 million in 1914; 6 million in 1915; 45 million in 1916; 76 million in 1917; and 67 million in 1918.

3. Curiously little has been written about Arras (although much about Vimy, mainly by Canadians). This section relies on Marble, *'The Infantry Cannot Do with a Gun Less'*, and Wynne, *If Germany Attacks*. Jack Sheldon, *The*

German Army on Vimy Ridge 1914–1917 (Pen & Sword, 2008), is excellent on that section of the battle.

4. Roy MacLeod, 'Sight and Sound on the Western Front: Surveyors, Scientists and the Battlefield Laboratory, 1915–1918', *War & Society*, vol. 18, no. 1 (May 2000), offers a superb summary; William Van der Kloot, 'Lawrence Bragg's role in the development of sound-ranging in World War I', *Notes & Records of the Royal Society*, vol. 59 (2005), pp. 273–84. The Allies were able to coordinate the work of Charles Nordmann, William Tucker, Lucian Bull and Lawrence Bragg, enabling Allied gunners to accurately calculate German battery positions in minutes while the Germans floundered for 'almost an hour'.

5. A number of histories cover this, but this section is largely based on the British General Staff's 'Summary of Recent Information Regarding the German Army and its Methods', January 1917, available at www.archive.org/details/summaryofrecenti00grearich; *German and Austrian Tactical Studies* and *Evolution of the Organisation of the German Artillery During the War*, trans. R.A. Wargin (US Army Military History Institute).

6. Lucas, *The Evolution of Tactical Ideas*, p. 123; *Manual of Position Warfare for All Arms, Part 8, 'The Principles of Command in the Defensive Battle in Position Warfare'*, issued by the Chief of the General Staff in March 1917 and translated by British General Staff (Intelligence) in May 1917.

7. Sheldon, *The German Army on Vimy Ridge*, pp. 252–3, 256, 260–1, 267.

8. Major von Dittelsbach, I/1st Bavarian Reserve Infantry Regiment, quoted in Sheldon, *The German Army on Vimy Ridge*, p. 273.

9. Sheldon, *The German Army on Vimy Ridge*, pp. 340–1.

10. Doughty, *Pyrrhic Victory*, pp. 324–5.

11. Clayton, *Paths of Glory*, p. 105.

12. Doughty, *Pyrrhic Victory*, p. 330.

13. Lucas, *The Evolution of Tactical Ideas*, p. 101.

14. Doughty, *Pyrrhic Victory*, pp. 350–1, quoting the CO of II Colonial Corps.

15. *Ibid.*, pp. 338–9, 342–3, 348. A number of senior French commanders had concerns. The French fired 11 million shells in the offensives, of which 2.5 million were heavy.

16. Clayton, *Paths of Glory*, pp. 133–40.

17. *Ibid.*, p. 142. One cry was that 'l'artillerie nous tire dans le dos' ('the artillery shoots us in the back').

18. *Ibid.*, p. 148.

19. Doughty, *Pyrrhic Victory*, p. 366.

20. *Ibid.*, pp. 369–70.

21. See 'The Battle of Malmaison (23 October 1917) as seen by the Germans', in *German and Austrian Tactical Studies*, pp. 193–202, for a French assessment

based on interrogations and captured documents. Available at www.archive.org/details/germanaustrianta00germiala.

22. Doughty, *Pyrrhic Victory*, pp. 387–9.

23. Lucas, *The Evolution of Tactical Ideas*, p. 114.

24. This section draws heavily on Ian Passingham, *Pillars of Fire: The Battle of Messines Ridge, June 1917* (Sutton, 1998) and Marble, '*The Infantry Cannot Do with a Gun Less*'.

25. WO106/399 at the National Archives, Kew, has the 42-page Canadian Corps artillery plan.

26. Quoted in Passingham, *Pillars of Fire*, p. 94.

27. There is an immense literature on Passchendaele. This section draws on Robin Prior and Trevor Wilson, *Passchendaele: The untold story* (Yale, 1996); Marble, '*The Infantry Cannot Do with a Gun Less*', pp. 97–102, 139–42, 176–8; Farndale, *Western Front*, pp. 195–214; and several of the chapters in Peter Liddle (ed.), *Passchendaele in Perspective: The Third Battle of Ypres* (Leo Cooper, 1997).

28. It is possible that some of the venom apparent in his memoirs is due to reflecting on his own pusillanimity.

29. Quoted in Ian Beckett, 'The Plans and Conduct of Battle', in Liddle (ed.), *Passchendaele in Perspective*, p. 107.

30. Peter Oldham, *Pillboxes on the Western Front: a guide to the design, construction and use of concrete pillboxes 1914–1918* (Leo Cooper, 1995), is the best book on the subject so far.

31. Herwig, *The First World War*, p. 331.

32. Quoted in Asprey, *The German High Command at War*, p. 336.

33. *The War Diary of the Master of Belhaven*, by Lt-Col. Ralph Hamilton, quoted in Farndale, History of the Royal Regiment of Artillery: Western Front 1914–18, p. 201.

34. Quoted in Passingham, *All the Kaiser's Men*, p. 177.

35. Allain Bernede, 'Third Ypres and the Restoration of Confidence in the Ranks of the French Army', in Liddle (ed.), *Passchendaele in Perspective*, p. 91.

36. R.B. Talbot-Kelly, *A Subaltern's Odyssey* (London, 1980), cited in Johnson, *Stalemate*, p. 145.

37. 'Accompanying and Infantry Batteries, German Army', *Field Artillery Journal* (July–September 1918), pp. 422–6.

38. Robert Foley, 'The Other Side of the Wire: The German Army in 1917', in Peter Dennis and Jeffrey Grey (eds), *1917: Tactics, Training, and Technology* (Australian History Military Publications, 2007), pp. 173–5.

39. On Lens, see Marble, '*The Infantry Cannot Do with a Gun Less*', pp. 101–2.

40. Quoted in Farndale, *History of the Royal Regiment of Artillery: Western Front 1914–18*, p. 205.

41. Quoted in *The Economist*, 19 December 2009, p. 94.

42. Heinz Hagenlucke, 'The German High Command', in Liddle (ed.), *Passchendaele in Perspective*, p. 53.

43. Peter Liddle, 'Passchendaele Experienced: Soldiering in the Salient during the Third Battle of Ypres', in Liddle (ed.), *Passchendaele in Perspective*, p. 307.

44. Quoted in Prior and Wilson, *Passchendaele*, p. 180.

45. Lucas, *The Evolution of Tactical Ideas*, p. 117.

46. *Ibid.*, p. 124.

47. *Ibid.*, pp. 121–2, quoting the 1918 regulations on the defence in position warfare.

48. Clayton, *Paths of Glory*, p. 152.

49. This operation is beautifully described in David T. Zabecki, *Steel Wind: Colonel Georg Bruchmüller and the Birth of Modern Artillery* (Preager, 1994), p. 24.

50. Zabecki, *Steel Wind*, p. 24.

51. *Ibid.*, pp. 21–5.

52. Springfield, *Firepower*, pp. 1–27. Springfield described his interpreter as 'a very nasty piece of work'. General Poole warned him not to trust the Russians, noting that 'everyone in this country, from a grand duke downwards, has his price. You may find people trying to bribe you to do or get something they want. The one thing in the English reputation is that we are not bribe-able – foster that reputation.'

53. *Ibid.*, pp. 1–27.

54. Headlam, 'Headlam Papers'. See also papers in the Liddell Hart Centre for Military Archives.

55. Cornish, *The Russian Army and the First World War*, pp. 227–34.

56. MacLeod, 'Sight and Sound on the Western Front', pp. 23–46.

57. Bryn Hammond, *Cambrai 1917: The Myth of the First Great Tank Battle* (Weidenfeld & Nicholson, 2008), pp. 57–8.

58. Hammond, *Cambrai 1917*, p. 111.

59. *Ibid.*, p. 326.

60. Georg Bruchmüller, *Die Deutsche Artillerie in den Durchbruchschlachten des Weltkrieges* (Berlin, Mittler & Son, 1922), p. 90. XX*III Korps* included a number of veterans from the Eastern Front.

61. Jack Sheldon, *The German Army at Cambrai* (Pen & Sword, 2009), pp. 207–8.

62. Hammond, *Cambrai 1917*, p. 362.

63. Sheldon, *The German Army at Cambrai*, p. 258.

64. Hammond, *Cambrai 1917*, p. 373.

65. Sheldon, *The German Army at Cambrai*, p. 219.

66. A.H. Maude, *The 47th (London) Division 1914–1919* (London, 1922), cited in Johnson, *Stalemate*, p. 193.

67. Lucas, *The Evolution of Tactical Ideas*, pp. 121–2, quoting the 1918 regulations on the defence in position warfare.

68. *Ibid.*, p. 121.

69. Mark Thompson, *The White War. Life and Death on the Italian Front, 1915–1919* (Faber & Faber, 2008), p. 245. The total was 52 new field batteries, 44 mountain batteries and 166 heavy batteries.

70. Schindler, *Isonzo*, p. 202.

71. *Ibid.*, p. 202.

72. The rugged terrain meant that specialist assault troops were essential for making and exploiting breakthroughs; during 1917 the Austrians had created *Sturmtruppen* battalions and the Italians *Reparto d'Assalto*, better known as the *Arditi* or the *Fiamme Nere* ('black flames', due to the feathers on their hats). These units were full-strength elite infantry battalions with generous allocations of support weapons and their own artillery support, and the Austrians were particularly skilled at using these elite troops in counter-attacks.

73. Thompson, *The White War*, p. 260.

74. *Ibid.*, rightly dedicates an entire chapter to Cadorna's wilfully counter-productive policy of decimation.

75. *Ibid.*, p. 277. Even with this disparity in firepower and the challenging terrain, some critics also suggested that Cadorna still did not understand how to mass his guns effectively; Fortunato Marazzi, a former divisional commander, was one of these critics.

76. *Ibid.*, p. 282.

77. Dalton, *With the British Guns*, pp. 139, 179. The rates of fire were *lento, normale, vivace, celere* and *double vivace*.

78. *Ibid.*, p. 142.

79. In contrast to the Italian artillery units, the British attempted to establish close liaison with nearby infantry units and regularly monitored developments in their sector. As a result few of the local infantry used the common term of abuse, *imboscato* ('risk avoider'), to describe the RA.

80. Thompson, *The White War*, pp. 299–301.

81. Erwin Rommel, *Infantry Attacks* (Greenhill, 1995), pp. 195, 205.

82. *Ibid.*, pp. 169–72, 183.

83. *Ibid.*, p. 178. Rommel's detachment captured seventeen guns, including twelve heavies.

84. *Ibid.*, p. 219.

85. *Ibid.*, pp. 186–93.

86. Sheldon, *The German Army at Cambrai*, p. 304.

87. MacLeod, 'Sight and Sound on the Western Front', pp. 23–46.

Chapter Five

1. Lupfer, *The Dynamics of Doctrine*. A number of senior officers believed that accurate firing was only possible with registration but Ludendorff recognised

that the British lead in 'map firing' could be matched by similar advances in German gunnery.

2. The literature on the Kaiserschlacht is substantial. The most important here are Zabecki, *Steel Wind*, especially pp. 42–56, 67–78; Zabecki, *The German 1918 Offensives: A case study in the operational level of war* (Routledge, 2006) takes a wider and deeper look. Martin Kitchen, *The German Offensives of 1918* (Tempus, 2001) is a good summary. Farndale, *History of the Royal Regiment of Artillery: Western Front 1914–18*, covers the March fighting on pp. 259–79, Marble, *'The Infantry Cannot Do with a Gun Less'*, pp. 202–10. Martin Middlebrook, *The Kaiser's Battle. 21 March 1918: The First Day of the German Spring Offensive* (London, Penguin, 1983) has some background and covers the first day with many personal accounts.

3. Quoted in Zabecki, *German 1918 Offensives*, p. 108.

4. Zabecki, *German 1918 Offensives*, p. 135.

5. The Allies would capture documents about this through the year and published 'The Scientific Preparation of Fire in the German Artillery', *Field Artillery Journal* (October–December 1918), pp. 527–34.

6. Zabecki, *German 1918 Offensives*, p. 46.

7. *Ibid.*, p. 70. Lucas, *The Evolution of Tactical Ideas*, pp. 133–5, 155, discusses German artillery doctrine changes for this period.

8. See 'Current Notes – Barrage' and 'Organization of a Rolling Barrage in the German Army', *Field Artillery Journal* (July–September 1918), pp. 439–41, 417–21, for details on some *feuerwalze*.

9. Von Berendt had far more Western Front experience, and had also planned artillery support at Caporetto.

10. See 'Measures Taken by the German Artillery to carry out preparations for attack without betraying the intentions of the command', *Field Artillery Journal* (October–December 1918), pp. 504–12; 'German Precautions to Disguise Intentions', *Field Artillery Journal* (October–December 1918), pp. 553–9; and Zabecki, *German 1918 Offensives*, pp. 125–6.

11. 'Attack in Position Warfare' noted that 'this mission is the most important and the most difficult during the breakthrough. The artillery that has taken part in the preparation of the initial breakthrough can only be partially charged with this mission. An additional and mobile force of artillery must be available.' Lucas, *The Evolution of Tactical Ideas*, p. 155. On 20 April Ludendorff summarised the role of the artillery as 1. counter-battery fire, 2. bombardment and 3. harassing fire, including gas shelling. 'Accurate firing has much greater value than firing a great number of projectiles. The most important objectives are living objectives, and full consideration must be given to good observation. An automatic and non-observed fire, fired in response to a signal from our infantry, cannot be considered. Such fire cannot be put down in an unbroken line and without gaps over the whole front of

our infantry, as was done in the old barrage; it must be concentrated upon the zones which the enemy occupies when the fire is opened. Counter-preparation fire, which is opened at a tactically opportune time in response to a definite order, fires which are well adjusted and observed, are of greater benefit to the infantry.'

12. Herbert Sulzbach, *With the German Guns: Four Years on the Western Front, 1914–1918*, trans. Richards Thonger (Pen & Sword, 2003), pp. 148–9.
13. Ernst Junger, *Storm of Steel* (Penguin, 2003), p. 243.
14. Middlebrook, *The Kaiser's Battle*, p. 108, gives more details.
15. Quoted in Middlebrook, *The Kaiser's Battle*, p. 138.
16. Arthur Behrend, *As From Kemmel Hill: An Adjutant in France and Flanders* (Eyre & Spottiswoode, 1963), p. 63.
17. Sources for the British are W.H.F. Weber's excellent series of articles headed 'Being a Tactical Study of the Field Artillery Group in Retreat', published in the *Field Artillery Journal:* (May–June 1920), pp. 243–72; (July–August 1920), pp. 382–401; (September–October 1920), pp. 501–21; (November–December 1920), pp. 567–98; and (January–February 1921), pp. 27–48.
18. Quoted in Middlebrook, *The Kaiser's Battle*, p. 147.
19. Quoted in Middlebrook, *The Kaiser's Battle*, p. 151.
20. Quoted in Middlebrook, *The Kaiser's Battle*, p. 225.
21. Farndale's history of the battle, *History of the Royal Regiment of Artillery: Western Front 1914–18*, is largely gallant stories; this one is from p. 264.
22. Quoted in Kitchen, *The German Offensives of 1918*, p. 77.
23. Zabecki, *German 1918 Offensives*, p. 151.
24. Sulzbach, *With the German Guns*, pp. 150–60, covers this period.
25. Lucas, *The Evolution of Tactical Ideas*, pp. 132–3.
26. Hindenburg, *Out of My Life* (London, 1920), pp. 350, 357.
27. Quoted in Michael Neiberg, *The Second Battle of the Marne* (Indiana University Press, 2008), p. 67. Jünger's unit was facing one of the two British divisions in a mainly French sector.
28. Sulzbach, *With the German Guns*, pp. 197–203.
29. Pétain disagreed and wanted to continue to conduct only limited operations after the Germans were contained.
30. Doughty, *Pyrrhic Victory*, p. 425.
31. Lucas, *The Evolution of Tactical Ideas*, p. 148.
32. The *minenwerfers* bombarded the front-line positions while the rest of the artillery fired a sophisticated *feuerwalze* across the entire defensive system immediately preceding the attack and in support of infantry when targets were identified by forward observers. In theory, even the creeping barrage would be partly 'subordinated to the infantry' using signals to control its progress, if required, once it penetrated 3 to 4 kilometres into the defensive

system (the attack on 15 July was regulated up to 9 kilometres into the French defences).

33. See Neiberg, *The Second Battle of the Marne*.
34. Ludendorff dismissively noted that 'the tank is easy prey for guns of all calibres', including *minenwerfers*.
35. Lucas, *The Evolution of Tactical Ideas*, p. 150.
36. *Ibid.*, pp. 132–3, discusses this for the French; an example of British lessons is at http://www.gutenberg-e.org/mas01/archive/app33.html, or see IWM Misc 9 (181), War Diary of Eagle Troop RHA, 24th Division, 21–30 March 1918.
37. Foch, *Memoirs*, pp. 348–50; Lucas, *The Evolution of Tactical Ideas*, p. 154.
38. This period is covered in several general histories of the war, and there are several books on Amiens and some attention to the breaking of the Hindenburg Line, but the best coverage of the whole period is Paul Harris (with Niall Barr), *Amiens to the Armistice: The BEF in the Hundred Days' Campaign, 8 August–11 November 1918* (Brassey's, 2003). Marble, *'The Infantry Cannot Do with a Gun Less'*, covers these operations on pp. 107–11, 148–51, 182–9. Farndale, *History of the Royal Regiment of Artillery: Western Front 1914–18*, covers this period on pp. 287–99.
39. 'Notes on Tactical Organisation of German Artillery', *Field Artillery Journal* (July–September 1918), pp. 432–5.
40. Sulzbach, *With the German Guns*, p. 223.
41. Two articles on German artillery measures in late 1918 are 'Action of the Artillery in Battle' and 'Artillery Fire of Protection', both reprinted in *Field Artillery Journal* (January–March 1919), pp. 99–106.
42. Sulzbach, *With the German Guns*, p. 224, et seq. for some details.
43. Farndale, *History of the Royal Regiment of Artillery: Western Front 1914–18*, pp. 292–3, describes the Fourth Army's methods at this period. W.H.F. Weber, 'A Field Artillery Group in the General Advance', *Field Artillery Journal* (January–February 1923), pp. 41–60, gives a brigade's view from 13–30 September, while Part II, with the same title, *Field Artillery Journal* (March–April 1923), pp. 99–129, covers 5 October–11 November. Available online at http://sill-www.army.mil/FAMAG/archives.htm.
44. This refers to an Australian attack on 18 September around Epehy, quoted in Farndale, *History of the Royal Regiment of Artillery: Western Front 1914–18*, p. 297.
45. Quoted in Marble, *'The Infantry Cannot Do with a Gun Less'*, p. 188.
46. Weber, 'A Field Artillery Group in the General Advance', part I, p. 57.
47. The whole report is in Marble, http://www.gutenberg-e.org/mas01/archive/app35.html.
48. 'The Principles of Command in Defensive Battle', reprinted in *Field Artillery Journal* (January–March 1919), pp. 89–95.

49. It was 'Forces' because command of troops sent to Murmansk was also put under Pershing. While it is now rather dated, the best overview of the American war effort is Edward Coffman, *The War to End All Wars: The American Military Experience in World War I* (Oxford University Press, 1968). Publications focusing on combat include: Paul Braim, *The Test of Battle: The American Expeditionary Forces in the Meuse–Argonne Campaign*, 2nd edn (White Mane Books, 1998); Mark Grotelueschen, *The AEF Way of War: The American Army and Combat in World War I* (Cambridge, 2006); idem, *Doctrine Under Trial: American Artillery Employment in World War I* (Greenwood, 2000); and Boyd Dastrup, *King of Battle: A Branch History of the US Army's Field Artillery* (Fort Monroe, Virginia, 1993), pp. 160–76. A number of articles published in the *Field Artillery Journal* shortly after the war, and a series by Colonel Conrad Lanza through the mid-1930s contain all sorts of details.

50. Dastrup, *King of Battle*, p. 165, and Coffman, *The War to End All Wars*, pp. 40–2 cover this. See also ch. 6 of Leonard Ayres, *The War With Germany: A Statistical Summary* (Washington, DC, 1919) – available at www.archive.org/details/warwithgermanyst00unit – for as positive a view as the US Army could put together.

51. The Report of the Chief of Field Artillery to the Secretary of War, 1919 (Washington, DC, 1919) is surprisingly honest and critical for a published government report.

52. Quoted in Grotelueschen, *Doctrine Under Trial*, p. 23.

53. *Artillery Operations of the 9th British Corps at Messines, June 1917* (US Army War College edition, August 1917).

54. Discussed in Grotelueschen, *Doctrine Under Trial*, pp. 79–81; 'Pirate Guns' comes from Braim, *The Test of Battle*.

55. Quoted in Braim, *The Test of Battle*, p. 71.

56. Quoted in Braim, *The Test of Battle*, p. 105.

57. Major-General Charles Summerall, quoted in Grotelueschen, *Doctrine Under Trial*, p. 115.

58. Quoted in Braim, *The Test of Battle*, p. 131.

59. Quoted in Grotelueschen, *Doctrine Under Trial*, p. 123. This commander was from one of the most experienced American regiments.

60. William Campsey, 'The Birth of Modern Counter-fire: The British and American Experience in World War I', MA thesis (Fort Leavenworth, Kansas, 1991); http://cgsc.cdmhost.com/cgi-bin/showfile.exe?CISO-ROOT=/p4013coll2&CISOPTR=1338&filename=1339.pdf covers counter-battery work in good detail.

61. Alan Palmer, *The Gardeners of Salonika: The Macedonian Campaign 1915–1918* (New York, 1965); and Alan Wakefield and Simon Moody, *Under the Devil's Eye: Britain's Forgotten Army at Salonika, 1915–1918* (Stroud,

2004) are the main English-language histories. Wakefield and Moody focus on the British, while Palmer's is more a diplomatic and political history than an operational one. Otherwise, relatively little has been written about the campaign. Doughty, *Pyrrhic Victory*, also discusses Allied strategy. Sir Martin Farndale, *History of the Royal Regiment of Artillery: The Forgotten Fronts and the Home Base, 1914–1918* (Woolwich, 1988), has two chapters on Salonika. Sanders is obliged to Mr Wakefield, President of the Salonika Campaign Society, for sending some of the sparse material.

62. The British Official History is unusually candid in discussing material short-comings and problems.

63. On the Bulgarians, War Office, *Military Notes on the Balkan States* (London, 1915) is useful, as are two papers (Holger Afflerbach, 'Greece and the Balkan Area in German Strategy, 1914–1918' and Dimitre Minchev, 'The Bulgarian Army at the Salonica Front') in the compendium *The Salonica Theatre of Operations and the Outcome of the Great War* (Institute for Balkan Studies, Thessaloniki, 2005).

64. Quoted in Alan Wakefield, 'Soldiers of a lesser Tsar: The Bulgarian Armed Forces 1915–1918', part 2.

65. To trace the fighting over the years, see Major Nedeff, 'Operations on the Doiran Front – Macedonia, 1915–1918' (held at the Imperial War Museum). Nedeff was chief of staff of the Bulgarian 9th Division, which held the key Grand Couronne (Devil's Eye) sector.

66. See Richard Hall, 'The Enemy is Behind Us: The Morale Crisis in the Bulgarian Army during the Summer of 1918', *War In History*, vol. 11, no. 2. The same author's *Balkan Breakthrough: The Battle of Dobro Pole, 1918* (Indiana University Press, 2010) was published too late to be consulted.

67. See Paul Cassou, 'The Breaking of the Dobro-Pole Front, Conclusions', trans. Captain J. McBride, US Army (*Revue Militaire General*, 15 May 1923).

68. Quoted in Palmer, *The Gardeners of Salonika*, p. 200.

69. Schindler, *Isonzo*, p. 270. The Habsburg arsenal produced 2,285 pieces in the first six months of 1917 but only 1,296 in the first six months of 1918. Boroević's army was only a third of its paper strength.

70. Cyril Falls, *Caporetto: 1917* (Weidenfeld & Nicholson, 1966), p. 151.

71. Ortner, *The Austro-Hungarian Artillery from 1867 to 1918*, pp. 605–23.

72. Falls, *Caporetto: 1917*, p. 151.

73. Thompson, *The White War*, p. 358.

74. Harris, *Amiens to the Armistice*, covers Valenciennes well, esp. pp. 263–72. J.F.B. Livesay, *Canada's Hundred Days: With the Canadian Corps from Amiens to Mons, Aug. 8–Nov. 11 1918* (Toronto, 1919) is a contemporary account; and the Commonwealth War Graves Commission website has a nice section on the battle. See also Major-General A.G.L. McNaughton (Commander, Heavy Artillery, Canadian Corps for the battle), 'The Capture of

Valenciennes: A Study in Co-Ordination', *Canadian Defence Quarterly,* vol. 10, no. 3 (1933), pp. 279–94. Philip Gibbs' report about Valenciennes made the front page of the *New York Times* on 2 November.

75. McNaughton, 'The Capture of Valenciennes', p. 279.

76. Afterwards one German would tell Gibbs, 'We have been betrayed and that is why we have lost the war.' The idea of the German army failing because of being 'stabbed in the back' at home does not originate in the post-war period.

77. McNaughton was quite proud of his bombardment and noted that for this one action he had fired almost as much shell as during the whole Boer War (1899–1902), vastly more than during Waterloo (37 tons), and more than the Germans at the Battle of Jutland.

78. McNaughton gives 420, but multiple other sources quote 501.

79. Foch, *Memoirs,* p. 202.

80. Bidwell and Graham, *Firepower.* Jeremy Black, *Rethinking Military History* (Routledge, 2004); Albert Palazzo, *Seeking Victory on the Western Front: The British Army and Chemical Warfare in World War One* (Nebraska, 2000).

81. M.C. Ford, 'Operational Research, Military Judgement and the Politics of Technical Change in the British Infantry, 1943–1953', *Journal of Strategic Studies,* vol. 32, issue 6 (December 2009), pp. 871–97.

Bibliography

Primary Sources

Anon, 'The Principles of Command in the Defensive Battle in Position Warfare', Issued by the Chief of the General Staff in March 1917 and translated by British General Staff (Intelligence) in May 1917

Anon, 'Artillery Operations of the 9th British Corps at Messines, June 1917', US Army War College edition (August 1917)

Anon, 'The Attack in Position Warfare', issued by the Chief of the General Staff in January 1918 and translated by British General Staff (Intelligence) in May 1917

Anon, 'German and Austrian Tactical Studies' and 'Evolution of the Organisation of the German Artillery During the War,' trans. R.A. Wargin (US Army Military History Institute, 1931)

Balck, Generalleutnant Wilhelm, *Development of Tactics – World War*, trans. Harry Bell (General Service School's Press, Fort Leavenworth, 1922)

Bates, A.G., *To Ypres for a Haircut, The War Diaries and Letters of Lieutenant A.G. Bates RA* (Winkfield, 2006)

Behrend, Arthur, *As From Kemmel Hill: An Adjutant in France and Flanders* (Eyre & Spottiswoode, 1963)

Birdwood, William, *Khaki and Gown: an Autobiography* (Ward Lock, 1941)

Bruchmüller, Georg, *Die Deutsche Artillerie in den Durchbruchschlachten des Weltkrieges* (Berlin, Mittler & Son, 1922)

Brusilov, Alexei, *A Soldier's Note-Book* (Macmillan, 1930)

Budworth, C.E.D., 'Artillery in Co-operation with Infantry', *Journal of the Royal Artillery*, vol. 37, no. 1 (1910), pp. 1–14.

Canadian Corps artillery plan at the National Archives, Kew (WO106/399)

Dalton, Hugh, *With the British Guns in Italy* (London, Leonaur, 2007)

Elmannsberger, Ludwig, 'The Austro-Hungarian Artillery in the World War', *Coast Artillery Journal*, vol. 62 (1925)

Field Artillery Training 1914 (London, HMSO, 1914)

Foch, Ferdinand, *The Principles of War*, trans. Hilaire Belloc (Paris, 1903; repr. London, Chapman & Hall, 1918)

Foch, Ferdinand, *The Memoirs of Marshal Foch* (London, Windmill, 1931)

François, Hermann von, *Gorlice 1915, The Piercing of the Carpathian Mountains and the Liberation of Galicia*, trans. Alfred R.W. Ronge (US Army Military History Institute, 1931)

Fraser-Tytler, Neil, *Field Guns in France* (Hutchinson, 1922)

Headlam, Sir John, Sir John Headlam Papers (RAHT Archive, Woolwich, MD183)

Helps, G.T., IWM Documents 86/41/1, Training Leaflet no. 6, Hints on Training for Artillery and Brigade Commanders (9/18)

Helps, G.T., IWM Documents 86/41/1, Notes on Artillery in the Present War (10/14)

Helps, G.T., IWM Documents 86/41/1, Further Notes on Artillery in the Present War (11/14)

Helps, G.T., IWM Documents 86/41/1, Co-operation of Aeroplanes with Artillery (12/14)

Helps, G.T., IWM Documents 86/41/1, Rough Notes on Calibration

Helps, G.T., IWM Documents 86/41/1, Rough Notes on Aeroplane Registration

Joffre, Joseph, *His Memoirs* (Harpers, 1932)

Jünger, Ernst, *Storm of Steel* (Penguin, 2003)

McNaughton, Major-General A.G.L., 'The Capture of Valenciennes: A Study in Co-Ordination', *Canadian Defence Quarterly*, vol. 10, no. 3 (1933), pp. 279–94

Marras, Efisio Luigi, 'Evolution of the Employment of Artillery in the World War', translated by the US Military Attaché in Rome for the Office of the Chief of Artillery (Army Military History Institute, 1924)

Moberly, Archibald H., 'Report on B1 Group Heavy Artillery, 1917' (RAHT Archive, Woolwich, 7/1)

Richards, Frank, *Old Soldiers Never Die* (Naval and Military Press, 2001)

Rommel, Erwin, *Infantry Attacks* (Greenhill, 1995)

Rose, C.A., *Three Years in France with the Guns* (London, Leonaur, 2007)

Severn, Mark, *The Gambardier: The Experiences of a Battery of Heavy Artillery on the Western Front during the First World War* (London, Leonaur, 2007)

Springfield, Charles, *Firepower* (Woolwich Arsenal Archive, MD2096)

Sulzbach, Herbert, *With the German Guns: Four Years on the Western Front 1914–1918*, trans. Richard Thonger (Pen & Sword, 2003)

Tudor, Henry Hugh, Papers (RAHT Archive, Woolwich, MD1060)

War Diary III Corps, Heavy Artillery Log Book, 1917 (Woolwich Archive, A.137)

Secondary Sources

Afflerbach, Holger, 'Greece and the Balkan Area in German Strategy, 1914–1918', in *The Salonica Theatre of Operations and the Outcome of the Great War* (Institute for Balkan Studies, Thessaloniki, 2005)

Anderson, Ross, 'The Battle of Tanga, 2–5 November 1914', *War In History*, vol. 8 (2001)

Anon, 'The French Artillery after August 1914, Armies of the First World War, Tactical Notebook' (Quantico, Institute for Tactical Education, August 1992)

Anon, 'French Trench Artillery, Tactical Notebook' (Quantico, Institute for Tactical Education, vol. I, October 1991–September 1992)

Arthur, Max, *Forgotten Voices of the Great War* (Globe Pequot, 2004)

Asprey, Robert, *The German High Command At War: Hindenburg and Ludendorff and the First World War* (New York, 1991)

Bailey, J.B.A., *Field Artillery and Firepower* (Naval Institute Press, 2004)

Barker, A.J., *The First Iraq War 1914–1918* (Enigma, 2009)

Becker, Captain, 'The 42cm Mortar: Fact and Fancy', *Field Artillery Journal* (May–June 1922), pp. 224–31

Beckett, Ian F.W., *Ypres: The First Battle, 1914* (Pearson Longman, 2004)

Beckett, Ian F.W., *The Great War: 1914–1918* (London, Longman, 2001)

Bellamy, Chris, *Red God of War: Soviet Artillery and Rocket Forces* (Brassey's, 1986)

Berendt, General von, 'Use of Heavy Artillery in Attacking Fortifications', *Field Artillery Journal* (November–December 1939)

Bidwell, Shelford and Graham, Dominick, *Firepower: British Army Weapons and Theories of War – 1904–1945* (Pen & Sword, 2004)

Bobbio, Laura and Illing, Stefano (eds), *The Great War on the Little Lagazuoi*, trans. Giacomel, Paolo and Striffler, Robert (Cortina d'Ampezzo, Belluno, Italy, 1998)

Braim, Paul, *The Test of Battle: The American Expeditionary Forces in the Meuse–Argonne Campaign*, 2nd edn (White Mane Books, 1998)

Brose, Eric, *The Kaiser's Army: the politics of military technology in Germany during the Machine Age, 1870–1918* (Oxford University Press, 2001)

Brown, Malcolm, *Verdun: 1916* (Tempus, 2000)

Bruce, Robert B., *Petain: Verdun to Vichy* (Washington DC, Potomac, 2008)

Campsey, William, 'The Birth of Modern Counter-fire: The British and American Experience in World War I', MA thesis (Kansas, Fort Leavenworth, 1991)

Carlyon, L.A., *Gallipoli* (Doubleday, 2002)

Cassou, Paul, 'The Breaking of the Dobro-Pole Front, Conclusions', trans. Captain J. McBride, US Army, *Revue Militaire General* (15 May 1923)

Cherry, Niall, *Most Unfavourable Ground: the Battle of Loos, 1915* (Helion, 2005)

Chickering, Roger, *Imperial Germany and the Great War, 1914–1918* (Cambridge University Press, 1998)

Clarke, Dale, *British Artillery 1914–18: Field Artillery* (Osprey Publishing, 2004)

Clarke, Dale, *British Artillery 1914–19: Heavy Artillery* (Osprey Publishing, 2005)

Clayton, Anthony, *Paths of Glory: The French Army 1914–1918* (New York, Cassell, 2003)

Coffman, Edward, *The War to End All Wars: The American Military Experience in World War I* (Oxford University Press, 1968)

Cornish, Nik, *The Russian Army and the First World War* (London, Spellmount, 2006)

Cornish, Paul, *Machine Guns and the Great War* (Pen & Sword, 2009)

Dastrup, Boyd, *King of Battle: A Branch History of the US Army's Field Artillery* (Fort Monroe, Virginia, 1993)

Deak, Istvan, 'The Habsburg Army in the First and Last Days of World War I: A Comparative Analysis', in Bela A. Kiraly, Nandor F. Dreisziger and Albert A. Nofi (eds), *East Central European Society in World War I* (Columbia University Press, 1985)

Decsy, Janos, 'The Habsburg Army on the Threshold of Total War', in Bela A. Kiraly, Nandor F. Dreisziger, and Albert A. Nofi (eds), *East Central European Society in World War I* (Columbia University Press, 1985)

Diest, Wilhelm, 'Strategy and Unlimited Warfare in Germany: Moltke, Falkenhayn and Ludendorff', in Roger Chickering and Stig Forster (eds), *Great War, Total War: Combat and Mobilisation on the Western Front, 1914–1918* (Cambridge University Press, 2000)

Djordgevic, Dimitrije, 'Vojvoda Putnik, The Serbian High Command, and Strategy in 1914', in Bela A. Kiraly, Nandor F. Dreisziger and Albert A. Nofi (eds), *East Central European Society in World War I* (Columbia University Press, 1985)

Doughty, Robert A., *Pyrrhic Victory: French Strategy and Operations in the Great War* (London, 2008)

Dowling, Timothy C., *The Brusilov Offensive* (Indiana University Press, 2008)

Duffy, Christopher, *Through German Eyes: The British and the Somme* (Weidenfeld & Nicholson, 2006)

Dunn, J.C., *The War the Infantry Knew: 1914–1918* (Cardinal, 1987)

Erickson, Edward J., *Ordered to Die: a History of the Ottoman Army in the First World War* (Greenwood, 2001)

Evera, Stephan van, 'The Cult of the Offensive and the Origins of the First World War', *International Security*, vol. 9, no. 1 (Summer 1984)

Falls, Cyril, *Caporetto: 1917* (Weidenfeld & Nicholson, 1966)

Falvey, Denis, *A Well Known Excellence: British Artillery and an Artilleryman in WWII* (London, Brassey's, 2002)

Farndale, Sir Martin, *History of the Royal Regiment of Artillery: Western Front 1914–18* (Royal Artillery Institution, 1986)

Farndale, Sir Martin, *History of the Royal Regiment of Artillery: The Forgotten Fronts and the Home Base, 1914-1918* (Royal Artillery Institution, 1988)

Farrar-Hockley, Anthony, *Death of an Army* (William Morrow, 1968)

Foley, Robert, *German Strategy and the Path to Verdun* (Cambridge University Press, 2005)

Foley, Robert, 'The Other Side of the Wire: The German Army in 1917', in Peter Dennis and Jeffrey Grey (eds), *1917: Tactics, Training, and Technology* (Australian History Military Publications, 2007)

Ford, M.C., 'Operational Research, Military Judgement and the Politics of Technical Change in the British Infantry, 1943–1953', *Journal of Strategic Studies*, vol. 32, issue 6 (December 2009)

Fryer, C.E.J., *The Destruction of Serbia in 1915* (New York, 1997)

Gentsch, James F., 'General Luigi Cadorna: Italy and the First World War', in Matthew Seligmann, *Leadership in Conflict 1914–1918* (Leo Cooper, 2000)

Golovin, N.N., *The Russian Army in the World War* (Yale University Press, 1931)

Greenhalgh, Elizabeth, 'The Experience of Fighting with Allies: The Case of the Capture of Falfemont Farm during the Battle of the Somme, 1916', *War In History*, vol. 10 (2003), p. 157

Griffith, Paddy, *Forward into Battle: Fighting Tactics from Waterloo to the Near Future* (Presidio Press, 1991)

Griffith, Paddy, *Battle Tactics of the Western Front: The British Army's Art of Attack, 1916–1918* (London, Yale University Press, 1994)

Grotelueschen, Mark, *Doctrine Under Trial: American Artillery Employment in World War I* (Greenwood, 2000)

Grotelueschen, Mark, *The AEF Way of War: The American Army and Combat in World War I* (Cambridge, 2006)

Gudmundsson, Bruce, *On Artillery* (Praeger, 1993)

Gudmundsson, Bruce, *Stormtroop Tactics: Innovation in the German Army, 1914–1918* (Praeger, 1995)

Hall, Richard, 'The Enemy is Behind Us: The Morale Crisis in the Bulgarian Army during the Summer of 1918', *War In History*, vol. 11, no. 2

Hammond, Bryn, *Cambrai 1917: The Myth of the First Great Tank Battle* (London, Weidenfeld & Nicholson, 2008)

Harris, J.P., *Douglas Haig and the First World War* (Cambridge, 2008)

Harris, Paul (with Niall Barr), *Amiens to the Armistice: The BEF in the Hundred Days' Campaign, 8 August–11 November 1918* (Brassey's, 2003)

Herwig, Holger H., *The Marne 1914: The Opening of World War I and the Battle that Changed the World* (Random House, 2009)

Herwig, Holger H., *The First World War: Germany and Austria-Hungary 1914–1918* (Arnold, 1997)

Hogg, Ian and Thurston, L.F., *British Artillery Weapons and Ammunition, 1914–1918* (Allan, 1972)

Hogue, James K., 'Puissance de Feu: The Struggle for New Artillery Doctrine in the French Army, 1914–1916', MA Thesis (Ohio State University, 1988)

Hindenburg, *Out of My Life* (London, 1920)

Holmes, Richard, *Tommy: The British Soldier on the Western Front 1914–1918* (Harper, 2005)

Horne, Alistair, *The Price of Glory: Verdun 1916* (London, Penguin, 1993)

Johnson, Douglas, *Battlefields of the World War: A Study in Military Geography* (Oxford University Press, 1921)

Johnson, J.H., *Stalemate: The Real Story of Trench Warfare* (London, 1995)

Kearsey, A., *A Study of the Strategy and Tactics of the East Prussian Campaign, 1914* (Sifton Praed, 1932)

Keegan, John, *August 1914: Opening Moves* (Ballantine, 1973)

Kitchen, Martin, *The German Offensives of 1918* (Tempus, 2001)

Lee, John, *A Soldier's Life: General Sir Ian Hamilton 1853–1947* (London, Pan Books, 2000)

Liddle, Peter (ed.), *Passchendaele in Perspective: The Third Battle of Ypres* (Leo Cooper, 1997)

Livesay, J.F.B., *Canada's Hundred Days: With the Canadian Corps from Amiens to Mons, Aug. 8–Nov. 11 1918* (Toronto, 1919)

Lloyd, Nick, *Loos 1915* (Tempus, 2006)

Lucas, Pascal M.H., *The Evolution of Tactical Ideas in France and Germany During the War of 1914–1918* (GCG, Paris, 1923; trans. by F.A. Kieffer, US Army, 1925)

Lupfer, Timothy, *Dynamics of Doctrine: the changes in German tactical doctrine during the First World War* (Kansas, Fort Leavenworth, 1981)

Lyon, James, '"A Peasant Mob": The Serbian Army on the Eve of the Great War', *Journal of Military History*, vol. 61, no. 3 (1997)

MacLeod, Roy, 'Sight and Sound on the Western Front: Surveyors, Scientists and the Battlefield Laboratory, 1915–1918', *War & Society*, vol. 18, no. 1 (May 2000)

McWilliams, James and Steel, James R., *Amiens: 1918* (History Press, 2001)

Marble, Sanders, *'The Infantry Cannot Do with a Gun Less': The Place of the Artillery in the British Expeditionary Force, 1914–1918* (Columbia University Press, 2003)

Middlebrook, Martin, *The Kaiser's Battle. 21 March 1918: The First Day of the German Spring Offensive* (London, Penguin, 1983)

Millett, Allan R. and Williamson, Murray (eds), *Military Effectiveness. Vol. 1: The First World War*, International Security and Foreign Policy (Allen & Unwin, 1989)

Minchev, Dimitre, 'The Bulgarian Army at the Salonica Front', in *The Salonica Theatre of Operations and the Outcome of the Great War* (Institute for Balkan Studies, Thessaloniki, 2005)

Mitrovic, Andrej, *Serbia's Great War, 1914–1918* (Perdue University Press, 2007)

Nash, David, *German Artillery, 1914–1918* (Altmark, 1970)

Neiberg, Michael, *The Second Battle of the Marne* (Indiana University Press, 2008)

Oldham, Peter, *Pillboxes on the Western Front: a guide to the design, construction and use of concrete pillboxes 1914—1918* (Leo Cooper, 1995)

Ortner, Christian, *The Austro-Hungarian Artillery from 1867 to 1918* (Verlag Militaria, 2007)

Paige, Edward, *Tip and Run: The Untold Tragedy of the Great War in Africa* (Weidenfeld & Nicholson, 2007)

Palmer, Alan, *The Gardeners of Salonika: The Macedonian Campaign 1915–1918* (New York, 1965)

Palmer, Alan, *The Salient: Ypres, 1914–1918* (Constable, 2007)

Passingham, Ian, *Pillars of Fire: The Battle of Messines Ridge, June 1917* (Sutton, 1998)

Passingham, Ian, *All The Kaiser's Men, The Life and Death of the German Army on the Western Front 1914–1918* (History Press, 2005)

Passingham, Ian, *The German Offensives of 1918: The Last Desperate Gamble* (Pen & Sword, 2008)

Philpott, William, *Bloody Victory: The Sacrifice on the Somme and the Making of the Twentieth Century* (London, Little Brown, 2009)

Prior, Robin and Wilson, Trevor, *Passchendaele: The untold story* (Yale, 1996)

Prior, Robin and Wilson, Trevor, *Command on the Western Front: The Military Career of Sir Henry Rawlinson 1914–1918* (Pen & Sword, 2004)

Prior, Robin and Wilson, Trevor, *The Somme* (New Haven, Connecticut, 2005)

Prodan, Costica and Preda, Dumitru, *The Romanian Army During the First World War* (Univers, 1998)

Ripperger, Robert M., 'The Development of the French Artillery for the Offensive, 1890–1914', *Journal of Military History*, 59 (October 1995)

Rohne, Lieutenant-General H., 'Concerning the Fall of the Belgian Forts', *Field Artillery Journal* (October–December 1914)

Rothenberg, Gunther, *The Army of Francis Joseph* (Perdue University Press, 1976)

Rothenberg, Gunther, 'The Austro-Hungarian Campaign Against Serbia in 1914', *Journal of Military History*, 53 (April 1989)

Schindler, John, R., *Isonzo: The Forgotten Sacrifice of the Great War* (Greenwood, 2001)

Schindler, John, 'Disaster on the Drina: The Austro-Hungarian Army in Serbia, 1914', *War in History*, 9/2 (2002)

Sheffield, Gary, *Forgotten Victory: The First World War – Myths and Realities* (Headline, 2001)

Sheldon, Jack, *The German Army on the Somme, 1914–1916* (Pen & Sword, 2005)

Sheldon, Jack, *The German Army at Passchendale* (Pen & Sword, 2007)

Sheldon, Jack, *The German Army on Vimy Ridge, 1914–1917* (Pen & Sword, 2008)

Sheldon, Jack, *The German Army at Cambrai* (Pen & Sword, 2009)

Showalter, Dennis E., *Tannenberg: clash of empires, 1914* (Brassey's, 2004)

Sondhaus, Lawrence, *Franz Conrad von Hötzendorf: architect of the apocalypse* (Humanities Press, 2000)

Stone, Norman, 'Army and Society in the Habsburg Monarchy, 1900–1914', *Past and Present*, 33 (April 1966)

Stone, Norman, *The Eastern Front, 1914 to 1917* (London, Penguin, 1998)

Strachan, Hew, *To Arms* (Oxford University Press, 2001)

Thompson, Mark, *The White War. Life and Death on the Italian Front: 1915–1919* (Faber & Faber, 2008)

Torrey, Glenn E., *Henri Mathias Berthelot: Soldier of France, Defender of Romania* (Centre for Romanian Studies, 2000)

Torrey, Glenn E., 'The Battle of Turtucaia (Tutrakan) (2-6 September 1916): Romania's Grief, Bulgaria's Glory', *East European Quarterly*, XXVII, no. 4 (Winter 2003/4)

Travers, Tim, *Gallipoli 1915* (London, History Press, 2001)

Tunstall, Graydon A., *Planning for War Against Russia and Serbia: Austro-Hungarian and German Military Strategies, 1871–1914* (Columbia University Press, 1993)

Tunstall, Graydon A., 'Austria-Hungary and the Brusilov Offensive of 1916', *The Historian*, vol. 70 (2008)

Van der Kloot, William, 'Lawrence Bragg's role in the development of sound-ranging in World War I', *Notes & Records of the Royal Society*, vol. 59 (2005)

Wakefield, Alan and Moody, Simon, *Under the Devil's Eye: Britain's Forgotten Army at Salonika, 1915–1918* (Stroud, 2004)

Wynne, G.C., *If Germany Attacks* (Faber, 1940)

Zabecki, David T., *Steel Wind: Colonel Georg Bruchmüller and the Birth of Modern Artillery* (Preager, 1994)

Zabecki, David T., *The German 1918 Offensives: A case study in the operational level of war* (Routledge, 2006)

Zuber, Terence, *Ardennes 1914: The Battle of the Frontiers* (Tempus, 2007)

Online Sources

Ayres, Leonard, *The War With Germany: A Statistical Summary* (Washington, DC, 1919), available at www.archive.org/details/warwithgermanyst00unit

Battle of Malmaison – French assessment based on interrogations and captured documents available at www.archive.org/details/germanaustrianta00germiala

Data at www.heroesofserbia.com/2009/08/battle-of-cer-first-allied-victory-of.html

British General Staff's 'Summary of Recent Information Regarding the German Army and its Methods,' January 1917, available at www.archive.org/details/summaryofrecenti00grearich

Fritz Kreisler's Memoir at http://net.lib.byu.edu/estu/wwi/memoir/Kreisler/Kreisler.htm

German and Austrian Tactical Studies (captured documents printed by the US General Staff, Washington, DC, 1918), www.archive.org/detailsgermanaus-trianta00germiala

Gorlice Podcast at http://bobrowen.com/nymas/podcasts/diNardo per cent20WWI per cent203.mp3

Maps at
http://cgsc.cdmhost.com/cdm4/item_viewer.php?CISOROOT=/p4013col
114&CISOPTR=927&CISOBOX=1&REC=1has

Notes On Recent Operations (captured documents printed by the US General Staff, Washington, DC, 1917), www.archive.org/details/notesonrecen-tope00unitrich

Index